MONEY LAUNDERING, FINANCING TERRORISM AND SUSPICIOUS ACTIVITIES

MONEY LAUNDERING, FINANCING TERRORISM AND SUSPICIOUS ACTIVITIES

BENTON E. GUP

Nova Science Publishers, Inc.
New York

For permission to use material from this book please contact us:
Telephone 631-231-7269; Fax 631-231-8175
Web Site: http://www.novapublishers.com

LIBRARY OF CONGRESS CATALOGING-IN-PUBLICATION DATA

Money laundering, financing terrorism, and suspicious activities / Benton E. Gup (editor).
p. cm.
Includes index.
ISBN 13 978-1-60021-387-8
ISBN 10 1-60021-387-1
1. Money laundering. 2. Money laundering--Prevention. 3. Banks and banking--Corrupt practices. 4. Terrorism--Finance. I. Gup, Benton E.
HV6768.M66 2006
364.16'8--dc22 2006024154

Published by Nova Science Publishers, Inc. ✦ New York

Dedication

To Jean, Lincoln, Andrew and Carol, and Jeremy

CONTENTS

INTRODUCTION

Money laundering is a global problem. It involves hundreds of billions of dollars, and it is proof that crime pays. According to the United Nations Office on Drugs and Crime, money laundering can erode a nation's economy and it can adversely affect the global stability of financial markets.[1] After the 9/11 terrorist attacks on the United States, the concept of money laundering was expanded to include the financing of terrorism.

Today, all financial institutions in the U.S. are required by law to have Bank Secrecy Act and Anti-Money Laundering (BSA/AML) compliance and training programs that are suitable for their particular institutions. Thus, a BSA/AML compliance and training program designed for Citicorp is not going to be suitable for a small community bank, a money transmitter, or a casino.

AML programs also have been established by international organizations. These include the United Nations, International Group Against Money Laundering, the Committee of the Council of Europe, Financial Action Task Force for South America, and others. Thus, there is international cooperation in fighting money laundering; but some countries are more cooperative than others.

A key part of all BSA/AML programs is to have some understanding of how money laundering and financing terrorism works. This book explains money laundering, financing terrorism, and suspicious activities. It provides numerous examples of each. However, money laundering and financing terrorism are like games in the following sense. As soon as the law enforcement authorities foil one method of laundering funds or financing terrorists, the bad guys figure out new methods. Interestingly, sometimes the bad guys are insiders.

The basic idea behind this book is that if you don't know what you are looking for, you are not going to find it. By way of illustration, few people realize that cigarette smuggling, certain charitable organizations, internet solicitations, as well as investments in legitimate businesses have been used to finance terrorists. This book will help you figure out what to look for in terms of money laundering and financing terrorism, but it cannot provide all of the answers in an ever changing setting.

The numerous examples and cases cited in the book come from a wide variety of sources that are cited in the chapters and listed in the references in the back of the book. A careful examination of the sources reveals that most of them are from domestic and international government and government related entities.

---

[1] United Nations Office on Drugs and Crime, "Global Programme Against Money Laundering," April 4, 2005.

For your convenience, online sources of information about money laundering and financing terrorism, references, abbreviations, and the definitions of selected terms that are used in Chapters 1-6, are listed in the back of the book.

It should be noted that the names of some foreign terrorist groups, such as al Qaeda and Hezbollah, are spelled in a variety of ways. To avoid confusion, one consistent spelling is used through out the book.

As I was writing this book, Mike Hardin and Raj Aggarwal wanted to contribute articles about money laundering:

1. Professor J. Michael Hardin at The University of Alabama is an expert in data mining. In addition, he is the Associate Dean for Research at The University of Alabama. Mike collaborated with Billie S. Anderson, a Ph.D. candidate in Applied Statistics at The University of Alabama; Tim Lutz, a Financial Behavior Expert at SAS; and David Stewart is the Program Manager, Anti-Money Laundering at SAS. Their article, "Overview of Analytical Methods for Money Laundering," (Chapter 7) provides easy to understand explanations of the data mining tools that can be used to detect money laundering.
2. Professor Raj Aggarwal holds the Firestone Chair in Corporate Finance at Kent State University. Raj has considerable international and domestic experience working with corporate boards and management. He serves on the Board for the Financial Executives Research Foundation (FERF), the research arm of the Financial Executives Institute (FEI). Raj and Assistant Professor Kamala Raghavan, Department Head of Accounting and Taxation at Robert Morris University, collaborated on writing "Management and Board Challenges Complying With Bank Secrecy Act and Anti Money Laundering Regulations (Chapter 8). Kamala is a former Senior Vice President of National City Corporation (Cleveland), Citizens and Southern Corporation (Atlanta), and a Vice President of First City Bank (Houston).

Chapter 1

MONEY LAUNDERING

Money laundering is the proof that crime pays. *Money laundering* is the conversion of the monetary proceeds of criminal activity into funds with an apparently legal source and without revealing the true nature, source, or ownership of those proceeds.[1] Stated otherwise, it is disguising illegal proceeds by introducing them into legitimate commerce and finance.[2] Money laundering also includes using legitimate funds for illegal purposes, such as financing terrorism. Thus, money laundering occurs in connection with bribery and kickbacks, drug trafficking, fraud, tax evasion, terrorism, and other illegal activities.

When illegal activities generate large profits, the perpetrators must find ways to move the funds without attracting attention to themselves. Therefore, in one sense, money laundering is a game. If the perpetrators are successful in laundering money they win, and society loses. The Financial Action Task Force said that money laundering has resulted in "inexplicable changes in the money demand, prudential risks to bank soundness, contamination effects on legal financial transactions, and increased volatility of international capital flows and exchange rates due to unanticipated cross-border asset transfers...Money laundering is inextricably linked to the underlying criminal activity that generated it. Laundering enables the criminal activity to continue."[3]

According to the United Nations Office on Drug and Crime, "money laundering empowers corruption and organized crime. Corrupt public officials need to be able to launder bribes, kick-backs, public funds, and on occasion, even development loans from financial institutions. Organized criminal groups need to be able to launder the proceeds of drug trafficking and commodity smuggling. Terrorist groups use money laundering channels to get cash to buy arms. The social consequences of allowing these three groups access to the capacity to launder money can be disastrous."[4] Society is worse off because of money laundering. Money laundering is not a victimless crime.

To put money laundering in perspective, estimates of the aggregate size of money laundering are somewhere between 2 and 5 percent of the world's gross domestic product

---

[1] U. S. Senate, Current Trends in Money Laundering, Report prepared for the Permanent Subcommittee on Investigations of the Committee on Government Affairs, 102ned Cong., 2nd Sess. S. Hrg. 102-123, December 1992, p. 1; Also see Gup (1995).

[2] U.S. Department of the Treasury, Program Performance Report, Fiscal Year 2000, 2001, 145.

[3] Financial Action Task Force, "Basic Facts about Money Laundering," February 7, 2004. pp. 3-4.

[4] United Nations Office on Drugs and Crime, "Global Programme Against Money Laundering,," April 4, 2005.

(GDP).[5] Stated otherwise, between $600 billion and $1.5 trillion is being laundered annually, and about half of that amount is in the United States.[6] In 1999, for example, the Black Market Peso Exchange laundered about $5 billion per year in the United States.[7] The Black Market Peso Exchange (BMPE) allows Colombian drug traffickers to convert the dollars they receive in the U.S. for selling cocaine and heroin into pesos in their Colombian bank accounts. More will be said about the BMPE in Chapter 3.

Because governments and law enforcement agencies are constantly shutting down existing money laundering activities, the perpetrators must find new means to launder money. Accordingly, the examples of money laundering presented in this book are only the proverbial "tip of the iceberg." Nevertheless, they provide important clues and insights about how to find the latest methods of money laundering in connection with criminal activities other than terrorism. Examples of financing terrorism are presented in Chapter 2.

THE PROCESS OF MONEY LAUNDERING

Money laundering is a business specialty, and like other business activities, has its own jargon. Some of the terms used by law enforcement authorities and drug traffickers include the following:[8]

Commingling

Obscuring the illegal funds by commingling (mixing) them with the proceeds of a legitimate business (front company) so that all of the funds appear to be income from the legitimate business.

Complicity

Money laundering facilitated by financial institution's employees or owners. It is not limited to one bank. Various domestic and foreign banks my jointly be involved in money laundering. The Bank of Commerce and Credit International (BCCI) is one example. The parent company, BCCI Holdings, was chartered in Luxembourg, and BCCI operated in 73 countries. In 1983, a Jordanian arms dealer was one of the largest customers of BCCI's office

---

[5] Money Laundering: A Bankers Guide to Avoiding Problems, Office of the Comptroller of the Currency, December 2002, 3; The International Money Laundering Abatement and Financial Anti-Terrorism Act of 2001, Pubic Law 107-56, Sec. 302, (31 USC 5311 note) October 26, 2001; Quirk, Peter J., "Macroeconomic Implications of Money Laundering," International Monetary Fund, Working Paper, WP/96/66-EA, June 1, 1996; Rodger, Ian, "Survey of Fraud – Prevention and Detection," Financial Times, October 18, 1994, 34.

[6] William R. Schroder, "Money Laundering, A Global Threat and the International Community's Response," FBI Law Enforcement Bulletin, May 2001, 1-9.

[7] U.S. Department of Treasury, "The National Money Laundering Report for 1999," September 1999, 21-22.

[8] U. S. Senate, Current Trends in Money Laundering, Report prepared for the Permanent Subcommittee on Investigations of the Committee on Government Affairs, 102nd Cong., 2nd Sess. S. Hrg. 102-579, February 27, 1992, pp. 215-216, 437,-434.

in Miami Florida.[9] He used fraudulent bills of lading and cargo manifests to carry out a massive smuggling operation. BCCI issued phony letters of credit to finance the smuggling. Other alleged BCCI crimes included fraud, arms trafficking including the procurement of nuclear weapons and technologies for Pakistan, smuggling, and support of terrorist organizations such as Abu Nidal - an international terrorist organization that has carried out attacks in 20 countries including the United States.[10]

Front/Shell Companies

The illegal funds are represented as income (commingled) of companies such as legitimate real estate agencies and pizzerias. Front companies also may be dummy corporations, such as jewelry stores and precious metals dealers that were established for the express purpose of laundering.

Shell companies or *international business corporations* (IBCs) are similar to front companies, but they are usually chartered offshore to hide their identity, and they may exist on paper only. They can be used to transfer funds in what appears to be a legitimate transaction.

Shell banks are institutions with no physical presence in the jurisdiction where they are incorporated. They are not affiliated with a regulated financial group.[11]

Integration

Integration is an attempt to provide apparent legitimacy to the illegally gained wealth. Stated otherwise, the money launderers are trying to integrate their funds into the financial system to give the appearance of legitimacy and hide their illicit origin.

Layering

Separating illegal proceeds from their source by creating multiple layers of financial transactions in various accounts at different banks in order to hinder the audit trail and hide the source of funds.

Placement

The physical disposal of illegally obtained bulk cash proceeds by converting it into money orders, traveler's checks, or bank deposits. Cash-based retail businesses, such as a grocery store or bar, are ideal for placing cash in the domestic financial system. Similarly,

---

[9] Gup (1995), pp. 31-38.

[10] U.S. Department of State, Patterns of Global Terrorism, 2003, April 2004. Appendix B.

[11] Financial Action Task Force on Money Laundering, "Report on Money Laundering Typologies, 2001-2002," February 1, 2002, 9. For information on IBCs see the Government of Antigua and Barbuda web site: http://www.antiguabarbuda.gov.ag/business/economy.htm

companies that deal in international trade, such as import/export and travel businesses, can be used for international placements.

Structuring/Smurfing/Straw Parties

Structuring is the process of converting bulk cash into small amounts to avoid Currency Transaction Reports (CTRs) and Suspicious Activity Reports (SARs). The typical CTR reporting threshold is $10,000, but in some cases it is less than that amount. SARs involve funds or other assets worth $5,000 or more when the institution suspects the transaction is designed to evade any of the requirements of the Bank Secrecy Act. Consider the following example involving $40,000 in cash. The $40,000 can be structured into ten deposits of $4,000 each. The individuals who "place" or carry out multiple, small transactions are called "smurfs." *Smurfing* is defined as two or more persons conducting related financial transactions that could have been completed in a single transaction.[12]

Similarly, individuals transmitting funds through Money Service Businesses frequently use *straw parties* to handle the transactions for them. The straw party that conducts the wire transfer may or may not know that they are assisting someone in a criminal activity. More will be said about Money Service Businesses shortly.

Three Steps in Money Laundering

The process of money laundering begins when cash is generated by an illegal activity such as drug trafficking. Then it involves three steps: 1) placement, 2) layering, and 3) integration. They may occur simultaneously, or they may overlap each other. The process

1. Placement may involve structuring and/or smurfing to place bulk cash in traditional or nontraditional financial institutions or selected businesses. This is the riskiest part of the process of money laundering because money is still close to its origins. This step is labor intensive and may involve hundreds of smurfs. Alternatively, the trafficker may get an exemption from a financial institution to engage in transactions in excess of $10,000. In either case, the deposited funds can be wire transferred or sent by some other means to another location. Detection of money laundering transactions becomes difficult once it moves beyond the placement stage.
2. During the second step, layering, the funds are usually placed in monetary instruments (cashier's checks, money orders, letters of credit, stocks, bonds, etc.), and wire transfers to other banks. Launderers prefer wire transfers because they are fast and impose no limits on the amount of funds that can be transferred. Multiple wire transfers occur through numerous institutions, front companies, and shell companies in order to deter detection.
3. Integration occurs when the laundered funds are put back in the economy in such a way that they appear to be legitimate. For example, the funds may be used to buy real estate, establish a business, or acquire cars, boats, and aircraft that can be used to

12 FinCEN, "The SAR Activity Review: Trends, Tips & Issues, Issue 8, April 2005, p. 11.

further money laundering activities. Then the funds are recycled back into criminal activity. One integration technique is overstating the value of exports and imports. For example, if imports to the United States are overvalued on the invoice, the difference between the actual value and the amount listed on the invoice is paid for from the proceeds from illegal activities. The overvaluation of exports provides justification to receive funds from abroad.

The choice of techniques used to launder money depends on the following factors:[13]

- The immediate business environment --- making the laundering look like a normal business.
- The dollar amount of the funds to be laundered. Small amounts require different techniques than large amounts.
- Time. Is it a one time deal or an on going operation?
- The amount of trust that can be placed in particular individuals and institutions.
- The record of law enforcement authorities – the stricter their track record, the higher the cost and complexity of laundering.
- The planned long-term disposition of funds. If the funds are needed now, for example, the launderer can use the funds to buy winning tickets, and then cash them in. In the case of long-term disposition, the funds could be invested in real estate.

Recovering Laundered Funds

Once the money has been laundered, a variety of techniques can be used to recover the funds. Some of the methods are listed below:[14]

- Loans. The launderer arranges for funds held in his offshore account to be lent to his domestic account. The loan can be repaid and the interest deducted for tax purposes.
- The money is received as business income for goods or services rendered.
- Receive or ship commodities. They can be overvalued if they are shipped out, and undervalue if they are being imported.
- Funds can be received as "consulting fees" from which "expenses" can be deducted for tax purposes.
- Bogus capital gains on option trading between domestic and foreign companies – especially those in places with secrecy laws.
- International real estate flips. Where the sale price of the foreign real estate is inflated, and is realized as a capital gain.
- Casino winnings from offshore casinos.
- The use of debit or credit cards to withdraw funds from offshore accounts.

---

[13] Blum, Jack A., Michael Levi, R. Thomas Naylor, and Phil Williams, "Financial Havens, Banking Secrecy and Money Laundering, New York, United Nations Office for Drug Control and Crime Prevention, 1999.

Selected U.S. Federal Legislation

Federal legislation has developed to address the fact that money laundering is a criminal activity. In order to detect the criminal activity, financial institutions and businesses must report money laundering and suspicious transactions to federal authorities. Those convicted of money laundering are subject to legal sanctions. Listed below are the principal laws dealing with money laundering that directly affect financial institutions.

The important point here is that the U.S. government relies on financial institutions in general, and banks in particular as their first line of defense – the primary "gatekeeper" - against money laundering and financing terrorism. Financial institutions must report the suspected illegal activities to the government that, in turn, investigates those activities.

Bank Secrecy Act of 1970

The Bank Records and Foreign Transaction Reporting Act is commonly referred to as the Bank Secrecy Act (BSA) of 1970.[15] BSA was the first federal legislation targeting money laundering and other white-collar crimes, including tax evasion. It is called the Bank Secrecy Act because it helps provide information to law enforcement agencies about the secret use of foreign accounts by U.S. customers by creating a "paper trail." While the BSA aided in tracking money launderers, it did not make money laundering illegal *per se*. Nevertheless, some money launderers were prosecuted for violating the BSA and under the Racketeer-Influenced and Corrupt Organizations (RICO) statutes.

The BSA requires banks to develop internal policies, procedures, and controls to carry out anti-money laundering programs. The law has been amended and updated. Financial institutions must 1) keep certain basic records; and 2) file *Currency Transaction Reports* (CTRs) for domestic currency transactions (deposits, withdrawals, exchanges) in excess of $10,000, and *Currency or Monetary Instruments Reports* (CIMRs) for international currency transactions in excess of $10,000. All of the reports are filed with the Department of Treasury's Financial Crimes Enforcement Network, which is known as FinCEN.[16] FinCEN facilitates information sharing among law enforcement, regulatory, and financial institutions.

The BSA defines financial institutions to include banks (e.g. commercial banks, savings and loan associations, and credit unions), federally regulated securities brokers, currency exchange houses, funds transmitters, check-cashing businesses, and persons subject to supervision by state or federal bank supervisory authority. In 1985, the BSA was amended to include casinos and card clubs in the definition of financial institutions. In 2005, rules were proposed to add Insurance companies offering selected products to the list.

---

[14] Blum, et. al. (1999), 19-22.

[15] For details on the implementation, see 12 C.F.R. Part 326; 12 C.F.R. 21.21; 31 C.F.R. Parts 103 and 353.

[16] For additional information see their web site, www.fincen.gov

Exemptions

Banks, subject to the approval of the Treasury and/or Internal Revenue Service, can grant exemptions to filing CTRs for certain legitimate firms that regularly engage in currency transactions that exceed $10,000. Bowling alleys, car washes, and dry cleaners are examples of such businesses. In addition, banks can unilaterally grant exemptions to certain retail businesses such as bars, restaurants, and hotels. The exemptions are for a specific time period and for stated dollar amounts.

Willful Blindness – The Bank of Boston

Banks must exercise caution in granting exemptions. In August 1980, the Bank of Boston exempted a deposit of $1.5 million that it handled as an international bank transfer, and did not file the required CTR.[17] It was one of a series of deposits from a front businesses that were laundering funds for an organized drug distribution network. The bank accepted large cash deposits from reputed mobsters with underworld connections. The bank had no direct knowledge of the source of funds, but it did not question their origin. The Bank of Boston pled guilty and was fined $500,000. A more important outcome of this case was the concept of "knowledge" of criminal activity was expanded from "actual knowledge" to include *"willful blindness," "deliberate ignorance,"* and *"conscious avoidance."*

Internal Revenue Service

The BSA, the Internal Revenue Code (Title 26), and the money laundering criminal statutes (Title 18) requires any person engaged in trade or business who receives more than $10,000 in a single transaction or related series of transactions to file a "Report of Cash Payments over $10,000 Received in Trade or Business" report with the Internal Revenue Service (IRS). The IRS also has responsibility for CTRs with Casinos. Finally, any person subject to U.S. jurisdiction who has a financial interest or signature authority in foreign accounts with a value of $10,000 or more must file a Report of Foreign Bank and Financial Accounts with the IRS.

Money Laundering Control Act of 1986

Money laundering became a federal crime when the BSA was amended by the Money Laundering Control Act of 1986, and again with the Money Laundering Prosecution Act of 1988 (part of the Omnibus Anti-Drug Abuse Act).

One outcome of the 1986 amendments was that financial institutions could no longer be "willfully blind" to money laundering activities of their customers. A bank can be found guilty of money laundering even if does not know the legal origins of the funds, but should

[17] Robert E. Powis, The Money Launderers, Chicago, Probus Publising Co., 1992, Chapter 1.

have suspected criminal activity based on the behavior of the customer. In other words, banks must "*know their customers*!"

Know Your Customers (KYC)

Banks must make reasonable efforts to determine who the borrower is, the credit history, the purpose of a loan, and other relevant information. Other relevant information includes the sources of income and expenditures.

Part of the KYC due diligence includes customer identification. Banks must verify that customers –individuals or non-individuals - are who they claim to be.[18] KYC also is known as the customer identification program (CIP) as part of the BSA compliance program. Consider the following case. A bank made a one-year $800,000 first mortgage loan to a Panamanian corporation. The loan was collateralized with a $1.1 million home owned by the corporation. After the loan was made, a government investigation revealed that the Panamanian corporation was owned by an illegal drug trafficker. The government seized the property claiming that it had probable cause to believe that the house was purchased with the proceeds from illegal drug sales. The government also claimed that the bank's president who made the loan, should have known that the owner of the property was a drug trafficker.

Under federal law, property that has been acquired with laundered money is subject to seizure and forfeiture, even if it is collateral for a bank loan. If the bank was an "innocent" lien holder, the court may "pardon" the property. However, in this case, the court ruled that the bank was "willfully blind" to the facts that it should have taken into account. These facts were that the Panamanian corporation was a shell corporation whose sole asset was the property, which was vacant, and up for sale. The bank did not know the purpose of the loan, or how it was going to be repaid. It did not do a title search on the property. The loan proceeds were transferred to Switzerland, and some funds were used to buy expensive gifts for the bank president's family. The bank lost $800,000 plus attorney fees.

The important point here is that banks must have appropriate procedures to detect and forestall money laundering activities. These include, but are not limited to BSA compliance programs that banks must establish and maintain adequate internal controls, independent testing, responsible personnel, and sufficient training to comply with the BSA.[19] Institutions that fail to comply with the laws have been fined and put on probation. [20] The Board of Governors of the Federal Reserve, the Office of the Comptroller of the Currency (OCC), the FDIC and other agencies regularly post on their web sites enforcement actions taken against financial institutions in connection with BSA violations. More will be said about fines and penalties later in this chapter.

---

[18] For additional details on KYC Policies and Procedures see 31 C.F.R. 103.121. Also see Customer Due Diligence for Banks, Basel Committee on Banking Supervision, Bank for International Settlements, October 2001; "ID-Defusing the Issue: A Progress Report," Financial Crime Sector Report, The Financial Services Authority, London, UK, October 2004.

[19] See Comptroller of the Currency, OCC Bulletin, Enforcement Guidance for BSA/AML Program Deficiencies, OCC 2004-50, November 10, 2004.

[20] National Banks also must comply with 12 C.F.R. 21.21. The Federal Reserve's rules for anti-money laundering programs are in Regulation H (12 C.F.R. 208.63).

Annuzio-Wylie-Anti-Money Laundering Act of 1992

The Housing Community Development Act of 1992, commonly referred to as the Annuzio-Wylie-Anti-Money Laundering Act, permits the Secretary of the Treasury to require any financial institution (including employees, officers, and directors) to file Suspicious Transaction Reports (STRs). The banks are prohibited from notifying the person who is the subject of the report. In addition, all businesses must keep customer identification records for currency transactions between $3,000 and $10,000, and report suspicious transactions regardless of their size. The suspicious transactions do not have to be linked to the drug trade.

Banks may not have "*flagrant organizational indifference*" to their obligations under the BSA or to report suspicious transactions. All employees, officers, and directors must comply with it. Under the doctrine of "*collective knowledge*," information known by employees, acting within the scope of their employment, can be attributed to that organization. Accordingly, a bank can face criminal charges if an employee suspects that a transaction may be involved in money laundering, but does not report it.

The Annuzio-Wiley Act provides a "safe harbor" for financial institutions and their employees that follow the prescribed regulations from civil liability for reporting known or suspected criminal offenses for by filing STR reports.[21]

The Act strengthens anti-money laundering efforts by giving federal bank regulators more latitude in their investigations, and allowing them to close or seize a bank, savings and loan association, or credit union under some circumstances; or terminate its insured status. In deciding whether an institution should be seized, they must consider whether employees, officers, and directors were involved in illegal activities, the bank's policies concerning money laundering, and other factors.

Finally, the Annuzio-Wiley Act made the operation of an illegal money transmitting business a crime.

Money Laundering Suppression Act of 1994

Beginning April 1,1996, all banks, thrifts, and credit unions were required to file Suspicious Activity Reports (SARs) with FinCEN.[22] SARs must be filed when there are known or suspected criminal violations of federal laws involving banks, money laundering, and/or the BSA. There is no minimum dollar amount when insiders are involved. The minimum dollar amount is $5,000 for BSA violations and/or when there is an identifiable suspect. The minimum dollar amount is $25,000 when there is no identifiable suspect. Some violations require immediate reporting, while others must be reported no later than 60 days from the date of detection.[23]

[21] "Federal Court Reaffirms Protections for Financial Institutions Filing Suspicious Activity Reports," Board of Governors of the Federal Reserve System, Interagency Advisory, May 24, 2004.

[22] 12 U.S.C. 1818, 1819; 31 U.S.C. 5318; Part 353 appears at 61 Fed. Reg. 6099, February 16, 1996, effective April 1, 1996.

[23] http://www.fdic.gov/regulations/laws/rules/2000-7500.html

Antiterrorism and Effective Death Penalty Act (AEDPA) of 1996

The Antiterrorism and Effective Death Penalty Act of 1996 makes it a crime to: 1) engage in financial transactions with governments or countries designated as supporting international terrorism; or 2) providing material support or resources to a designated Foreign Terrorist Organization (FTO).[24] Seven countries are on the original list of designated countries - Cuba, North Korea, Iran, Libya, Iraq, Sudan, and Syria. The sanctions against Libya were removed. The list of FTOs includes al Qaeda, Hamas, Hizballah, the Palestinian Islamic Jihad, and more than two dozen other organizations. Section 2339 B of that Act prohibits those subject to U.S. criminal laws from knowingly providing material support to FTOs.[25] Thus, the FTOs had to find other ways to raise funds.

USA Patriot Act of 2001

Following the September 11, 2001 terrorists attacks on the United States, Congress passed the USA Patriot Act (formally known as the Uniting and Strengthening America by Providing Appropriate Tools Required to Intercept and Obstruct Terrorism Act of 2001.[26] The intent of the law is to deter terrorists and others from using the U.S. financial system anonymously to launder money. And to deter and punish terrorists acts in the U.S. and around the world. Part of the Act made financing of terrorism a criminal activity, and it increased the civil and criminal penalties for money laundering. It expanded the anti-money laundering (AML) program requirements to all financial institutions including broker-dealers, casinos, as well as to futures commission merchants, introducing brokers, commodity pool operators, and commodity trading advisors. Also included in the definition of financial institutions are any individual or groups engaged in conducting, controlling, directing or owning informal value transfer systems (IVTS) in the United States.[27] The IVTS are examined in Chapter 3.

Other features of the USA Patriot Act include:

- Strengthened the requirements for customer identification when opening an account, and requires checks against government lists of known or suspected terrorists (customer identification program).
- Prohibited banks from engaging in business with foreign shell banks.
- Requires increased due diligence in dealing with foreign private banking and correspondent accounts.

---

[24] Newcomb, R. Richard, Director, Office of Foreign Asset Control, U.S. Department of Treasury, Statement before the U.S. Senate, Committee on Governmental Affairs, 108th Cong. 1st. Sess,, Terrorism Financing: Origination, Organization, and Prevention, S. Hrg. 108-245, July 31, 2003, p. 57.

[25] Saban, Barry, Chief, Counterterrorism Section, Criminal Division, Department of Justice, Testimony before The Committee on Financial Services Hearing entitled "The 9/11 Commission Report: Identifying and Preventing Terrorist Financing," August 23, 2004. Note that al Qaeda also has been spelled Al-Aq'ida, al-Qaida, etc. For consistency, it is spelled al Qaeda in this book.

[26] Public Law 107-56. A short title for the USA Patriot Act is the "International Money Laundering Abatement and Financial Anti-Terrorism Act of 2001."

[27] Section 359, USA Patriot Act. For information on IVTS, see: "The SAR Activity Review: Trends, Tips & Issues," Issue 5, FinCEN, February 2003; FinCEN Advisory, Informal Value Transfer Systems, Issue 33, March 2003.

- Requires banks to respond to regulatory requests for information within 120 hours.
- Increased the civil and criminal penalties for money laundering.
- Requires financial institutions to establish anti-money laundering programs and imposes various standards on money-transmitting businesses.

Prior to 2006, insurance companies were conspicuous by their absence on the listing of financial institutions. Nevertheless the International Association of Insurance Supervisors provided a "Guidance Paper on Anti-Money Laundering and Combating the Financing of Terrorism" that is discussed in Chapter 2.[28] In October 2005, rules were proposed concerning insurance companies offering life insurance policies, annuity contracts, property and casualty insurance, and health insurance that would be added to the list of financial institutions covered by the Bank Secrecy Act anti- money laundering programs and regulations[29]

ANTI-MONEY LAUNDERING PROGRAMS

All financial institutions must develop, administer, and maintain anti-money laundering (AML) programs that ensure compliance with the BSA. This includes the record keeping, reporting, and compliance with each federal financial institution's agencies rules. The federal financial institution regulators include the Federal Reserve Board, Federal Deposit Insurance Corporation, Office of the Comptroller of the Currency, Office of Thrift Supervision, National Credit Union Administration, Securities Exchange Commission, and the Commodity Futures Trading Commission.

The AML programs must be written, and approved by the board of directors (or its equivalent), and noted in the minutes of the board.[30] The BSA/AML programs must include:

1. Internal controls to assure compliance with the BSA.
2. Independent testing of the financial institutions compliance with BSA.
3. The designation of one individual who is responsible for coordinating and monitoring compliance on a daily basis.
4. Training personnel.
5. Customer identification programs (CID) including account opening procedures, and verifying the customer's identity. The customer due diligence (CDD) must include

---

[28] International Association of Insurance Supervisors, "Guidance Paper on Anti-Money Laundering and Combating the Financing of Terrorism," Guidance Paper No. 5, October 2004.

[29] 31 CFR Part 103, RIN 1506-AA36, Financial Crimes Enforcement Network: Amendment to the Bank Secrecy Act Regulations – Requirement that Insurance Companies Report Suspicious Activity. FinCEN Final Rule; 31 CFR Part 103, RIN 1506-AA70, Financial Crimes Enforcement Network: Amendment to the Bank Secrecy Act Regulations-Anti-Money Laundering Programs for Insurance Companies, Final Rule. The insurance sector is discussed in Chapter 5.

[30] Biern, Herbert A., Senior Associate Director, Division of Banking Supervision and Regulation. Testimony on The Bank Secrecy Act and U.S.A. Patriot Act, Before the Committee on International Relations, U.S. House of Representatives, November 17, 2004.
The Federal Financial Institutions Examination Council (FFIEC) is comprised of five banking agencies: The Board of Governors of the Federal Reserve System, Federal Deposit Insurance Corporation, National Credit Union Administration, Office of the Comptroller of the Currency, and Office of Thrift Supervision. See: Federal Financial Institutions Examination Council, Bank Secrecy Act/Anti-Money Laundering Examination Manual, June 2005, (FFIEC BSA/AML Examination Manual), www.ffiec.gov/pdf/bsamanual.pdf

risk assessment procedures in connection with the customer and or transactions, and have sufficient information to determine if the filing of a SAR is warranted.

The BSA/AML programs apply to all operational areas of the financial institutions including, but not limited to retail, credit, private banking, and trust.

Box 1-1
Financial Institutions Defined[31]

Financial institutions, in the context of BSA/AML, include banks (e.g. commercial banks, all subsidiaries of bank holding companies, Edge and Agreement corporations, U.S. branches and agencies of foreign banks, savings and loan associations, credit unions), federally regulated securities brokers, dealers, and investment companies, money service businesses (MSB's, currency dealers or exchangers; check cashers, issuers of traveler's checks, money orders, or stored value; sellers or redeemers of traveler's checks, money orders, or stored value; and funds transmitters), persons subject to supervision by state or federal bank supervisory authority, casinos, card clubs, futures commission merchants, introducing brokers, commodity pool operators, and commodity trading advisors. Also included in the definition of financial institutions are individuals or groups engaged in conducting, controlling, directing or owning informal value transfer systems (IVTS) in the United States. Insurance companies offering selected products and mutual funds were added to the list in 2006.

Office of Foreign Asset Control

The U.S. Department of Treasury's Office of Foreign Asset Control (OFAC) administers laws that impose economic sanctions against hostile targets to further U.S. Foreign policy and national security.[32] OFAC acts under Presidential wartime and national emergency powers, and by laws and statutes that grant it authority to impose controls on transactions and freeze foreign assets under U.S. jurisdiction. As part of its tasks, OFAC publishes lists of Specially Designated Narcotics Trafficker Kingpins (SDNTK) and Specially Designated Nationals and Blocked Persons (SDNs), lists of sanctioned countries, and rules about Cuba, North Korea, Iran, Libya, Iraq, Sudan, and Syria. Banks. It also publishes lists of designated foreign terrorist organizations, such as FARC, Fuerzas Armadas Revolusionaria de Colombia. Box 1-2 is an example of an OFAC Listing.

---

[31] For a discussion of the definition of financial institution, see Federal Register/Vol. 71, No. 2, January 4, 2006, 31 CFR Part 103, Financial Crimes Enforcement Network: Anti-Money Laundering Programs; Special Due Diligence Programs for Certain Foreign Accounts: Final Rule and Proposed Rule.

[32] U.S. Department of Treasury, "Foreign Asset Control Regulations for the Financial Community," November 24, 2004, 2. Also see OFAC's web page: http://www.treas.gov/offices/enforcement/ofac/

Box 1- 2
Office of Foreign Asset Control Specially Designated Nationals and Blocked Persons, March 17, 2005

- On March 3, 2005, the Department of the Treasury's Office of Foreign Assets Control (OFAC) added four names to its list of Specially Designated Narcotics Trafficker Kingpins and Specially Designated Nationals and Blocked Persons (SDNs).
- The new entries are: CARIBBEAN BEACH PARK, Rosehall Main Road, Rosehall, Jamaica; 1137 Sugar Mill Road, Montego Bay, Jamaica [SDNTK].
- CARIBBEAN SHOWPLACE LTD (f.k.a. FLAMINGO CLUB), Tropigala Night Club, Ironshore, Montego Bay, Jamaica; Rosehall Main Road, Rosehall, Jamaica [SDNTK].
- RAMCHARAN BROTHERS LTD, Rosehall Main Road, Rosehall, Jamaica [SDNTK].
- RAMCHARAN LTD, Rosehall Main Road, Rosehall, Jamaica [SDNTK].
- OFAC has asked that we distribute the information to all FDIC-supervised institutions so records can be checked for accounts that are required to be blocked.
- OFAC information also may be found on the Internet at http://www.treas.gov/offices/eotffc/ofac.
- Please distribute this information to the appropriate personnel in your institution.
- For further information about Executive Orders, the list of blocked accounts or the procedures to block accounts, please call OFAC's Compliance Programs Division at 1-800-540-6322.

Source: FDIC, Financial Institution Letters: Office of Foreign Asset Control Specially Designated Nationals and Blocked Persons, FIL-18-2005, March 17, 2005.

The complete list of SDNs and Blocked persons is more than 190 pages in length. It also is available in a computerized format to facilitate its use by financial institutions. Each entry is followed by a key that indicates under which program it has been designated, such as FTO for foreign terrorist organization, SDT for specially designated terrorist, and SDGT for specially designated global terrorist. For example, the Holy Land Foundation for Relief and Development was designated as an SDT and SDGT because it funneled money to the terrorist group Hamas.[33] Financial institutions must report all blockings of accounts to OFAC within ten days of the occurrence, or be subject to fines and criminal penalties.

Finally, the battle against money laundering and terrorism requires the coordination of a variety of U.S. government agencies and departments. The Treasury Department plays a key role in this process.[34]

---

[33] White House News Release, "Fact Sheet on Shutting Down the Terrorist Financial Network," December 4, 2001.

[34] For further discussion, see: Levey, Stuart A., Under Secretary Terrorism and Financial Intelligence, Testimony before The Committee on Financial Services Hearing entitled "The 9/11 Commission Report: Identifying and Preventing Terrorist Financing, August 23, 2004: Also see, U.S. Department of State, "Money Laundering and Financial Crimes," No date, www.state.gov/documents/organization/8703.pdf for a detailed discussion of international cooperation and detailed descriptions of the vulnerabilities of each country.

INTERNATIONAL COOPERATION

Financial Action Task Force

Money laundering and terrorism is international in scope, and there is substantial international cooperation in combating it. For example, in 1989, the *Financial Action Task Force (FATF)* was established at a G-7 Summit. It is an inter-governmental body of 33 countries, territories, and organizations whose purpose is the development and promotion of policies at national and international levels to combat money laundering and terrorist financing.[35] It is a "policy-making body" which works to bring about national legislative and regulatory reforms in these areas. The FATF members include: Argentina, Australia, Austria, Belgium, Brazil, Canada, Denmark, European Commission, Finland, France, Germany, Greece, Gulf Co-operation Council, Hong Kong, China, Iceland, Ireland, Italy, Japan, Luxembourg, Mexico, Kingdom of the Netherlands, New Zealand, Norway, Portugal, Russian Federation, Singapore, South Africa, Spain, Sweden, Switzerland, Turkey, United Kingdom, and the United States.

The secretariat of the FATF is housed in the Organization for Economic Co-Operation and Development (OECD), but the FATF is not part of the OECD. However, where the efforts of the OECD and FATF complement each other, such as on bribery and corruption or the functioning of the international financial system, the two secretariats consult with each other and exchange information.

"The FATF Forty Recommendations (2003)" lists "Designated categories of offences" that are conducive to money laundering.[36] These include but are not limited to:

- participation in an organized criminal group and racketeering;
- terrorism, including terrorist financing;
- trafficking in human beings and migrant smuggling;
- sexual exploitation, including sexual exploitation of children;
- illicit trafficking in narcotic drugs and psychotropic substances;
- illicit arms trafficking;
- illicit trafficking in stolen and other goods;
- corruption and bribery;
- fraud;
- counterfeiting currency;
- counterfeiting and piracy of products;
- environmental crime;
- murder, grievous bodily injury;
- kidnapping, illegal restraint and hostage-taking;
- robbery or theft;
- smuggling;

---

[35] See: http://www.fatf-gafi.org/index.htm for additional information about the FATF.

[36] "The FATF Forty Recommendations (2003)," http://www1.oecd.org/fatf/40Recs_en.htm#Other%20measures. This listing is not as comprehensive as the "Specified Unlawful Activities" in the U.S. under the money laundering laws. Aircraft piracy and Espionage are two examples. For additional information see: http://www.moneylaundering.com/freeresources/mlsualist.aspx

- extortion;
- forgery;
- piracy; and
- insider trading and market manipulation.

Surprisingly, tax evasion was not included on this list. Nevertheless, in the United States, tax evasion and money laundering are closely linked together.

Other international organizations combating money laundering include, but are not limited to the United Nations Office for Drug Control and Crime Prevention, the Council of Europe, the Asia-Pacific Group on Money Laundering, and the Caribbean Financial Action Task Force, Eastern and Southern Africa Anti-Money Laundering Group, Financial Action Task Force for South America, International Group Against Money Laundering, the organization comprised of West African states under the umbrella of (ECOWAS), and the Committee of the Council of Europe.

Although many countries have endorsed anti-money laundering programs and controls, not all of them have been instituted globally for a variety of reasons. One reason is that some countries fear that such controls would harm their economies, the banks that were required to make reports, or the bank's employees or customers. Another reason is that it takes time to make legislative changes and adopt an infrastructure necessary to carry out those changes. Some less developed countries may lack the resources or will to carry them out. It costs time and effort to file reports with government agencies, and additional costs to follow-up on those reports.

A 2004 KPMG survey of 209 banks from around the world revealed that 95 percent of banks surveyed considered anti-money laundering programs to be a high to moderate profile issue among senior management, but the figures varied widely by region.[37] It was ranked very high profile by 88 percent of the respondents in the Middle East, and by 87 percent of the respondents in Latin America, Only 60% of the respondents in Western Europe ranked it high profile, and the figures were less in the Asia-Pacific area (49%) and in Africa (50%).

Egmont Group

The Egmont Group is an informal organization of Financial Intelligence Units (FIUs) from 101countries (as of October 2005) that provide a forum in their fight against money laundering[38] FIUs are national agencies responsible for receiving and, as permitted requesting information concerning the financial proceeds of crime and money laundering, then analyzing and disseminating information to competent authorities.[39] International cooperation is required because of the international nature of money laundering.

---

[37] "Global Anti-Money Laundering Survey 2004: How Banks are Facing Up to the Challenge," KPMG International, 2004.

[38] See the Egmont Group of Financial Intelligence Units website for a listing of countries. http://www1.oecd.org/fatf/Ctry-orgpages/org-egmont_en.htm, or http://www.egmontgroup.org/. Egmont Group was named after Egmont-Arenberg Palace in Brussels where the group first met on June 9, 1995.

[39] "Statement of Purpose of the Egmont Group of Financial Intelligence Units," The Hague, June 13, 2001. Also see: Financial Intelligence Units: An Overview, Washington, D.C., The International Monetary Fund and The World Bank, 2004, 92-93.

Depriving criminals of their profits is the core of anti-money laundering strategies. Because terrorism is not a profit oriented crime, such strategies may not apply directly to terrorism, although financing terrorism may involve large amounts of money. Another issue is that the agencies involved with money laundering are not necessarily the same ones involved in fighting terrorism. Thus, the FIUs are facing some challenges in dealing with such issues.

Wolfsberg Group

This is a private association of twelve global banks, which aims to develop financial services industry standards, and related products, for Know Your Customer, Anti-Money Laundering and Counter Terrorist Financing policies.[40] The global banks are ABN AMRO Bank NV, Banco Santander Central Hispano, S.A., Bank of Tokyo-Mitsubishi, Ltd., Barclays Bank plc, Citigroup, Credit Suisse Group, Deutsche Bank AG, HSBC Holdings plc, J.P. Morgan Chase, Société Générale, and UBS AG. The Group has published anti-money laundering principles dealing with private banking, correspondent banking, financing terrorism, and related topics.

Common Traits of Money Launderers

The money laundering business is usually dominated by professional individual advisors whose laundering businesses are international in scope. Money launderers are generally intelligent, willing to take risks, overconfident, and they have the desire to outwit the system. Their backgrounds are in business, accounting, finance, and law. The leaders tend to specialize in particular fields such as precious metals, jewelry, and import/export. Even those who work as low-level couriers tend to have a good education and frequently have no prior criminal records. Some of the money launderers belong to groups that are bound by ethnic affiliations, nationality, family ties, and business connections. They are motivated by the tax-free profits that come from money laundering. These facts are consistent with the previously mentioned facts that most those convicted of money laundering in 2001 were male (80%), U.S. citizens (77%), 35 years or older (70%), and white (52%). Only about 33% had prior convictions.

High Intensity Financial Crime Area

In accordance with The Money Laundering and Financial Crimes Strategy Act of 1998, the Secretary of the Treasury and the Attorney General designated six High Intensity Financial Crime Areas (HIFCA) where money laundering and financial crimes tend to be

[40] For additional details, see the Wolfsberg website: http://www.wolfsberg-principles.com/

concentrated.[41] These areas also were designated High Intensity Drug Traffic Areas (HIDTAs):

- New York/ New Jersey
- San Juan, Puerto Rico
- Los Angeles
- Miami
- The Southwestern border including Arizona and Texas
- The Northern District of Illinois (Chicago)
- The Northern District of California (San Francisco).

CREATIVE MONEY LAUNDERING

Despite the existence of anti-money laundering laws and enforcement activities, not all financial institutions comply with the laws. To some extent, this is because money laundering is analogous to a balloon that has been squeezed in one place and bulges somewhere else. Thus, as the laws make it more difficult to launder money at banks, the money launderers have turned to "nonbank" financial institutions. These include the following:

- Businesses that exchange money.
- Businesses that wire transfer money, cash checks, sell money orders and traveler's checks.
- Brokers and dealers in art, metals, and jewelry.
- Casinos and gambling establishments (including internet gambling).
- Dealers in automobiles, airplanes, and boats.
- Real estate brokers and dealers.
- Commodity brokers and dealers.
- Professionals such as attorneys and accountants.
- Illegal banking institutions.
- Hawalas (an informal value transfer system, IVTS).

Casinos

There are about 800 casino and card clubs operating in the United States that are regulated by the states and tribal government regulatory authorities. All licensed/authorized casinos operating in the United States (including Puerto Rico, the U.S. Virgin Islands, and Tinian) with gross annual gaming revenue in excess of $1 million are subject to the

---

[41] U.S. General Accounting Office, Combating Money Laundering: Opportunities Exist to Improve the National Strategy, GAO-03-813, September 2003; Motivans (2004); For further discussion of HIFCAs, see FinCEN. Also see P.L. 105-310. http://www.FinCEN.gov/le_hifcadesign.html.

requirements of the BSA in addition to their existing state and tribal government regulations.[42] In some states, *racinos*, or racetracks with slot machines may be classified as casinos[43]

It is estimated that more than $812 billion was wagered at the casinos and card clubs in 2003. Because they are high cash volume businesses, they are vulnerable to manipulation by financial criminals such as money launderers and tax evaders. In addition, they provide other financial services such as check cashing, currency exchange, and transferring funds.

Some methods that can be used to launder money in casinos include, but are not limited to the following:[44]

- Buying chips or tokens with cash. Then not betting, or doing minimal betting and requesting repayment of the remaining funds by check from the casino, or a wire transfer to a bank account; or purchasing gift certificates, or converting the funds into Web currencies.
- Using an international chain of casinos, and asking for credit in a country other than where the funds were originally placed, in the form of a check or bank transfer;
- Asking that a winner's check be made out to a third party, or that it be made out without a nominee.
- Wire transfers or cashier's checks were deposited at Casinos for "front money" to be used by a customer for gambling. But only a small dollar amount was used and the remaining balance was transferred or withdrawn.

FinCEN enforcement actions against casinos usually involve failure to file Currency Transaction Reports by Casinos (CTRC) for currency transactions exceeding $10,000.[45] A partial listing of enforcement actions and civil money penalties (CMP) assessed by the Department of Treasury include:

- Greenville Riverboat, LLC, doing business as (d/b/a) Lighthouse Casino (No. 2003 - 03), CMP $350,000.
- Grand Casinos of Mississippi, Inc. Biloxi (No. CAS-99-007). CMP $160,000
- Riverboat Corporation of Mississippi, (No. CAS-99-005). $150,000
- Biloxi Casino Corp. (d/b/a) Casino Magic, Biloxi (No. CAS 99-02). CMP $145,000.
- Gulfside Casino Partnership (d/b/a) Copa Casino (No. CAS -99-001). CMP $101,000.

It should be noted that dollar amounts required for Suspicious Activity Reports may differ among the Federal bank regulatory agencies. For example, there is no dollar threshold if an insider is involved, but it the suspect cannot be identified it is $25,000. In addition,

[42] William J. Fox, Director, Financial Crimes Enforcement Network, United States Department of Treasury, Statement Before the Senate Committee on Banking, Housing, and Urban Affairs, September 28, 2004.

[43] For additional information about racinos, see: FinCEN, "The SAR Activity Review: Trends, Tips & Issues, Issue 8, April 2005, pp. 19-21.

[44] Financial Intelligence Units: An Overview, Washington, D.C., The International Monetary Fund and The World Bank, 2004, 38; FinCEN, "Suspicious Activities Reported by Casinos," SAR Bulletin, August 2000, Issue 2; FinCEN, "The SAR Activity Review: Trends, Tips & Issues, Issue 8, April 2005, pp 13-14.

[45] See 31 CFR 103.45(c)(1) and 31 CFR 103.55 (c)(1). For additional information, see Federal Register, Vol. 67, No. 187, September 26, 2002, 60722 -60730.

FinCEN's SAR reporting requirements for non-bank financial institutions have different thresholds.[46]

In 1985, the U.S. Department of Treasury made an agreement with the State of Nevada that Casinos in the state at that time were exempt from BSA requirements. The Secretary of Treasury may grant exceptions to any state whose regulatory system meets the reporting and record keeping requirements of this part of the code.

Internet casinos provide a way to transfer funds quickly and inexpensively, both on- and off-shore. Internet casinos are illegal in the United States, but they are legal in Europe and other areas. The 1961 Federal Wire Act, that outlawed betting on sports over state and international lines, makes internet casinos illegal. But some federal courts have ruled that internet casinos are not sports betting.[47] Only five states, (Illinois, Oregon, Nevada, and South Dakota) have laws that prohibit certain aspects of internet gambling, but laws in some other states that prohibit some types of gambling also may be applied to internet gaming.[48]

In 2002, there were about 1,800 internet gambling sites and more than 50 countries and jurisdictions allow internet gambling.[49] Sportingbet PLC claims to be the world's largest online betting and gaming group. It is based in London and the stock is listed on the London Stock Exchange.[50] The Sportingbet website advertises a wide range of sporting events worldwide as well as a casino, poker, backgammon, and games. Other internet casinos are headquartered in Antigua, Costa Rica, and Gibraltar. At the beginning of 2001, Antigua and Barbuda alone had licensed more than 80 internet gaming websites.[51]

One study estimated that internet gambling revenues would soar from about $651 million in 1998 to $3 billion in 2002.[52] Another reported the total number of internet gaming sites in early 2006 was estimated to be 2,400, and their revenue was about $12 billion – double the amount earned in Las Vegas.[53] Finally, a third study claims that online gambling will be worth $22.7 billion in 2009.[54]

Although internet gambling is illegal in the U.S. and for its citizens, the extraterritorial reach of U.S. laws on foreign owned and operated gambling sites is not clear. But it is clear in the U.S. For example, PayPal paid $10 million to settle charges of enabling online betting by transferring funds. And *Sporting News* agreed to a $7.2 million settlement with the government for advertising gambling cites.[55]

---

[46] See 12 CFR 21.11(c).

[47] Kesmodel, David, "Internet Casinos Get Creative With Ads," The Wall Street Journal, March 2, 2005, B2A.

[48] U.S. General Accounting Office, Interim Report on Internet Gambling, GAO-02-1101R, September 23, 2002, p.4; U.S. General Accounting Office, Internet Gambling: An Overview of the Issues, GAO—03-89, December, 2002, p.10.

[49] U.S. General Accounting Office, Internet Gambling: An Overview of the Issues, GAO—03-89, December, 2002, p.2.

[50] Sportingbet., Plc, http://www.sportingbet.com/content/home.asp. SBT is traded on the AIM, which is the London Stock Exchange's Alternative Investment Market for smaller growing companies.

[51] U.S. Department of State, "Money Laundering and Financial Crimes," No date, 9; For additional discussion of internet casinos, Financial Action Task Force on Money Laundering, "2000-2001 Report on Money Laundering Typologies," February 1, 2001.

[52] "Report on Correspondent Banking: A Gateway for Money Laundering," (2001), pp. 24-25; FinCEN, "The SAR Activity Review: Trends, Tips & Issues," Issue 8, April 2005, pp. 41-42; Comptroller of the Currency, OCC Bulletin, Interagency Guidance on Providing Banking Services to Money Services Businesses Operating in the United States, OCC 2005-19, May 6, 2005.

[53] Miller, Mathew, "Catch Me if You Can," Forbes, March 27, 2006, 113 – 125.

[54] Sportingbet., Plc, http://www.sportingbet.com/info/aboutus.asp cited a study by Christiansen Capital Advisors, LLC, 2004 (sited visited 12/25/05)

[55] Miller (2006), op. cit., p. 125.

Finally, internet gambling by using credit cards and offshore banks is used for both money laundering and tax evasion. Although major credit card companies and issuers have tried to block the use of credit and debit cards for gambling, their efforts have been circumvented by customers using on-line payment providers to pay for their gambling activities. On-line payment providers send and receive funds electronically to pay for goods and services. Customers also can pay for gambling using wire transfers and computer e-cash. E-cash exists only in cyberspace and it is used for virtual transactions. E-cash consists of electronic units that can be used in place of currency or credit cards for internet transactions.[56] For example, digital funds can be placed on a smart card or hard drive.

Money Service Business (MSB)

The Bank Secrecy Act/ USA Patriot Act (Sec. 359) defines Money Service Businesses (MSB) to include five distinct types of financial service providers and the U.S. Postal Service:

- Money transmitters,[57]
- Currency dealers or exchangers (*except* those who do not exchange more than $1,000 in currency or other monetary instruments for one person on any day in one or more transactions. A similar exception applies to 3, 4, and 5),
- Check cashers,
- Issuers of traveler's checks, money orders, or stored value.
- Sellers or redeemers of traveler's checks, money orders, or stored value.

Businesses that exchange money (casas de cambio), transfer money (giro houses), and money transmitters (agents of Western Union, American Express, PayPal) provide payment services. They are subject to the same anti-money laundering laws and regulations as banks. However, the activities of many small non-bank financial entities are not regularly supervised or monitored by federal and state authorities. For example, many small casas de cambio and giros do not register in the states in which they operate. Some of these two- and three-person operations are mobile, and they are easily moved from one location to another if they are bothered by authorities.

MSBs are not regulated by Federal Banking Agencies or *de facto* by banking institutions. Nevertheless, banking institutions that open or maintain accounts with MSBs must apply the requirements of the BSA to all of its customers including MSBs.[58] As previously noted, financial institutions are the first line of defense against money laundering.

The services provided by five types of MSBs are complimentary and are often provided by one firm. For example, an individual can take a paycheck and convert it to cash. The cash can be used to purchase money orders to pay bills. Alternatively, the funds can be sent

[56] U.S. General Accounting Office, Internet Gambling: An Overview of the Issues, GAO—03-89, December, 2002, p.33; For additional details about MSBs, see: FinCEN, "The SAR Activity Review: Trend, Tips, & Issues, Issue 10, May 2006.

[57] Fox (2004); Also see 31 CFR 103.11(uu). For additional information, see: FDIC, Bank Secrecy Act: Registration and De-registration of Money Service Businesses, FIL-20-2006, March 1, 2006.

[58] Board of Governors of the Federal Reserve System, "Joint Statement on Providing Banking Services to Money Services Businesses," March 30, 2005.

overseas by a money transmitter. The major point is that all of these services that were traditionally provided by banks, can now be performed by MSBs. A 1997 study that Coopers and Lybrand conducted for FinCEN found that there were more than 158,000 money service business *outlets* (not including U.S. Post Offices), and their financial services were about $200 billion annually.[59] Only 21,058 MSBs were registered with FinCEN as of September 2004. About 80 percent of all money orders are issued by the U.S. Post Office, Western Union, and Traveler's Express/MoneyGram.[60] Small regional companies account for the remainder.

Many MSBs act as agents for large companies such as Western Union and MoneyGram that handles the actual transfer of the funds, especially the larger dollar amounts. For outgoing transfers, the check casher collects the funds and transfer information and receives a fee for its services. For incoming transfers, the check casher pays out the funds. It is estimated that check cashers transfer about $4 billion per year. Other MSBs may be small businesses that provide financial services and unrelated products or services to their customers. Travel agencies, courier services, convenience stores, "mom and pop" grocery stores, and liquor stores are examples of such firms.

Even the big companies have problems with the rules. FinCEN filed an enforcement action against Western Union Financial Services, Inc., Greenwood Village, Colorado (No. 2003-03) for not filing CTRs for transactions greater than $10,000 in a single day.

Next, we examine check cashers and money transmitters that have established bank accounts. A check casher's primary role is to cash payroll and government checks for those who do have regular bank accounts. Many of them operate 24 hours per day, they service non-English speaking populations, there is no client relationship, and immediate funds are available.[61] The Internal Revenue Service (IRS) defines a "check casher is a person engaged in the business of a check casher (other than a person who does not cash checks in an amount greater than $1,000 in currency or monetary or other instruments for any person on any day in one or more transactions). A check casher is a type of money services business, and is regulated by Title 31."[62] The IRS goes on to say that "Multiple currency transactions must be aggregated and a CTR is required, if the entity knows or has reason to know that multiple transactions are by or on behalf of any person and result in either cash in or cash out totaling more than $10,000 in one business (gaming) day."

One way to launder money is for a drug trafficker to buy relatively small money orders and travelers checks from several check cashers, and then deposit them in different banks in order to avoid the CTRs. Thus, the check cashing business is considered a "high risk" business in terms of money laundering. The money orders and travelers checks can pass through many hands, leaving no clear money trail.

---

[59] Fox (2004). The outlets include principal MSBs and their agents. Only the principal MSBs – not their agents – are required to register with FinCEN.

[60] U.S. Department of Treasury (and other U.S. Government agencies, bureaus, and offices), U.S. Money Laundering Threat Assessment, December, 2005, p. 17.

[61] Stahlmann, Chatherine, "Check Cashers and Money Transmitters, Serious Risks or Just Misunderstood?" International Supervision and Regulation, Federal Reserve Bank of Atlanta, May 2003.

[62] "FAQs regarding Check Cashers," Internal Revenue Service, IRS.gov, http://www.irs.gov/govt/tribes/article/0,,id=108295,00.html.

New York, Los Angeles, Dallas, Houston, Phoenix, Tucson, Seattle, and San Juan have been identified as the origin of many money transfers.[63] What is surprising is that a large amount of the funds being laundered thorough MSBs are sent to the Southwest border of the U.S. Cities such as Roma, McAllen, Brownsville, and Dallas are common destinations. In Southern Arizona, $12 dollars are received for every $1 dollar sent. The most common predicate crimes along the Southwest border and narcotics are alien trafficking. From the Southwest border, funds are frequently bulk shipped to the South.

The Wall Street Journal reported that an MSB in Uruguay, called Lespan SA and its affiliates, "moved hundreds of millions of dollars between New York and Uruguay, Paraguay and Brazil at the behest of obscure firms in the British Virgin Islands, a well-known secrecy haven..... The money to have come from a lawless enclave known as the Tri-Border Area, a free-trade zone on the borders of Argentina, Brazil, and Paraguay. The officials say the area is dominated by organized criminal groups including narcotics traffickers and people raising money...for the Lebanese terrorist group Hezbollah."[64] Robert Morganthau, Manhattan District Attorney was investigating banks that participated in the transfers.

Giro Houses

Giro is Spanish for "wire," as in the term wire transfer. Giro's and Casas de Cambios, which are discussed next, are Currency exchangers. A giro house's primary business is to facilitate international business transactions by coordinating and arranging for the transfer of funds between the United State and say Colombia. It is usually done by wire transfer or other electronic means. They also provide other services including cell phones, fax machines, answering services, private postal boxes, and automobiles. Giros are usually located in major cities such (e.g. New York and Houston), operating within other businesses, such as travel agencies.

Suppose that an illegal drug trafficker in the U.S. has $50,000 that he wants to launder through a giro to obtain Colombian pesos. The giro will contact by fax or phone its Colombian counterpart, which has the equivalent amount in pesos that it is willing to convert into dollars. The two giros trade for a small fee that is split between them. In this case, the dollars stay in the U.S. and the pesos in Colombia.

Sometimes the giros deposit laundered funds in U.S. banks. Commercial banks account for most of the wire transfer traffic, both legal and illegal. CHIPS, Clearing House Interbank Payments System, is the bank-owned payments system for clearing and settling large value payments. It processes over 267,000 payments a day with a gross value of over $1.37 trillion.[65] It is a payments platform serving the largest banks from around the world, representing 21 countries world wide.

---

[63] U.S. Department of Treasury (and other U.S. Government agencies, bureaus, and offices), U.S. Money Laundering Threat Assessment, December, 2005, pp. 12-13.

[64] Glen R. Simson, "As Investigations Proliferate, Big Banks Feel Under the Gun," The Wall Street Journal, December 20, 2004, A1, A4. Additional information from is source about MSBs and terrorist financing appears in Chapter 2.

[65] For additional information see the Clearing House Interbank Payments System, http://www.chips.org/

Casas De Cambio

Casas de Cambio are currency exchange houses that specialize in Latin American currencies and transactions, and more than 1,000 of them are along the Southwest border.[66] They can lauder as much as $5 million per month for drug traffickers. Some are run out of cars and telephone booths, making them difficult to catch.

Money laundering schemes involving casas de cambio can be simple. For example, an illegal trafficker gives the owner of a casa de cambio $100,000 to launder. The owner deposits that amount in the name of the company in a commercial bank. The bank fills out the required CTR, listing the casa de cambio as the owner of the funds. This breaks the like between the trafficker and the money because most casa de cambios do not keep records of where they got their cash, and the bank records the cambio as the owner. Once the funds have been deposited in a commercial bank, they can be wire transferred anywhere in the world. The laundering is complete because the CTRs are not required on wire transfers.

Some illegal drug traffickers use "smurfs'' to smuggle U.S. currency into Mexico. It is unlikely that they will be stopped at the border when going South. On the return trip, the smurfs file Custom's CMIR forms asserting that the money was earned in a legitimate business activity in Mexico. Now the funds can be deposited in a commercial bank for wire transfer to other destinations.

An alternative is to deposit the funds in a casa de cambio in Mexico and have the funds deposited in a Mexican bank, and then transferred to the U.S. The funds can then be used to purchase real estate in the name of a nominee of the drug trafficker. There, there would be no records in the U.S. linking the drug trafficker to the laundered money.

On January 12, 2005, the U.S. Department of Treasury identified 15 companies and 24 individuals associated with Arellano Felix Organization, a violent drug trafficking ring operating out of Mexico.[67] Over a three year period, the cell laundered more than $120 million in proceeds from the sale of narcotics.

The money laundering scheme centered on the use of casas de cambio. These front houses were used to launder the U.S. currency obtained from narcotics sales in the U.S. and bulk smuggled into Mexico. In addition to casas de cambio, the ring also used a pawn shop, a restaurant and bar, and a restaurant and bar supply company, all located in Tijuana, Mexico.

Against this background, the following financial institutions are required to comply with the various BSA/AML programs. In addition to financial institutions that must comply with the BSA/AML programs, "*dealers*" who have bought and sold at least $50,000 in *precious metals, stones or jewels* in the previous year are required to establish anti-money laundering programs.[68] Most "retailers" are not required to establish anti-money laundering programs.

As previously noted, not all financial institutions comply with the BSA/AML programs as evidenced by numerous and continuous enforcement actions by bank regulators. "The Federal Reserve takes formal *enforcement actions* against the above entities for violations of

---

[66] U.S. Department of Treasury (and other U.S. Government agencies, bureaus, and offices), U.S. Money Laundering Threat Assessment, December, 2005, p. 15.

[67] U.S. Department of Treasury, "Treasury Designates Mexican Money Laundering Cell," Press Release JS-2191, January 12, 2005. http://www.treas.gov/press/releases/js2191.htm

[68] FinCENnews, "Dealers in Precious Metals, Stones or Jewels Required to Establish Anti-Money Laundering Programs," June 3 2005. For additional details, see the "Interim Final Rule," and "Frequently Asked Questions" concerning the Rule.

laws, rules, or regulations, unsafe or unsound practices, breaches of fiduciary duty, and violations of final orders. Formal enforcement actions include Cease and Desist orders, written agreements, removal and prohibition orders, and orders assessing civil money penalties"[69]

TOOLS OF THE TRADE

Bearer Securities

The Financial Action Task Force on Money Laundering (FAFT) reports that bearer checks and securities are used in some money laundering schemes.[70] Bearer bonds and stocks are examples of such securities. There is no owner of record in the case of bearer securities or checks. In an investigation involving the importation of $1.7 million in illicit drugs, investigators found bearer shares in three off-shore companies that were used in the money laundering scheme. The names of the shareholders were not required to be registered at the corporate registry office or anywhere else. The only names on the articles of incorporation were the names of the original incorporators, the names of nominee directors and officers, and the lawyer who set it up. The use of professional intermediaries, such as lawyers, and bearer shares provided absolute anonymity to the holders of those shares, and were a power tool in concealing the proceeds of the crimes.

Bearer checks are negotiable instruments payable to the holder of that instrument when it is presented at a financial institution. The financial institution is not obligated to verify the identity of the holder unless the transaction exceeds a certain threshold.[71] Also, a non-bearer check becomes a bearer check when the original payee endorses it. Finally, *bank drafts*, or "*certified or registered* "*checks* in the U.S., also have been used in money laundering schemes. Certified checks are an unconditional order to pay a fixed amount to the named party.

Travelers checks have been used to launder money. The cases have involved large cash purchases of traveler's checks which are used to reduce the bulk of cash movements overseas. In addition, they have been used to purchase high value item, and as direct payment for narcotics or contraband.

Bulk Cash, Precious Stones, and Gold

U.S. dollars are an internationally accepted currency, and they can be converted into foreign currencies. Cash is bulky and heavy. It is commonly shipped across borders in containers, vehicles, and aircraft.

---

[69] Board of Governors of the Federal Reserve System, "Federal Reserve Enforcement Actions," September 19, 2002. http://www.federalreserve.gov/boarddocs/enforcement/

[70] Financial Action Task Force on Money Laundering, "Report on Money Laundering Typologies, 2001-2002," February 1, 2002, 15.

[71] Article 5, Convention on the uniform law of checques, Geneva, March 19, 1931.

Nevertheless, some cash couriers prefer commercial airliners because they can reach foreign destinations quickly, and little preplanning is involved. Others prefer sending it by mail.[72]

The major advantages of smuggling bulk cash is that there is no "paper trail" associated with it, and no financial institutions to report on it. The disadvantages are the costs and risks associated with transferring large amounts of cash across border. Between October 2001 and August 2003, The Bureau of Immigration and Custom's Enforcement's (ICE) Operation Oasis resulted in the seizure of more than $28 million in bulk cash. Another risk is theft by the couriers.

Precious stones, such as diamonds are used in lieu of cash in arms deals, money laundering, and financing terrorism because they are small, and easy to smuggle. In 2002, a pound of diamonds was worth about $225,000, while a pound of cash was worth $45,000 and a pound of gold was worth $4,800.[73] Antwerp, is the world's largest trading center were diamonds are sold on the black market, and no records are kept.

In the 1990s, al Qaeda had set up diamond mining and trading companies, was reportedly buying diamonds from rebel groups in Kenya and Tanzania, and they did diamond trading in Sierra Leone.[74] They also reportedly bought diamonds from rebel groups in Africa prior to the September 11 attacks on the United States.

Gold serves as both a commodity and a medium of exchange in laundering funds between Latin America, the U.S., and Europe. In this cycle, gold bullion from Switzerland is sent to Italy where it is made into jewelry which is then shipped to Latin America.[75] There it is used as a commodity, like electronic equipment and consumer goods, as part of the Black Market Peso Exchange which is explained in Chapter 3. In addition, gold can be smelted into many forms to disguise the metal, and then smuggled across borders. For example, gold can be molded into tools, belt buckles, light switches, etc. Like diamonds, gold leave no paper trails.

False Invoicing

In some cases, money launderers involved in buying and selling goods overseas may use over invoicing to balance books or move assets. For example, if a container of goods is worth $100,000 and it invoiced for $175,000, the payment will facilitate the illegal movement of $75,000 across borders.

Stored Value Cards

Stored value and prepaid cards operate in "open" and "closed" systems. Open systems can be used at automated teller machines (ATMs), and do not require a bank account. Closed

---

72 Financial Action Task Force on Money Laundering, Detecting and Preventing Cross-Border Transportation of Cash by Terrorists and Other Criminals, International Best Practices, February 12, 2005.

73 U.S. General Accounting Office, Terrorist Financing: U.S. Agencies Should Systematically Assess Terrorists' Use of Alternative Financing Mechanisms," GAO v4-163, November, 2003, p. 20.

74 Ibid. p. 21.

75 Financial Action Task Force on Money Laundering, "1998-1999 Report on Money Laundering Typologies," February 10, 1999, p.10.

systems can only be used with a select group of merchants, such as using a gift card. Open stored value cards have been used in connection with bulk cash smuggling (See Box 1-3). The drug dealers load cash on to an open/prepaid cash card, and then send the card to their overseas suppliers. The funds can then be withdrawn from local ATMs.[76]

Box 1-3
Bulk Cash Smuggling

In August 2002, the Mississippi Highway Patrol stopped a new Porsche Boxer, with temporary Mexican registration. The driver, Jorge Javier Magallanes-Vallarreal, was on his way back to Mexico. He gave the Highway Patrol permission to search the car, and they discovered a storage area under the hood. It contained $1,103,125 dollars stacked in plastic wraps with the dollar amounts written on the outside. The car had been brought into the U.S. containing a controlled substance in the storage area under the hood. The following day, another Porsche Boxer with temporary Mexican registration was stopped in Mississippi, and it contained 55.6 kilograms of cocaine.

In October 2002, Magallanes-Vallarreal pled guilty to bulk cash smuggling in or out of the United States, and was sentenced to 42 months in Federal Prison.

Source: U.S. Department of State, "International Narcotics Control Strategy Report – 2003, Released by the Bureau for International Narcotics and Law Enforcement Affairs, March 2004.

Online/Digital Payments

PayPal is registered as an MSB, and it is the largest online payment system. In addition, there are other online systems are "digital currency" dealers. Some of them purportedly use gold, silver, platinum, and other precious metals as a store of value for their online transactions. The best known digital currency system is "e-gold, Ltd," which has about 2 million customers.[77] It is licensed in Nevis, a small island that lies near the top of the Lesser Antilles archipelago, about 200 miles south of Puerto Rico. Nevis does not adhere to our BSA/AML laws. Because E-gold's monetary payment system operator – Gold and Silver Reserve, Inc., d/b/a Omnipay – operated as an "unlicensed money transmitter business," the U.S. District Court for the District of Columbia authorized the seizure $815,625 of their funds.[78] Gold and Silver Reserve, Inc. claim that they did nothing wrong and sought to reclaim their funds.

WebMoney, based in Moscow, USSR, is another large digital currency system that claims to have more than 1 million customers.[79] Digital currency systems can send funds

[76] U.S. Department of Treasury (and other U.S. Government agencies, bureaus, and offices), U.S. Money Laundering Threat Assessment, December, 2005. p. 21.

[77] Ibid. pp 25-26.

[78] U.S. District Court for the District of Columbia, United States of America v. All funds seized from or on deposit in SunTrust account number xxxxx8359, in the name of Gold and Silver Reserve, Inc., and al funds on deposit in Regions Bank account number xxxxx4851 in the name of Gold and Silver Reserve, Inc., filed 13/30/2005.

[79] Grow, Brian, and Bryon MacWilliams, "OnLine Extra: WebMoney and its Customers," BusinessWeek Online, Investigative Report, January 9, 2006.

anywhere throughout the world, and they are "becoming the currency of choice for cybercrooks."[80]

Lawyers, Accountants and Other Professionals

Lawyers, accountants, and other professionals provide valuable services in organizing and managing the financial affairs. As financial experts, or "gatekeepers," they are sought after by organized crime groups and criminals to facilitate laundering money. Their status as gatekeepers provides a veneer of legitimacy to their operations. By way of illustration, a 71 year-old lawyer, who was known and respected as an international lawyer, a good neighbor, and president of his church parish was also part of a money laundering network that involved Colombians.[81] When a Los Angeles County SWAT team executed a search and arrest warrant and entered the bedroom of his home, the attorney fired a 9-millemeter handgun at them. They returned fire and he was mortally wounded. He had 61 weapons and $450,000 in cash in his house, as well as files on money laundering and drug dealers. His money laundering scheme used front businesses, including a liquor store. Money generated from the sale of drugs was used to cash customer's checks, which were then deposited in the store's bank account. Those funds were then wire transferred to Colombia. The liquor store laundered $1.85 million, and his other businesses laundered over $5 million. The scheme was brought to the attention of law enforcement authorities when the bank became suspicious of the transactions.

Gary S. Kimmel, a Chicago dentist, provides another example.[82] He was indicted on federal money laundering charges linking him to a nationwide prostitution ring. He allegedly accepted $405,000 from two pimps to buy, finance, insure and maintain about a dozen luxury cars in connection with their prostitution activities. The money laundering count of the indictment alleges that Kimmel attempted to conceal the fact that the cars were for a pimp, Robert Lewis Young, and several prostitutes by making false statements to credit companies, insurance companies, and law enforcement officials concerning his relationship with Young and his role with the cars. The indictment also alleges that Kimmel accepted cash for dental care on some pimps and prostitutes, and did not report the payments as income to his dental practice.

---

[80] Grow, Brian, John Cady, Susann Rutledge, and David Polek, "Gold Rush," Business Week, January 9, 2006, p. 69.

[81] U. S. Senate, Current Trends in Money Laundering, Report prepared for the Permanent Subcommittee on Investigations of the Committee on Government Affairs, 102nd Cong., 2nd Sess. S. Hrg. 102-579, February 27, 1992, pp 169-70, 437-444.

[82] U.S. Department of Justice United States Attorney Northern District of Illinois, "U.S. Indicts Chicago Dentist Allegedly Linked to Providing Luxury Autos and Marina Towers Condos to Nationwide Prostitution Ring," January 18, 2005.

Correspondent Banks

Correspondent banking is one bank (the correspondent bank) providing services to another bank (the respondent bank).[83]

Large banks may act as correspondent banks for thousands of other banks around the word where the respondent banks have no physical presence. The correspondent banks provide a wide range of banking services in both domestic and international markets. Such services may include cash management services, letters of credit, wire transfers, and so on.

In essence, correspondent banks carry out financial transactions for the customers of the respondent bank. The basic issue is that the correspondent bank may not have first hand knowledge of those customers, and it must rely on the respondent bank for the due diligence evaluation. This becomes a problem when the foreign correspondent bank does not vigorously apply anti-money laundering standards or internal controls. The existence of sub-respondents – in which case the respondent bank is a correspondent bank for another respondent – complicates the matter further.

The degree of due diligence exercised by some correspondent banks depends on whether they extend credit or provide services for a fee. Greater due diligence is more commonly extended with credit services than with fee based services such as wire transfers. Nevertheless, enhanced due diligence is required when "high-risk" foreign banks are involved. High-risk foreign banks are those operating under an offshore banking license, or under a license granted specially designated countries.

FinCEN had an enforcement action against Hartsfield Capital Securities, Inc. of Alpharetta Georgia.[84] FinCEN determined that Hartsfield Capital Securities – a broker dealer - failed to take reasonable actions to prevent foreign shell banks from indirectly using correspondent accounts at Hartsfield. The bank was assessed a CMP of $10,000 and required to either close ten correspondent accounts, or obtain complete certification and documentation concerning them.

More will be said about correspondent and private banking in Chapter 5.

Private Banking

Private banking is the term used for "preferential treatment and services" given to high net worth individuals. In some cases these are "politically exposed persons" (PEPs) who are public figures including heads of states, politicians, senior executives of corporations, and political figures. For example, Raul Salinas, brother of Carlos Salinas who was the former president of Mexico, transferred $90 to $100 millions of dollars in alleged public corruption money though Citibank accounts.[85]

---

[83] Financial Action Task Force on Money Laundering, "Report on Money Laundering Typologies, 2001-2002," (2002), Chapter 2.

[84] FinCEN Enforcement Action in the matter of Hartsfield Capital Securities, Inc., No. 2003-05.

[85] National Commission on Terrorist Attacks Upon the United States, Monograph on Terrorist Financing, 2004, Chapter 4, 54; U.S. General Accounting Office, Private Banking: Raul Salinas, Citibank, and Alleged Money Laundering, Statement for the Record of Robert H. Hast, Acting Assistant Comptroller General for Investigations, Office of Special Investigations, Testimony Before the Permanent Subcommittee on Investigations, Committee on Governmental Affairs, U.S. Senate, GAO/T-OSI-003, November 9, 1999. See Chapter 4 for additional details.

Criminals and PEPs may seek out private banking services to facilitate the laundering of their illicit assets. In addition, they may use relatives or other government officials to set up bank accounts for them to launder their illicit funds. Thus, private banks that fail to apply due diligence could find itself in trouble.

In October 2000, a group of 11 international banks agreed to "Global Anti-Money-Laundering Guidelines for Private Banking" operations called the "Wolfsberg AML Principles."[86] These banks include ABN AMRO Bank NV; Banco Santander Central Hispano,SA; Barclays Bank; Chase Manhattan Corporation; Citibank, NA; Credit Suisse Group; Deutsche Bank AG;; HSBC; J. P. Morgan Inc.; Société Générale; and UBS AG. Some of these same organizations received enforcement actions by bank regulators for AML/BSA violations in other banking areas. In July 2004, ABN AMRO reached an agreement with the Federal Reserve to shed some of its correspondent relationships with certain banks in Eastern Europe and Russia. J. P. Morgan Chase transferred millions of dollars in connection with an al Qaeda fund raising operation.[87]

MONEY LAUNDERING RED FLAGS

Red flags are warning signs that a potential problem exists. The Office of the Comptroller of the Currency (OCC) has published several lists of red flags that bankers should look for in connection with money laundering.[88]

The existence of red flags does not mean that money laundering is occurring, but it may be one explanation for the unusual activities.

1. *Activities not consistent with the customer's business.* One example is a retail business that deposits large dollar volumes of checks, but does not withdraw sufficient cash to run that business. Another example when the currency transactions of a business show a sudden change that is inconsistent with the firm's normal pattern of transactions.
2. *Unusual characteristics.* Unusual characteristics include accounts outside the bank's normal service area. For example, the accounts may have foreign addresses in Colombia, Luxembourg, etc.
3. *Attempts to avoid reporting and or record keeping requirements.* The customer makes frequent deposits of cash just below the CTR reporting thresholds. The customer is reluctant to provide information, or they provide insufficient or suspicious information needed to file mandatory reports or to open accounts.
4. *Unusual funds transfer activities.* Wire transfer activity to or from high risk foreign countries without any apparent business reason.
5. *Bank employees.* Sudden changes in lifestyle of certain bank employees may not be due to winning the Florida lottery. In addition, employees who are not willing to take vacations may have sinister reasons for not doing so.

---

[86] Wolfsberg is the location in Switzerland where the guidelines were formulated in October, 30, 2000.

[87] Simson, Glen R., "As Investigations Proliferate, Big Banks Feel Under the Gun," The Wall Street Journal, December 20, 2004, A1, A4.

[88] Money Laundering: A Bankers Guide to Avoiding Problems, (2002); Also December 2002; Comptroller of the Currency, "A Pocket Guide to Detecting Red Flags in Board Reports," October, 2003.

6. *Changes in bank transactions.* Significant changes in currency shipment patterns between correspondent banks, or increases in the amount of cash handled with no increase in non-cash deposits are reasons to be suspicious.
7. *Other suspicious customer activity.* Frequent exchanges of small dollar denominations for larger denominations. Suspicious movement of funds from one domestic and or foreign bank to another in a short period of time.
8. The volume of SARS or CTRs is very high, or very low.
9. Inadequate training of bank personnel on the BSA and how to identify possible suspicious activity.
10. The bank acquires large deposit relationships, but bank management is not familiar with the depositor's business or line of work.

Along the same line of reasoning as red flags, money laundering most likely occurs in:[89]

1. High-intensity drug trafficking and/or high-intensity financial crime areas.
2. Where there are excessive currency flows.
3. Where there is significant international, private banking, fiduciary, and other high-risk activities.
4. Where there are unusual SAR/CTR reporting patterns.
5. Where there are funds transfers or account relationships with drug source countries, or countries with less stringent secrecy laws.

Regulatory and Law Enforcement

Bank regulators take BSA/AML offenses seriously, and have assessed large civil money penalties (CMP) on various banks (see Table 1). The fact that the fines and penalties applied to foreign banks reveals the "extraterritorial jurisdiction" of the BSA/AML laws. In addition, they also required banks to cease certain lines of business. For example, UBS bank, Zurich Switzerland, lost a profitable contract to act as a custodian for U.S. currency (extended custodial inventory, ECI). Similarly, the Financial Services Agency of Japan required Citibank to close its private banking operations in Japan due to poor AML practices and other misconduct. Finally, Arab Bank, PLC was required to close their branch bank in New York when it was revealed that they had deficiencies in the BSA/AML compliance in connection with wire transfers.

Law enforcement officials also take money laundering seriously. Between 1994-2001, 18,500 defendants were charged in U.S. District courts with money laundering and other offenses. They violated the Bank Secrecy Act of 1970 (monetary record and reporting violations) and the Money Laundering and Control Act of 1986 (prohibits criminal activity that generates the funds used in laundering). Of that total number of defendants, money

[89] Stipano, Daniel P., Deputy Counsel, OCC, Testimony Before the Subcommittee on Oversight and Investigations of the Committee on Financial Services, U.S. House of Representatives, June 2, 2004.

laundering was the most serious offense in 10,610 cases, and 9,169 defendants were convicted.[90]

Table 1.1. Large Fines and Penalties

Banks	Fines and Penalties	Case Discussed in Chapter #
UBS, AG, Switzerland	$100 million CMP Lost ECI contract	4
ABN AMRO Bank N.V.	$80 million CMP, Improve internal controls	4
AmSouth Bank	$50 million CMP	6
Riggs Bank N.A.	$25 million CMP $16 million (criminal, U.S.) $8 million (Spain)	5
Citibank	Closed private bank in Japan	1 also see 5
Arab Bank PLC, Jordon	Closed U.S branch, $24 mill CMP	4

In 2001, there were 1,420 money laundering cases. Of that total, 1,243 defendants were convicted of money laundering/racketeering offenses where the amounts ranged from less than $2,000 to more than $100 million.[91] About 20% of the cases involved less than $1 million.

Offenders may face penalties of up to 20 years in jail, and fines up to $500,000, or twice the value of the property involved. In addition, the may be criminal and civil forfeiture of the value of the property or funds involved in the transaction. For example, Antonio Giraldi, a former private banker to American Express, Bankers Trust, and Citibank, was convicted of money laundering because of his willful blindness to the fact that his client was a drug trafficker. He was sentenced to 10 years in jail.[92]

More than 98% of those convicted in 2001 were individuals rather than commercial defendants. The 22 convicted commercial defendants included auto dealerships, grocery stores, banks, furniture stores, construction firms, and beauty shops.

About 75% of the convicted defendants received a prison term that averaged 4 years. Offenders of the money laundering laws face prison terms up to 20 years and fines. Most of those convicted were male (80%), U.S. citizens (77%), 35 years or older (70%), and white (52%). Only about 33% had prior convictions.

The most shocking statistics about the convictions are that in 2001, financial institutions monetary record and reporting offenses accounted for 16% of the money laundering violations --- the same percentage as drug trafficking. Various laws require financial institutions to report cash transactions involving $10,000 or more, to report suspicious

[90] U.S. Department of Justice, Mark Motivans, "Money Laundering Offenders, 1994-2001," Bureau of Justice Statistics, Special Report, July 2003; U.S. Department of Justice, Bureau of Justice Statistics, Press Release, "Over 18,000 Charged with Federal Money Laundering From 1994 Through 2001," July 17, 2003.

[91] U.S. Department of Justice, Motivans (2003), where money laundering offenses are defined in Title 18 (Chapter 95, Racketeering), and Title 31 (Chapter 53, Monetary Transactions) of the Federal Criminal code. See 18 U.S.C. 1956, 1957, 1960, and 31 U.S.C. 5313, 5324.

[92] United States Senate, Permanent Subcommittee on Investigations, Committee on Governmental Affairs, "Private Banking and Money Laundering: A Case Study of Opportunities and Vulnerabilities," S. Hrg. 106-428, November 9, 10, 1999, p. 90.

activities, and they cannot engage in transactions with prohibited persons. One possible explanation of why financial institutions offenses are so high, is that many institutions provide ineffective training in recognizing suspicious activities related to money laundering.[93]

Finally, as previously noted, tax evasion and money laundering are closely linked in the United States. In 2004, The Internal Revenue Service reported that 687 individuals were sentenced to jail with 63 months average time to sever.[94] The incarceration rate was 89.1%.

93 "Report on Correspondent Banking: A Gateway for Money Laundering," Minority Staff of the Permanent Subcommittee on Investigations, U.S. Senate Committee on Governmental Affairs, February 5, 2001, p. 33.

94 U.S. Department of the Treasury, Internal Revenue Service, "Criminal Enforcement: Statistical Data-Money Laundering Enforcement." http://www.irs.gov/compliance/enforcement/article/0,,id=113002,00.html

Chapter 2

FINANCING TERRORISM

Terrorism can be defined as premeditated, politically motivated violence perpetrated against noncombatant targets by sub-national groups or clandestine agents, usually intended to influence an audience.[1] Terrorist groups are motivated by domestic and international politics, social causes, and extreme religious beliefs, Thus terrorism is a complex and diverse phenomenon.[2]

International terrorism refers to citizens in more than one country, and a *terrorist group* refers to any group or subgroup that practices international terrorism. The acts have to be "significant," causing death or injury or damage in excess of $10,000. Terrorism is a tactic to achieve some goal, such as destabilizing a government, economic disruption, or promoting extremist political or religious beliefs. The Red Brigades and Bader-Meinhof gang in Europe, Marxist guerrillas in Latin America, and al Qaeda in Pakistan and elsewhere in the Middle East and worldwide, are examples of terrorist groups. The U.S. Department of State's *Patterns of Global Terrorism, 2003* listed 21 terrorist attacks in that year alone.[3] Specific examples of terrorist attacks include, but are not limited to the following:[4]

- Iran Embassy Hostages, 1979;
- Beirut, Lebanon Embassy 1983;
- Beirut, Lebanon Marine Barracks 1983;
- Lockerbie, Scotland Pan-Am flight to New York 1988;
- First New York World Trade Center attack 1993;
- Riyadh, Saudi Arabia, Military facilities, 1995;
- Dhahran, Saudi Arabia Khobar Towers Military complex 1996;

---

[1] These definitions appear in Title 22 U.S.C. 2656f(d), and were adapted from "Patterns of Global Terrorism 2003," United States Department of State, April 2003. xii; Noncombatant includes civilians and military personnel who were not on duty or were unarmed at the time of the terrorist incidents.

[2] For a discussion of the psychology of terrorism, see Post, Jerold M, "Psychology," appears in Confronting Terrorism: The Club de Madrid Series on Democracy and Terrorism, Volume I; The International Summit on Democracy, Terrorism and Security, Madrid, Spain, March 8-11, 2005,

[3] U.S. Department of State, Patterns of Global Terrorism 2003, 2004, http://www.state.gov/s/ct/rls/pgtrpt/2003/ This annual report provides profiles of the major terrorist organizations, incidents, and other useful information.

[4] For a listing of more than al Qaeda terrorist attacks, see "List of Al Qaeda Inspired Attacks Released," Directgov, July 13, 2005, www.direct.gov.uk/output/Page7930.asp.

- Nairobi, Kenya US Embassy 1998;
- Dares Salaam, Tanzania US Embassy 1998;
- Aden, Yemen USS Cole 2000;
- New York World Trade Center 2001;
- Pentagon 2001;
- Bali, Indonesia, U.S. Consulate, Clubs, 2002;
- Casablanca, Morocco, Spanish Club, Hotels, 2003;
- Riyadh, Saudi Arabia, Military housing compound, 2003;
- Madrid, Spain, Trains, 2004;
- London, England, Train, 2005;
- Amman, Jordan, Hotel, 2005

The USA Patriot Act of 2001 and the Suppression of the Financing of Terrorism Convention Implementation Act of 2002 makes it a crime to provide or collect funds with the intention of funding terrorist activities.[5] Terrorism depends on three major factors: recruitment, indoctrination, and financing.[6] Reducing the financing to terrorist organizations may disrupt their organizations and lessen their chances for success. Unfortunately, most terrorist acts are low-cost which makes them difficult to detect.

Box 2-1
Problems Defining International Terrorism

By definition, some horrific acts are not considered to be "international terrorism," because all of the participants are from the same country. For example, in 2004, someone from the Abu Sayyaf Group in the Philippines, a terrorist group, sank a Superferry boat killing more than 100 people. Because the perpetrator and the victims were all Filipino, the act was not considered "international terrorism." Similarly, two Chechen suicide bombers blew up two Aeroflot flights. One flight contained all Russian citizens, and that act did not qualify as an international terrorist act. The other flight had Russians and one Israeli citizen onboard, and it did qualify as an international terrorist act.

The acts also have to be "significant." On two separate occasions, bombs exploded outside four HSBC banks in Turkey on the same day. However, since no single bomb caused more than $10,000 in damage, the attacks were not considered significant.

Source: U.S. Department of State, Philip Zelikow, Counselor for the Department; John Brennan, National Counterterrorism Center Interim Director, "Remarks on Release of 'Country Reports on Terrorism' for 2004, April 27, 2005.

Terrorism is an international phenomenon, and many nations around the world are cooperating in the fight against it. In the previous chapter, the section on "International

[5] Public Law No. 107-197, title II (June 25, 2002); 18 U.S.C. 2339C(a)(1)

[6] Testimony of Steven Emerson, U.S. Senate, Committee on Governmental Affairs, "Terrorism Financing: Origination, Organization, and Prevention," S. Hrg. 108-245, July 31, 2003, p. 132.

Cooperation" listed the countries involved with the Financial Action Task Force and other international bodies fighting money laundering and terrorism. It follows that new laws and regulations are being enacted. For example, September 2005, the Council of the European Union endorsed a "Directive on Money Laundering and Terrorist Financing."[7] It involves individuals who sell goods for cash of €15,000 or more, and it applies to financial institutions, auditors, accountants, tax advisors, lawyers, company service providers, real estate agents, and casinos.

Demographics

Terrorist groups are frequently associated with countries that have low income per capita, high infant mortality, a large "youth bulge" (unemployed youths), and the absence of political freedoms and participatory government.[8] Many of these nations are in the Muslim world – Pakistan, Iran, Sudan, Syria, etc. They have a potentially large labor force, but no jobs. Demographic projections suggest that rural workers will continue to flow into cities to create mega cities with populations greater than 5 million, and most of that growth will be in developing nations. While some cities may be vibrant commercial centers, others will be crime zones and ripe for the development of terrorist groups. Examples of the later group include Mumbai, Dhaka, Karachi, Manila, Jakarta, and Lagos.[9] Along this line, Lagos Nigeria is considered a hub for money laundering and financial crimes. They are best known for advanced fee frauds that were described in Chapter 1.

In one sense, terrorism can be seen as a battle between the haves and have nots. The U.S. and other large, prosperous industrialized states are the "haves." Robert Hutchings (January 12, 2004), Chairman of the National Intelligence Council, said "The terrorists and their supporters rage against the inequities and degradation brought on by globalization." Nevertheless, the leaders of some of the terrorist groups are wealthy, educated individuals, such as Osama bin Landen.

Terrorism also occurs in connection with the *propagation of Islamic extremism*. This refers to "the spread of Islamic ideology that denies the legitimacy of nonbelievers and practitioners of other forms of Islam and that explicitly promotes hatred, intolerance, and violence that could lead to future terrorist activities that threaten U.S. national security interests."[10] For example, the World Assembly of Muslim Youth (WAMY) promoted the view that Islam is a religion of jihad, and that they should teach their youngsters to love taking revenge on the Jews and other oppressors.[11] More will be said about WAMY later in this chapter. Similarly, a Saudi government appointed imam called Jews the "scum of the

---

7 Council of the European Union, "Directive on Money Laundering and Terrorist Financing," September 20, 2005 (Presse 240), http://ue.eu.int/ueDocs/cms_Data/docs/pressData/en/misc/86283.pdf

8 Hutchings, Robert L., Chairman, National Intelligence Council, "Terrorism and Economic Security," Speech before the International Security Management Association, Scottsdale, AZ, January 14, 2004.

9 For a discussion of demographic trends, see: Laudicina, Paul A, *World Out of Balance: Navigating Global Risks to Seize Competitive Advantage,*" New York, McGraw-Hill, 2005.

10 U.S. General Accounting Office, International Affairs: Information on U.S. Agencies' Efforts to Address Islamic Extremism, GAO-05-853, September 2005, Footnote 5.

11 Emerson, Steven, "Saudi Arabia: Friend or Foe in the War on Terror," Testimony before the U.S. Senate Judiciary Committee, November 8, 2005.

earth" who should be annihilated. He also referred to other enemies of Islam as "worshippers of the cross" and idol worshipping Hindus."[12] The imam also said that Muslims worldwide should "defeat all their occupiers and oppressors"[13]

Small Groups and Their Supporters

Unlike a traditional ground war where large armies face each other, terrorists can and do carryout their activities worldwide using a few individuals to do their dirty work.[14] The September 11, 2001 terrorist attacks by al Qaeda, the Lebanese Hezbollah attacks against Jewish targets in Argentina, Algerians hijacking a French airliner, and the Kurdistan Workers Party (a.k.a. PPK) attacks on Turkish targets in Europe are just a few such examples of international terrorism. Finally, the 1993 truck bombing of the World Trade Center was carried out by a local terrorist, Ramzi Yousef, and his associates – not by an international group.[15]

Al Qaeda, for example, has been described as a coalition of various groups rather than a unified group; and that it is this diversity that gives al Qaeda its global reach. For example, the following incomplete list includes groups that have been or are part of the al Qaeda coalition:[16]

- the Islamic Group and Al Jihad (Egypt)
- the Armed Islamic Group and the Salafist Group for Call and Combat (Algeria)
- the Islamic Movement of Uzbekistan
- the Jemaah Islamiyah (Indonesia)
- the Lybian Islamic Fighting Group (Libya)
- Harakat-ul-Mujahedin, Jaish-e-Mohammed, Lashkar-e-Tayyiba, and Lashkar-e-Jhangvi (Kashmir and Pakistan)
- Asbat al-Ansar (Lebanon).

Some 350 terrorist entities and individuals were designated by President George W. Bush under Executive Order 13224 (Executive Order on Terrorist Financing: Blocking Property and Prohibiting Transactions With Persons Who Commit, Threaten to Commit, or Support Terrorism) to freeze their U.S. based assets, as well as the assets of those who provide financial support to them.[17] As of December, 2004, more than more than 387 individuals and

---

[12] Ibid.

[13] Ibid.

[14] Pillar, Paul, "Fighting International Terrorism: Beyond September 11th," National Intelligence Council, November 28, 2001.

[15] After the bombing of the World Trade Center, Ramzi Yousef fled to Manila and then to Pakistan where he was captured. Evidence from Manila and Pakistan revealed the he was planning to launch a wave of attacks on the U.S., by putting twelve bombs on airliners. For additional details about him, see Garcia, Michael J., Assistant Secretary for Immigration and Customs Enforcement, "Meeting the Threat: A Symposium on Counter-Terrorism, " Duke University Law School, February 4, 2004.

[16] Katzman, Kenneth, "Al Qaeda: Profile and Threat Assessment," CRS Report for Congress, August 17, 2005. This source provides an interesting history of al Qaeda, and Osama bin Laden.

[17] To view Executive Order 13224, see: http://www.whitehouse.gov/news/releases/2001/09/print/20010924-1.html

entities have been designated under EO 12334, and more than $200 million in terrorist related funds have been seized and frozen.[18] The blocking of terrorist's assets helps to disrupt the flow of funds to terrorist organizations. It also discourages those who might help finance terrorism because they might be considered part of the "money trail."

Similarly, the United Nations 1267 Sanctions Committee has a list of designated terrorists which requires all member states and regional organizations to freeze their assets, block their travel, and the sales of arms and military equipment.[19] The U.N. Security Council established the 1267 Committee, under Resolution 1267 (1999) concerning al Qaeda and the Taliban and associated individuals and entities.

In addition to the Specially Designated Global Terrorists, seven countries were designated in 2001 as state sponsors of terrorism: Cuba, Iran, Iraq, Libya, North Korea, Sudan, and Syria. Sanctions against Iraq have been suspended.

Financial transactions involving terrorism are illegal because the intent is for funds to be used to finance terrorism which is illegal.[20] Financing terrorism is not a profit-motivated crime – it is politically motivated. Financing terrorism involves both legitimate and illegitimate sources of financing, which is a key difference between it and traditional money laundering.[21]

Funding terrorist attacks does not always require large sums, and the transactions may not be complex. The financial connections between the September 11th hijackers and their foreign accounts showed that most of the individual transactions were small sums (e.g. less than $10,000), and consisted of a few wire transfers. The individuals were ostensibly foreign students who received funds from their parents, or in the form of educational grants.[22] Thus, the laundering of small amounts of money for terrorist purposes may be difficult to detect. The total cost of this terrorist attack is estimated to be $400,000-$500,000, of which about $300,000 was passed through U.S. banks over a two year period.[23] The money was spent primarily on living expenses and flight training and first-class airfares. Some of the funds came from the United Arab Emirates, from Germany, and from Khalid Sheikh Mohamed in the form of wire transfers that ranged from $5,000 to $7,000, not large enough to report to FinCEN. They also carried cash and travelers checks.

The cost of the bombings of the U.S. Embassy in East Africa in 1998 was estimated to be $10,000.[24]

---

18 Zarte, Juan Carlos, Assistant Secretary Terrorist Financing and Financial Crimes, U.S. Department of Treasury, Testimony before the House Financial Services Committee on Domestic and International Monetary Policy, Trade and Technology And Oversight and Investigations," September 30, 2004.

19 For additional information, see: http://www.un.org/Docs/sc/committees/1267Template.htm

20 Financial Intelligence Units: An Overview, Washington, D.C., The International Monetary Fund and The World Bank, 2004. 49, 93.

21 Herbert A. Biern,, Senior Associate Director, Division of Banking Supervision and Regulation. Testimony on The Bank Secrecy Act and U.S.A. Patriot Act, Before the Committee on International Relations, U.S. House of Representatives, November 17, 2004.

22 Financial Action Task Force on Money Laundering, "Report on Money Laundering Typologies, 2001-2002," February 1, 2002.

23 National Commission on Terrorist Attacks Upon the United States, 2004, Terrorist Financing, Staff Monograph, Chapter 4. http://www.9-11commission.gov; Hamilton, Lee H., Vice Chair, National Commission on Terrorist Attacks, Testimony before The Committee on Financial Services Hearing entitled "The 9/11 Commission Report: Identifying and Preventing Terrorist Financing, August 23, 2004.

24 National Commission on Terrorist Attacks Upon the United States, 2004, Terrorist Financing, Staff Monograph Chapter 4.

Although individual attacks may not cost much, terrorist groups such as al Qaeda must spend large sums for recruiting, training, transportation, paying bribes, and so on. Therefore, reducing their sources of funds impedes their ability to operate.

The al Qaeda Training Manual says nothing about financing terrorist operations, but it does provide limited guidance for terrorists in managing their funds.[25] It instructs them to divide their operational funds into two parts: One part is to be invested in projects that offer financial returns. The other part is to be saved and not spent except during operations. It cautions them about putting all of the operational funds in one place, having protection when carrying large amounts of money, and leaving the money with non-members and spending it as needed. The method used for funding al Qaeda will be discussed shortly.

"An analysis of global and regional terrorist funding shows that *Jihadist* funding networks have little or no form structures in the Western sense, and the informal, personal initiatives are the bloodlines of terrorist financing. For this and other reasons, confronting terrorist financing in the Muslim world has been an uphill struggle.[26]

PRIMARY SOURCES OF FUNDING

There are three primary sources for financing terrorism: States and organizations, revenue generating activities, and criminal acts.[27]

States

The first source involves States or structures with large enough organizations to collect the necessary funds. Some national states, including Cuba, Iran, Iraq, Libya, North Korea, Saudi Arabia, Sudan, and Syria have provided financial support and other resources to terrorist groups.[28]

The FATF "Report on Money Laundering Typologies, 2001-2002," claims that Osama bin Laden is an example of one individual whose personal fortune was used to establish and support the al Qaeda terrorist network that was responsible for the September 11 terrorist attacks on the United States. However, Lee Hamilton, Vice Chair of the National Commission on Terrorist Attacks said that contrary to popular belief, after Osama bin Laden moved from Sudan to Pakistan, he no longer had access to any significant amounts of personal wealth.[29] Most of al Qaeda's $30 million per year funds came from Islamic charities and individuals

---

[25] United States Department of Justice, "Al Qaeda Training Manual," February 23, 2004.

[26] Napoleoni, Loretta, and Rico Carish, "Terrorist Financing," appears in Confronting Terrorism: The Club de Madrid Series on Democracy and Terrorism, Volume II; The International Summit on Democracy, Terrorism and Security, Madrid, Spain, March 8-11, 2005,

[27] "Report on Money Laundering Typologies, 2001-2002, (2002).

[28] "Money Laundering and Financial Crimes," U.S. Department of State, No date, www.state.gov/documents/organization/8703.pdf, 6; Prados, Alfred B., and Christopher M. Blanchard, Saudi Arabia: Terrorist Financing Issues, CRS Report to Congress, RL32499, Updated March 1, 2005. It should be noted that Saudi Arabia has made significant progress in curtailing terrorist financing. Also see: Prados, Alfred B., Saudi Arabia: Current Issues and U.S. Relations, CRS Issue Brief for Congress, IB93113, Updated August 4, 2003.

[29] Hamilton (2004).

based mainly in Saudi Arabia. "And for years, Saudi officials turned a blind eye to this problem."[30] Because al Qaeda is "financially robust," it is free from control of any government, and it can operate from failed or dysfunctional states.[31]

John Helgerson, Chairman of the National Intelligence Council, said that while state sponsored terrorism has been on the decline, the proportion of terrorists that identify themselves with religion – particularly Islam – has increased over the last two decades.[32] Therefore it is not surprising that they take advantage of charities.

Revenue Generating Activities

The second method is to obtain funds from various "revenue generating" activities. Some of the legal fund raising methods include:

- Membership dues and subscriptions;
- Sale of publications;
- Speaking tours, cultural and social events;
- Door-to-door solicitations;
- Appeals to wealthy individuals;
- Donations.

The most effective way of raising funds is through charities and relief organizations, where the community believes that the funds are going for a good cause. But in reality, the funds are used to finance terrorism. For example, a group of individuals (Group Y) who belong to religious extremist groups living in Country C (not the U.S.) convinced wealthy foreign nationals living in that country to finance the construction of a place of worship.[33] A businessman "B" had bought the building intended to be the place of worship, and renovated it with his own funds. He transferred the building to Group Y for a very large profit. The place of worship was completed and a "foundation" was established to collect funds without attracting attention from local authorities.

The businessman "B" was the head of a multinational financial network that has assets of about U.S. $53 million that was used to provide financial support for a terrorist network. B had made a number of trips to Pakistan and to the U.S. He also bought property in another country. When country C government authorities tried to block the transactions based on foreign investment regulations, B had his bank transfer the funds to a country that did not have laws against money laundering. The regulators suspect that part of the money was used to finance terrorists abroad.

---

30 Greenberg, Maurice M., "Terrorist Financing," Report of an Independent Task Force Sponsored by the Council on Foreign Relations, New York, Council on Foreign Relations Press, 2002. Page 1.

31 Ibid. P. 5.

32 Helgerson, John L., Chairman, National Intelligence Council, "The Terrorist Challenge to US National Security," Speech before the Tenth Cosmos Club Spring Symposium, March 23, 2002.

33 Adapted from "Report on Money Laundering Typologies, 2001-2002, (2002), 4.

In February 2005, the U.S. had designated five U.S. based charities and 35 international based charities for funding terrorist activities.[34] Other charities were under investigation.

The key point here is that some charities provide services to enhance the well being of their communities as well as finance certain terrorist activities.

Criminal Acts

The third way to raise funds involves illegal methods and include criminal acts such as commercial frauds, drug trafficking, extortion, kidnapping, large-scale smuggling operations (e.g. bulk cash,[35] commodities such as precious stones [see Box 2-2] and gold, silver, humans, and narcotics), thefts, and robbery, etc. The methods may vary by geographic region. In South Asia, al Qaeda is reported to have trafficked heroin to support their activities.[36]

In Latin America, terrorists have used drugs and arms to finance their activities. The tri-border area, where Argentina, Brazil, and Paraguay converge, joined at the cities of Puerto Iguazu, Foz de Iguazu, and Ciudad del Este respectively, has been a safe haven for Hezbollah and Hamas to fund their activities in the Middle East. The area has a relatively large Arab population, most of whom are Muslim Lebanese.

Some of the crimes are relatively small scale operations. Lieutenant John Stedman of the Los Angeles County Sheriff's Department testified before the Senate in May 2005 regarding the Intellectual Property Rights (IPR) crimes, and how they are used by criminals and terrorist organizations, such as Hezbollah, to raise funds.[37] The counterfeit items include Coach purses, CDs, DVDs, cigarettes, food items, toys, sun glasses, and more. In a little more than a one year period, the L.A. Sheriff's Department made 125 arrests and seized $16 million in counterfeit products.

The majority of counterfeit goods are manufactured in China, South Korea, Taiwan, and Mexico. They are shipped into the United States in large shipping containers. Counterfeiters often pack the counterfeit goods in the back of containers andĐnhe authentic merchandise in the front. In the case of counterfeit handbags, the counterfeiter can make about $500,000 per container. The counterfeit goods are sold in chain department stores, boutique shops, flea markets, and other locations.

---

[34] Zarte, Juan Carlos, Assistant Secretary Terrorist Financing and Financial Crimes, U.S. Department of Treasury, Testimony before the House Financial Services Committee on Domestic and International Monetary Policy, Trade and Technology And Oversight and Investigations," February 16, 2005.

[35] Bulk currency refers to smuggling cash, travelers, or other instruments across national borders; Passas, Nikos, "Informal Value Transfer Systems, Terrorism and Money Laundering: A Report to the National Institute of Justice," November 2003

[36] U.S. General Accounting Office, Terrorist Financing: U.S. Agencies Should Systematically Assess Terrorists' Use of Alternative Financing Mechanisms," GAO-04-163, November, 2003, p. 11.

[37] Stedman John, Kris Buckner, and Matthew Levitt, Testimony Before the U.S. Senate Committee on Homeland Security and Governmental Affairs, "Counterfeit Goods, Easy Cash for Criminals and Terrorists," May 25, 2005.

Box 2-2
Smuggling Precious Stones

Executive Order 13312, that implements the Clean Diamond Trade Act, prohibits the importation/exportation into/from the United States of any rough diamonds that are not controlled through the United Nation's *Kimberley Process Certification Scheme* (KPCS). The KPCS concerns global trafficking in so-called "conflict diamonds," "blood diamonds," or "rough diamonds" that are mined in war zones, and have been used to help fund armed conflicts in Angola, the Democratic Republic of the Congo, and Sierra Leone. The funds were used to overthrow governments and to buy weapons.

The KPCS certificate of origin provides assurance to diamond consumers that the stone that they purchase have not contributed to violent conflicts and human rights abuses in their countries of origin.

Sources: United Nations, "General Assembly Reaffirms Strong Support for Global Certification Scheme," Press Release GA/10319, December 15, 2004;
U.S. Department of Treasury, Office of Foreign Asset Control, "Diamond Trading: What You Need to Know About U.S. Sanctions, An Overview of the Rough Diamonds Control Regulations, Title 31 Part 592 of the U.S. Code of Federal Regulations," November 5, 2004; White House Executive Order 13312, Implementing the Clean Diamond Trading Act, July 29, 2003; National Commission on Terrorist Attacks Upon the United States, Staff Monograph on Terrorist Financing, 2004, p. 32.

Table 2. 1. Examples of Alternative Financing Methods for Terrorists

Alternative Financing Mechanisms	Earning	Moving	Storing
Trade in Commodities			
Illicit drugs	x		
Weapons	x		
Cigarettes	x		
Diamonds	x	x	X
Gold		x	X
Systems			
Charities	x	x	
Informal banking		x	
Currency			
Bulk cash		x	X

Source: U.S. General Accounting Office, Terrorist Financing: U.S. Agencies Should Systematically Assess Terrorists' Use of Alternative Financing Mechanisms," GAO-04-163, November, 2003, Table 2.

The funds raised from selling the counterfeit goods are often sent to Lebanon and Paraguay – part of the tri-border area between Brazil, Argentina, and Paraguay. As previously noted, the tri-border area is an important source of funding for Hezbollah.

In essence, terrorists use the same money laundering techniques as other criminal groups. These methods include, but are not limited to smuggling cash, structured deposits, purchases of various types of monetary instruments, and various forms of underground banking, such as the hawala system that will be explained shortly.

Monitoring terrorist's use of alternative methods of financing, such as using precious stones, is difficult because if they suspect they are being monitored, they switch to some other means, such as metals, to move funds.

Another way to look at financing terrorism is that they use various techniques to earn, move and store their assets, as shown in Table 2-1.

TOOLS OF THE TRADE

Wire Transfers

As previously noted, wire transfers were used by the terrorists who attacked the U.S. on September 11, 2001. Wire transfers refers to any financial transaction carried out for a person through a financial institution by electronic means, and making that amount of money available to a person at another financial institution. Advances in payment system technology have made wire transfers an attractive tool for terrorists and money launderers. In addition, the transfers may take place through Money Service Businesses (MSBs) that were discussed in Chapter 1. Terrorists frequently use false identities, or "straw men" to avoid detection. In general, the transfer payments are structured to avoid detection by keeping them below the mandatory reporting requirements. Some have been reported to be $500 or less.

Internet

Terrorists and their organizations use the internet to communicate with each other, to solicit funds through charities, to move funds, to commit crimes such as identity theft, and to run front businesses.[38] The internet provides efficient global communications and anonymity. Because it is largely unregulated and decentralized, it is an ideal tool for terrorists and a nightmare for law enforcement authorities.

By way of illustration, InfoCom was a Texas based internet service provider (ISP) that was indicted for providing in kind support and funds to HAMAS and the Holy Land Foundation for Relief and Development. It also exported advanced computer technology to two designated terrorist states – Libya and Syria. The firm was funded mainly by capital provided by the wife of a HAMAS figurehead who was a designated terrorist.[39]

Hezbollah, a designated terrorist organization, had a television station Al-Manaar, that urges contributions for the Intifadah, and lists bank accounts in Lebanon where the donations should be sent. Similarly, the HAMAS military wing had a web site recruiting suicide bombers.[40]

---

[38] U.S. Department of Justice and U.S. Department of Treasury, 2003 National Money Laundering Strategy, 2003, p. 56.

[39] Ibid. p. 64.

[40] Ibid, p. 59.

Correspondent Bank Accounts

The U.S. Department of Treasury issued a rule that U.S. financial institutions must terminate correspondent accounts at the Commercial Bank of Syria and its subsidiary, Syrian Lebanese Commercial Bank.[41] The Commercial Bank of Syria is owned and controlled by the Syrian government, a designated state sponsor of terrorism. The Syrian government provides support to Hezbollah, HAMAS, and other terrorist organizations. The Bank of Syria has been used to by terrorists to move funds for their international terrorist activities.

Automatic Teller Machines

Funds deposited in bank accounts in the U.S. can be withdrawn from ATM machines in foreign countries. About 66% of the suspicious ATM withdrawals occurred in the Middle East.[42] Europe accounted for 19%, Asia 11%, and the remainder of the suspicious ATM withdrawals were in the U.S.

Signed Blank Checks

U.S. Customs and Border Protection (CBP) inspectors have reported that signed blank checks are being taken out of the U.S. to avoid border reporting requirements. The payor signs the check, but the name of the payee and the dollar amount to be paid are filled in after crossing the border. CBP requires that individuals bringing in or taking out $10,000 or more must report the funds on FinCEN's Currency Reporting Form (FinCEN 105).[43] Because the dollar amount is blank, no report is required. Generally there were multiple bank checks signed by someone other than the person who was holding them.

Non-Profit Organizations

Non-governmental organizations (NGO), including some non-profit organizations (NPO) have been linked to terrorist financing. In some cases they may have charitable or tax exempt status. They have used aggressive fund raising techniques and target particular ethnic and religious communities. Although most of the funds that they collect are for legitimate purposes, the potential for abuse exists. The cash collections can be used to facilitate the integration of laundered funds into the financial system.

---

41 U.S. Department of Treasury, "Treasury Issues Final Rule Against Bank of Syria, U.S. Financial Institutions Must Terminate Correspondent Accounts," Press Release, JS4105, March 9, 2006. For additional details, see: FinCEN Network: "Amendment; to the Bank Secrecy Act Regulations-Imposition of Special Measure Against Commercial Bank of Syria, Including it Subsidiary Syrian Lebanese Commercial Bank, as a Financial Institution of Primary Money Laundering Concern," Federal Register, Vol. 71, No. 50, March 15, 2006, 13260-13267.

42 FinCEN, "The SAR Activity Review: Trends, Tips & Issues, Issue 8, April 2005. p. 17.

43 Ibid; Also see U.S. Customs and Border Protection, www.cbp.gov.

The NPOs also can be used to move funds across borders. They also can provide logistical support and cover for terrorists. For example, an NPO was registered in Country X as a tax-exempt charity whose purpose was to conduct humanitarian relief projects around the world. However, the Chief Executive Officer was convicted for fraud and organized crime, and diverting more than $315,000 of charitable donations to terrorist organizations.[44]

The Benevolence International Foundation, an Islamic charity located in suburban Chicago had been designated by the U.S. Government in 2002 as a supporter of terrorism received more than $15 million in donations between 1995 and 2000.[45] Enaam M. Arnaout, the director of the Benevolence International Foundation plead guilty to operating a charity as a Racketeer Influence Corrupt Organization (RICO), and failing to tell donors that their money was used to finance terrorist operations. He provided material support to al Qaeda, and diverted charitable contributions to militant groups in Bosnia and Chechnya.[46] Arnaout was sentenced to more than 11 years in prison, and to pay $315,000 in restitution to the United National High Commission on Refugees.

Similarly, the Global Relief Foundation, another Illinois charity and designated terrorist supporter, sent over $7 million dollars overseas to Bosnia, Kashmir, Pakistan, Lebanon, and Chechnya. The money goes to an overseas office of the charity or an affiliated charity. Then it is diverted to terrorist groups.

Some of the warning signs include large amounts of funds being raised by funds located in communities that have modest standards of living. Mismatches between the size of financial transactions and the stated purposes of the NPO. For example, a local cultural NPO that after ten years of existence opens a bank account for handling a music festival, and deposits disproportionately large sums into that account. Several NPOs transferring funds to each other, or sharing the same addresses, managers, or personnel. The office director of a branch office of an NPO defrauded the donors to fund terrorism. The branch office padded the number of orphans it claimed to care for by using false names as well as those of dead children. The funds intended for the orphans were sent to al Qaeda.

In July 2005, Stuart Levey, U.S. Treasury, testified before Congress that the Saudi Government has taken steps to deal with charities and NGOs – The Islamic Relief Organization, the World Assembly of Muslim Youth (WAMY), and the Muslim World League.[47] They were prohibited from sending funds abroad, and created a commission to oversee the charitable sector. However, it is not clear that the prohibitions are working. These same concerns were expressed again in November 2005 by another Treasury official, Daniel Glaser, in interviews in January 16, 2006.[48]

---

[44] Financial Action Task Force on Money Laundering, "Report on Money Laundering Typologies, 2002-2003," February 14, 2003; Financial Action Task Force on Money Laundering, Report on Money Laundering Typologies, 2003-2004, 2004, 9. Also see: "Financial Action Task Force on Money Laundering Combating the Abuse of Non-Profit Organizations: International Best Practices," October 11, 2002.

[45] National Commission on Terrorist Attacks Upon the United States, 2004, Terrorist Financing Staff Monograph, 53; U.S. Department of State, "International Narcotics Control Strategy Report – 2003, Released by the Bureau for International Narcotics and Law Enforcement Affairs, March 2004.

[46] U.S. Department of Justice and U.S. Department of Treasury, 2003 National Money Laundering Strategy, 2003. 63-64.

[47] Levey, Stuart A., Under Secretary Terrorism and Financial Intelligence, U.S. Department of Treasury, Testimony before the Senate Committee on Banking, Housing, and Urban Affairs, July 13, 2005.

[48] Glaser, Daniel, L., Deputy Assistant Secretary Office of Terrorist Financing and Financial Crimes, U.S. Department of Treasury, Testimony before the Senate Committee on the Judiciary, November 8, 2005; Meyer,

Additional examples of the misuse of NPOs by terrorists are presented as case studies later in this chapter.

Insurance

Insurance can be used in the layering and integrating laundered funds into the financial systems. Thus, the launderer may seek insurance brokers who are not aware of the rules, or money laundering, or does not conform to the rules. In one case, a money launderer bought marine property and casualty insurance for a phantom ocean-going vessel.[49] He paid large premiums, and made regular claims, always being careful that the claims were less than the premium payments so the insurer made a profit. He received checks from the insurer that could be used to launder funds. Few questioned the checks or wire transfers from a reputable insurance company.

In another case, narcotics traffickers laundered funds through an off-shore insurance company that offered investment products similar to mutual funds.[50] The account holders would over-fund the policies, moving funds in and out of the funds for the cost of the penalties of an early withdrawal. The withdrawn funds were disbursed though wire transfers or checks from the insurance company that appeared to be clean. Over $29 million was laundered in this fashion.

Finally, electronic commerce poses some threats to the insurance industry.[51] Customer's identities can be difficult to authenticate over the internet, and that opens the door for criminal activity such as money laundering and insurance fraud.

Additional ways that insurance can be used in laundering funds are discussed in Chapter 5.

Bulk Cash

It is easier to smuggle $100 bills than smaller denominations. One pound of $100 dollar bills is worth about $45,000. And $2.2 million in $100 bills weighs about 60 pounds. Interestingly, the cash used to pay for cocaine and other drugs often weighs substantially more than the drugs themselves.[52]

Bulk cash is a widely used source of funding terrorism. Bulk cash carriers may bribe or threaten airport security guards and others with bodily harm so that they can carry the bulk cash onboard aircraft. As previously noted, many terrorist acts do not require a lot of cash.

Josh, "U.S. Faults Saudi Efforts on Terrorism," Latimes.com. (from the Los Angeles Times), January 15, 2006.

49 Financial Action Task Force on Money Laundering, "Report on Money Laundering Typologies, 2003-2004, (2004), 15-16.

50 Financial Action Task Force on Money Laundering, "Report on Money Laundering Typologies, 2003-2004, (2004), 16. For additional indicators on money laundering in the insurance industry, see the International Association of Insurance Supervisors: http://www.iaisweb.org/.

51 "Risks to Insurers Posed by Electronic Commerce," Issue Paper, International Association of Insurance Supervisors, October, 2002. http://www.iaisweb.org/187riskstoinsurers.pdf

52 U.S. Department of Treasury, "Treasury Department Assistant Secretary David Medina, House Banking Subcommittee on Financial Services and Consumer Credit," Press Release, LS-623, May 15, 2000.

Bulk cash is also used in connection with other criminal acts. In early 2006, FinCEN issued an Advisory concerning the increased use of bulk cash from drug trafficking being smuggled into Mexico[53]. Once in Mexico, numerous layered transactions are used to hide the source of the funds. Then the funds can be returned to the United States.

Economic Citizenship

Some offshore centers, such as Dominica, Nauru, and others, sell improperly controlled economic citizenship. The lack of controls allows buyers of economic citizenship in a jurisdiction that may not have an extradition agreement with the buyers' home country to avoid extradition. Also, it allows them to change their names to go along with their new passports. In Belize, two suspected Middle Eastern terrorists acquired economic citizenship to enter the U.S. as citizens from Belize. They were denied entry visas by the U.S. Embassy and in 2002 Belize stopped selling the citizenships.[54]

Informal Value Transfer Systems

Informal value transfer systems (IVTS) refers to any non-bank system where someone receives money for the purpose of making those funds, or an equivalent value, available to someone else in a different geographic location. Hawalas are a common form of IVTS. They are widely used for both legitimate and illegitimate purposes. The legitimate uses are closely linked to immigrants and expatriates sending funds to their countries of origin. The illegitimate uses are typically associated with drug trafficking and financing terrorism. Various types of IVTS are discussed in Chapter 3.

CASE STUDIES OF FINANCING TERRORISM

Financing Al Qaeda

Congressional testimony by Jonathan Winer (2003), former U.S. Deputy Assistant Secretary of State, International Law Enforcement, provides unique insights on the funds used to finance the al Qaeda terrorist organization.[55] The CIA estimates that it cost al Qaeda about $30 million per year before the 9/11 attack to support its activities. Most of the funds came from contributions including charitable and religious organizations. Charitable giving, also known as zakat, is one of the five pillars of Islamic faith. The charitable giving also serves as

---

[53] FinCEN, Advisory, Guidance to Financial Institutions on the Repatriation of Currency Smuggled into Mexico from the United States, FIN-2006-A003, April 28, 2006.

[54] U.S. Department of State, "Money Laundering and Financial Crimes," No date. 9.

[55] Winer, Jonathan M., Alston & Bird LLP, Testimony, "Terrorism Financing: Origination, Organization, and Prevention," Hearing before the Committee on Governmental Affairs, U.S. Senate, (S. Hrg. 108-245), July 31, 2003; Also see the National Commission on Terrorist Attacks Upon the United States, Staff Monograph on Terrorist Financing, 2004, pp. 19 – 22.http://www.9-11commission.gov

a form of taxation, educational assistance, foreign aid, and political influence. Simply stated, it is part of the Islamic culture.

The Jamiat al-Ikhwan al-Muslim organization, also called the Muslim Brotherhood ("Brotherhood") was founded in Egypt in 1928 as a religious organization. It grew into a political organization that threatened the Egyptian government and was banned from that country in 1954. Elements of the Brotherhood reached Saudi Arabia, Kuwait, and other Gulf states. Over time, it became clandestine and a militant group that was supporting Islamic fundamentalism and it was against Western influences. The Brotherhood has been characterized by the U.S. Treasury as the parent of the Hamas terrorist organization, and linked to terrorist groups such as the Tamil Tigers, the Afghan mujahidin, the Indonesian Jemaah Islamiya, and others. It was one of the most significant sources of financing al Qaeda.

Furthermore, charitable organizations from Saudi Arabia, Kuwait, and other Gulf countries sent money to Afghanistan and neighboring countries to create schools, seminaries, and networks that fed terrorism. They provided funds for Osama Bin Ladin, and for military training camps in Afghanistan, Pakistan, Kashmir, and Chechnya, that were under Bin Ladin's control. Between the 1998 U.S. Embassy bombing in East Africa and the 9/11 attack, Al Qaeda used hawalas to move funds into Afghanistan.[56]

Investments in legitimate businesses, such as the East African Somalian based Al Barakaat's financial services and Telecommunications Empire provided additional funds for al Qaeda. Al Barakaat is considered a money remitter (e.g. Money Service Business) relying on wire transfers and correspondent banking. AL Barakaat also operated a hawala that was founded with a large investment from Osama Bin Ladin, and it was channeling millions of dollars for al Qaeda.[57]

In addition, al Qaeda operatives have used extortion, forcing businessmen to pay them or face attacks on their businesses in the Middle East. Similarly, Bin Ladin reportedly threatened attacks on Jordan and Saudi Arabia. Al Qaeda also received millions of dollars per year from the production and distribution of opium that was smuggled though Central Asian states to distribution networks in East Africa.

According to former U.S. Deputy Assistant Secretary of State Winer (2003, p.119), since the September 11 attacks, Saudi Arabians provided "the preponderant sources of funds for the development of al Qaeda, and a major source of funds for many other terrorist organizations." For example, in a March 2002 FBI raid of the Saudi charity Benevolence International in Sarajevo, a handwritten note purports to name 20 wealthy donors to al Qaeda, the bin Laden brothers, and Adel Batterjee. Battterjee was the initial president and secretary of Benevolence International, an Islamic charity, was founded in Chicago in 1987. In 2000-2001, the charity spent a reported $3.4 on relief operations. Benevolence International also had interlocking directors and senior offficers in the Muslim World League – Saudi Arabia's largest state funded charity.

Following the May 2003 terrorist attacks in Saudi Arabia, the Saudi government has taken a number of steps to combat terrorism. However, there is the problem of the fox guarding the chicken coop. For example, a task force established by the Jeddah Chamber of

---

56 National Commission on Terrorist Attacks Upon the United States, Staff Monograph on Terrorist Financing, 2004, p 25.

57 U.S. General Accounting Office, Terrorist Financing: U.S. Agencies Should Systematically Assess Terrorists' Use of Alternative Financing Mechanisms," GAO-04-163, November, 2003, p. 19; National Commission on Terrorist Attacks Upon the United States, Staff Monograph on Terrorist Financing, 2004, pp. 67-69 .

Commerce and Industry to develop the administrative system for Saudi charities, was funded and overseen by the Muslim World League. The Rabita Trust, a member of the Muslim World League, is on the U.S. Treasury list of specially designated terrorist organizations.

Box 2-3
Funding the 9/11 Highjackers

"The 9/11 plot cost al Qaeda approximately $400,000 - $500,000, of which approximately $300,000 was deposited into U.S. bank accounts of 19 highjackers. Al Qaeda funded the highjackers in the United States by three primary and unexceptional means: (1) wire transfers from overseas to the United States, (2) the physical transport of cash or traveler's checks into the United States, and (3) the accessing of funds held in foreign financial institutions by debit or credit cards. Once here, all of the highjackers used the U.S. banking system to store their funds and facilitate their transactions." " ...the highjackers opened bank accounts in their real names at U.S. banks....The highjackers used branches of both large national banks and smaller regional banks."

Source: National Commission on Terrorist Attacks Upon the United States, Staff Monograph on Terrorist Financing, 2004, pp. 13, 53. http://www.9-11commission.gov

Carnival French Ice Cream

The Wall Street Journal reported that Carnival French Ice Cream was primarily an unlicensed Money Service Business (MSB) for Yemeni immigrants.[58] They also set up other small businesses and at least 10 accounts giving the appearance of a network owned by a group of immigrants. The accounts were "feeder accounts" used to avoid suspiciously large deposits into Carnival's account at J.P. Morgan Chase. Carnival's gross receipts were less than $200,000 annually. Nevertheless, between September 11, 2001 and 2003 when it was closed, Carnival sent at least $5.3 million out of the country though J.P. Morgan Chase. Some of the funds came from charities and mosques. The money was sent to an al Qaeda ally in Yemen.

J.P. Morgan Chase did not suspect Carnival. On an average day, the bank processes more than 320,000 wire payments valued at $2.3 trillion.

Cigarette Smuggling

In 2002, a federal jury in North Carolina convicted Mohammad Hammoud and his brother Chawki, Lebanese immigrants, of providing material support for the Hezbollah terrorist group though racketeering, and conspiracy to commit money laundering by funneling

58 Glen R. Simson, "As Investigations Proliferate, Big Banks Feel Under the Gun," *The Wall Street Journal*, December 20, 2004, A1, A4.

profits though a cigarette smuggling operation.[59] Seven other defendants pled guilty to related charges including conspiracy to provide material support to terrorists, money laundering, and immigration violations. In 2003, Mohammad Hammoud, the lead defendant in this case was sentenced to 155 years in prison.[60]

Family and religious ties enabled the smugglers to move the cigarettes from Charlotte, North Carolina, and then sell them at a network of small convenience stores in Michigan. Cigarette prices and state sales taxes were low in North Carolina ($0.05/pack), and high in Michigan ($0.75/pack) and other states. Hezbollah earned an estimated $1.5 million between 1996 and 2000. The funds were used to buy weapons.

There is a growing trend of counterfeit cigarettes and internet cigarette sales. The Phillip Morris Company estimated that the revenue loss to New York City from one shipping container of counterfeit cigarettes sales is about $1.6 million.[61]

Cigarette smuggling is not limited to the United States. It is widespread in Eastern Europe, and the cigarettes are commonly used as currency.

Part of this cigarette smuggling operation involved two Canadians, Mohammed Hassan Dbouk and his brother-in-law, Ali Adam Amhaz. Their operations were funded, in part, by funds sent to them by Haj Hasan Hilu Laqis who was Hezbollah's chief military procurement officer. They sent stun guns, night vision goggles, laser range finders and other equipment to Lebanon.

It should be noted that cigarette smuggling is not limited to those financing terrorists. It is widespread in states, such as California, that have high taxes per pack of cigarettes.[62]

The leaders of one California cigarette smuggling ring were sentenced to two years in prison for defrauding the state out of more than $4.7 million in tax revenues. They brought truckloads of cigarettes into the state, and put counterfeit tax stamps on 5 million packs, and then sold them to retailers.

Other smugglers counterfeited cigarettes to look like the major American brands, and sold them California, China, Mexico, and elsewhere.

Holy Land Foundation for Relief and Development (HLF)

In December 2001, President Bush announced that the HLF, the largest Muslim charitable foundation in the United States, had provided millions in financial and material support that were used by Hamas terrorist organization, and blocked all of its assets.[63] Not all

---

[59] U.S. Department of Treasury and U.S. Department of Justice, 2002 National Money Laundering Strategy, July 2002, Appendix 7; U.S. General Accounting Office, Terrorist Financing: U.S. Agencies Should Systematically Assess Terrorists' Use of Alternative Financing Mechanisms," GAO-04-163, November, 2003. p.3, 11-13; Levitt, Matthew,Testimony Before the U.S. Senate Committee on Homeland Security and Governmental Affairs, "Counterfeit Goods, Easy Cash for Criminals and Terrorists," May 25, 2005.

[60] U.S. Department of Justice and U.S. Department of Treasury, 2003 National Money Laundering Strategy, 2003, p.3.

[61] U.S. General Accounting Office, Terrorist Financing: U.S. Agencies Should Systematically Assess Terrorists' Use of Alternative Financing Mechanisms," GAO-04-163, November, 2003, p 12.

[62] Halper, Evan, "State's Tobacco Revenue Surges," *Los Angeles Times*, December 27, 2005.

[63] White House News Release, "Fact Sheet on Shutting Down the Terrorist Financial Network," December 4, 2001; U.S. Department of Justice, News Release, "Holy Land Foundation, Leaders, Accused of Providing Material Support to Hamas Terrorist Organization," July 27, 2004; U.S. Immigration and Customs Enforcement, News

donors were aware of how their funds were used. One estimate is that in 2000, the HLF provided $13 million in aid to Hamas to support suicide bombers and their families.[64] Two additional entities were named as part of the terrorist financial network: Beitel el-Mal Holdings (an investment company controlled by Hamas) and Al-Aqsa Islamic Bank (a financial arm of Hamas that was substantially owned by Beitel el-Mal). Hamas espouses an extremist Islamic fundamentalist ideology, calling for the creation of an Islamic Palestinian State by destroying the State of Israel thought violent jihad.

The Occupied Land fund was established in California in 1989 as a tax-exempt charity, but not as a religious organization. Subsequently, it changed its name to the Holy Land Foundation for Relief and Development (HLF), and moved its headquarters to Richardson, Texas in 1993. It also had offices in California, New Jersey, and Illinois, and representatives in other states, the West Bank, and Gaza. HLF became designated as the primary fund raising agency for Hamas in the United States. It provided funds to Hamas through direct transfers from its offices in the West Bank and Gaza to Islamic charity committees (zakat committees) and to other charitable organizations that were owned or controlled by Hamas. Most of the funds were to be used to enhance Hamas and undermine Israel.[65]

Hamas used some of the funds to support schools that encouraged children to become suicide bombers, and to recruit suicide bombers by offering their families financial support. Between October 1, 2000 and September 10, 2001, Hamas claimed responsibility for 20 or more bombings, shootings, and mortar attacks were 77 people died and more than 540 were injured.

In July 2004, the U.S. Department of Justice handed down a 42 count indictment against the HLF and its top leaders for conspiracy to provide aid to a terrorist organization and the families of suicide bombers, and money laundering. In February 2005, former HLF leader Abdel Jabbar Hamdan was ordered removed from the United States. Arrest warrants were issued for others connected with the HLF.

Charitable Fund Raising for Terrorists

Solicitors asked travelers at Los Angeles International Airport to donate funds to the Committee on Human Rights. The Committee on Human Rights was a front organization for the Mujahedin-e Khalq (MEK), a designated terrorist organization.[66] The Committee on Human Rights gave the MEK money and credit cards, and wired funds to an MEK bank account in Turkey. In a conference call between the Committee and an MEK leader, they were instructed to continue to provide financial support. They provided several hundred thousand dollars.

Release, "Former High-Ranking Official from Holy Land Foundation Ordered Removed from the United States," February 8, 2005; "The Holy Land Foundation for Relief and Development, Update," Anti-Defamation League, July 27, 2006. Http://www.adl.org/israel/holyland.asp.

64 U.S. General Accounting Office, Terrorist Financing: U.S. Agencies Should Systematically Assess Terrorists' Use of Alternative Financing Mechanisms," GAO-04-163, November, 2003, p14.

65 Emerson, Steven," Fund-Raising Methods and Procedures for International Terrorist Organizations," Testimony before the House Committee on Financial Services Subcommittee on Oversight and Investigation, Patriot Act Oversight, February 12, 2002. This source also discusses other charities linked to terrorist organizations and al Qaeda.

66 US V. Afshari, U.S. 9th Circuit Court of Appeals, Case number 02-50355, 12/20/04.

The MEK was founded in the 1960s, and was an Iranian Marxist group seeking to overthrow the regime in Iran. The MEK was also known as the People's Mojahedin Organization for Iraq. The MEK took American embassy personnel hostage in 1979, and they carried out terrorist activities with the support of Saddam Hussein's regime.

Seven individuals, including those who knowingly collected money for the MEK, where charged with a 59 count indictment and found guilty for providing and conspiring to provide material support for a foreign terrorist organization.

Other charities with appealing names also have been associated with terrorist financing by sending funds abroad. The Global Relief Foundation, an Illinois based charity sends more than 90% of its donations abroad.[67] Some of the funds that were sent abroad have been linked to the HLF and to al Qaeda. Similarly, the Illinois based Benevolence International Foundation also moved funds overseas to support terrorist activities. In the case of the U.S. v. Benevolence International Foundation, Inc., it was revealed that a key associate of Osama bin Ladin kept thousands of dollars of various currencies in his apartment. The Benevolence International Foundation has offices in Afghanistan, Azerbaijan, Bangladesh, Bosnia/Herz., China, Croatia, Gaza Strip, U.K, U.S., Canada, Netherlands, Saudi Arabia, Pakistan, Russia, Sudan, Tajikistan, and Yemen. In 2003, the U.S. Executive Director of the Benevolence International foundation was indicted for supporting al Qaeda and other terrorist organizations, and he plead guilty to racketeering conspiracy, and admitted to fraudulently using a charitable organization to provide financial assistance to persons engaged in violent activities overseas. He was sentenced to 11 years in prison.[68]

Steven Emerson, testifying about financing terrorism before a Senate Committee in 2003, listed numerous charities that contributed funds to terrorist organizations.[69] For example, he cited the World Assembly of Muslim Youth (WAMY) which is the largest Muslim youth organization in the world. It was established by Osama bin Laden's brother, Abdullah bin Laden in Falls Church, Virginia, in 1992. Emerson states that there are strong links between this organization, Saudi Government officials, and financing terrorism. In 1992, the *Arab News* reported that WAMY was increasing its monthly contribution to the Palestinian Infitada from $800,000 to $2.7 million, in addition to the more than $70 million that had already been sent to that cause though WAMY offices abroad. WAMY also was active in Pakistan, supporting both Afghan warlords and Kashmiri terrorists. In 2001, a joint FBI-Pakistani intelligence operation raided WAMY's Peshwar office. They questioned one of WAMY's employees about a tape with a recorded message from Osama bin Laden to the local media. Osama bin Laden praised various terrorist attacks.

---

67 U.S. General Accounting Office, Terrorist Financing: U.S. Agencies Should Systematically Assess Terrorists' Use of Alternative Financing Mechanisms," GAO-04-163, November, 2003, p15 (Global Relief Foundation v. Paul H. O'Neil, et. al., 207 F. Supp. 2d 779, U.S. District Court, Northern District of Illinois, Eastern Division, June 11, 2002; U.S. v. Enaam Arnaout, Case No. 02 CR. 892, U. S. District Court, Northern District of Illinois, Eastern Division, April 2002; U.S. v. Benevolence International Foundation, Inc., and Enaam Arnaout, Case No. 02 CR. 0414, U. S. District Court, Northern District of Illinois, Eastern Division, April 2002). For additional information on the Global Relief Foundation and the Benevolence International Foundation, see: National Commission on Terrorist Attacks Upon the United States, Monograph on Terrorist Financing, Staff Report by John Roth, Douglas Greenburg, and Serena Wille, 2004, Chapter 6.

68 U.S. General Accounting Office, Terrorist Financing: U.S. Agencies Should Systematically Assess Terrorists' Use of Alternative Financing Mechanisms," GAO-04-163, November, 2003, 30.

69 Emerson, Steven, "Terrorism Financing: Origination, Organization, and Prevention," U.S. Senate, Committee on Governmental Affairs, S. Hrg. 108-245, July 31, 2003, pp. 163-170

In the U.S., WAMY provided financial support for the Council on American-Islamic Relations that allegedly received some of its initial funding from the HLF. In addition, the Council on American-Islamic Relations had previously defended individuals involved in terrorist attacks. Not surprisingly, the Council on American-Islamic Relations denied any allegations of wrongdoing.

In 2005, Steven Emerson questioned whether Saudi Arabia was a friend or foe. "The basic problem is that the interests of the two most powerful strata of Saudi society, the Saudi ruling elite (a family business) and the religious establishment – are intrinsically not comparable with ours. The U.S. believes in capitalism, democracy, freedom, separation of church and state, and for most of our citizens, a constant progress to a world of greater equality between people of different backgrounds. The Saudi elites and religious establishment do not believe in capitalism, or democracy or gender equality. What we call freedom they think of as chaos. We believe in progress, both material and moral. But large segments of Saudi society see the secular western world as a warped construction of a conspiracy of Jews, socialists, Christian missionaries and what-have-you. Only in one area do our interests concord. They sell oil; we buy it."[70]

PROFILING

The National Commission on Terrorist Attacks Upon the United States (2004, p.52) had the following to say about profiling:

"The inability to develop meaningful indicia of a terrorist cell or terrorist fund-rains operation creates a risk that financial institutions could rely primarily on religious, geographic, or ethnic profiling in an attempt to find some criteria helpful for identifying terrorist financing. Such profiling raises a number of problems. Fundamentally, it will not be an effective means to combat terrorist financing. The vast majority of Islamic or Arab bank customers are not terrorists or terrorist supporters, so indiscriminately filing SARs on them will do nothing but waste resources and cause bad will. Similarly, reporting that an Islamic charity is sending money to Pakistan will not be particularly effective in finding terrorist financiers; there are certainly many legitimate humanitarian needs there. In addition to doing little good, this type of profiling may subject customers to heightened scrutiny without legitimate basis, and could even extend to refusing service to customers meeting a certain profile. Of course, religion, nation of origin, or ethnicity can and should be taken into consideration, along with other factors, in the subjective judgment as to whether a certain transaction or account is suspicious. Our point is that profiling-by itself-is both unfair and an ineffective way for financial institutions to attack terrorist financing."

[70] Emerson, Steven, "Saudi Arabia: Friend or Foe in the War on Terror," Testimony before the U.S. Senate Judiciary Committee, November 8, 2005.

RED FLAGS

The following activities are red flags for financing terrorism or other illegal activities:[71]

- The use of multiple accounts to collect and funnel funds to a small number of foreign beneficiaries
- Deposits followed by wire transfers
- Beneficiaries located in problematic foreign jurisdictions
- Small deposits structured to circumvent Currency Transaction Reports
- Mixing cash and monetary instruments
- Mixing deposits with monetary instruments that are atypical of legitimate business activity
- Occupations of those engaging in transactions/depositors not commensurate with level of activity (students, unemployed, etc.)
- Large cash withdrawals from businesses that do not normally have such transactions
- Movement of funds to "non-cooperative countries."
- Involvement of multiple individuals from the same country or community.

FINANCIAL ACTION TASK FORCE'S "GUIDANCE FOR FINANCIAL INSTITUTIONS IN DETECTING TERRORIST FINANCING"[72]

Financial institutions should pay particular attention to:

Accounts

(1) Accounts that receive relevant periodical deposits and are dormant at other periods. These accounts are then used in creating a legitimate appearing financial background through which additional fraudulent activities may be carried out.

(2) A dormant account containing a minimal sum suddenly receives a deposit or series of deposits followed by daily cash withdrawals that continue until the transferred sum has been removed.

(3) When opening an account, the customer refuses to provide information required by the financial institution, attempts to reduce the level of information provided to the minimum or provides information that is misleading or difficult to verify.

(4) An account for which several persons have signature authority, yet these persons appear to have no relation among each other (either family ties or business relationship).

---

[71] U.S. Department of State, "Money Laundering and Financial Crimes," No date, 21.

[72] This section taken directly is from: Financial Action Task Force on Money Laundering, "Guidance for Financial Institutions in Detecting Terrorist Financing," April 24, 2002, Appendix A, and it is reprinted with permission. The material is copyright @ FATF. All rights reserved. The spelling of cheques and organisation were changed to checks and organization.

(5) An account opened by a legal entity»lr an organization that has the same address as other legal entities or organizations but for which the same person or persons have signature authority, when there is no apparent economic or legal reason for such an arrangement (for example, individuals serving as company directors for multiple companies headquartered at the same location, etc.).

(6) An account opened in the name of a recently formed legal entity and in which a higher than expected level of deposits are made in comparison with the income of the founders of the entity.

(7) The opening by the same person of multiple accounts into which numerous small deposits are made that in aggregate are not commensurate with the expected income of the customer.

(8) An account opened in the name of the legal entity that is involved in the activities of an association or foundation whose aims are related to the claims or demands of a terrorist organization.

(9) An account opened in the name of a legal entity, a foundation or an association, which may be linked to a terrorist organization and that shows movements of funds above the expected level of income.

Deposits and Withdrawals

(1) Deposits for a business entity in combinations of monetary instruments that are atypical of the activity normally associated with such a business (for example, deposits that include a mix of business, payroll and social security checks).

(2) Large cash withdrawals made from a business account not normally associated with cash transactions.

(3) Large cash deposits made to the account of an individual or legal entity when the apparent business activity of the individual or entity would normally be conducted in checks or other payment instruments.

(4) Mixing of cash deposits and monetary instruments in an account in which such transactions do not appear to have any relation to the normal use of the account.

(5) Multiple transactions carried out on the same day at the same branch of a financial institution but with an apparent attempt to use different tellers.

(6) The structuring of deposits through multiple branches of the same financial institution or by groups of individuals who enter a single branch at the same time.

(7) The deposit or withdrawal of cash in amounts which fall consistently just below identification or reporting thresholds.

(8) The presentation of uncounted funds for a transaction. Upon counting, the transaction is reduced to an amount just below that which would trigger reporting or identification requirements.

(9) The deposit or withdrawal of multiple monetary instruments at amounts which fall consistently just below identification or reporting thresholds, particularly if the instruments are sequentially numbered.

Wire Transfers

(1) Wire transfers ordered in small amounts in an apparent effort to avoid triggering identification or reporting requirements.

(2) Wire transfers to or for an individual where information on the originator, or the person on whose behalf the transaction is conducted, is not provided with the wire transfer, when the inclusion of such information would be expected.

(3) Use of multiple personal and business accounts or the accounts of non-profit organizations or charities to collect and then funnel funds immediately or after a short time to a small number of foreign beneficiaries.

(4) foreign exchange transactions that are performed on behalf of a customer by a third party followed by wire transfers of the funds to locations having no apparent business connection with the customer or to countries of specific concern.

Characteristics of the Customer or His/Her Business Activity

(1) Funds generated by a business owned by individuals of the same origin or involvement of multiple individuals of the same origin from countries of specific concern acting on behalf of similar business types.

(2) Shared address for individuals involved in cash transactions, particularly when the address is also a business location and/or does not seem to correspond to the stated occupation (for example student, unemployed, self-employed, etc.).

(3) Stated occupation of the transactor is not commensurate with the level or type of activity (for example, a student or unemployed individual who receives or sends large numbers of wire transfers, or who makes daily maximum cash withdrawals at multiple locations over a wide geographic area).

(4) Regarding non-profit or charitable organizations, financial transactions for which there appears to be no logical economic purpose or in which there appears to be no link between the stated activity or the organization and the other parties in the transaction.

(5) A safe deposit box is opened on behalf of a commercial entity when the business activity of the customer is unknown or such activity does not appear to justify the use of a safe deposit box.

(6) Unexplained inconsistencies arising from the process of identifying or verifying the customer (for example, regarding previous or current country of residence, country of issue of the passport, countries visited according to the passport, and documents furnished to confirm name, address and date of birth.

Transactions Linked to Locations of Concern

(1) Transactions involving foreign currency exchanges that are followed within a short time by wire transfers to locations of specific concern (for example, countries designated by national authorities, FATF non-cooperative countries and territories, etc.).

(2) Deposits are followed within a short time by wire transfers of funds, particularly to or through a location of specific concern (for example, countries designated by national authorities, FATF non-cooperative countries and territories, etc.).

(3) A business account through which a large number of incoming or outgoing wire transfers take place and for which there appears to be no logical business or other economic purpose, particularly when this activity is to, through or from locations of specific concern.

(4) The use of multiple accounts to collect and then funnel funds to a small number of foreign beneficiaries, both individuals and businesses, particularly when these are on locations of specific concern.

(5) A customer obtains a credit instrument or engages in commercial financial transactions involving movement of funds to or from locations of specific concern when there appears to be no logical business reasons for dealing with those locations.

(6) The opening of accounts of financial institutions from locations of specific concern.

(7) Sending or receiving funds by international transfers from and/or to locations of specific concern.

Chapter 3

INFORMAL VALUE TRANSFER SYSTEMS

Informal value transfer systems (IVTS). IVTS refer to any refers to any non-bank system where someone receives money for the purpose of making those funds, or an equivalent value, available to someone else in a different geographic location. IVTS are also referred to as "Alternative Remittance Systems (ARS). The term *remittance* refers to funds being sent by someone living in one country to someone else in a different country. However, the IVTS is different than sending funds though Money Service Business, or by some other conventional means. IVTS systems date back to 5,800 BC, and they are called by a variety of names: "hawala" (Middle East, Pakistan, Afghanistan), "hundi" (India), "fei-ch'ien" (China), "phoe kuan" (Thailand), and "underground banking." These systems also are called "transfer" (hawala), "collect" (hundi), "flying money or coin (fei-ch'ien), and chits and chops. The latter name comes from the fact that the recipient sometimes has to show a chit or token to receive the remittance. The majority of transactions using IVTS are legitimate. However, the IVTS also are used to facilitate both criminal activities and the funding of terrorism.

In recent years the "Black Market Peso Exchange - BMPE (South America) was added to the list if IVTS.[1] However, the BMPE is an asset sale rather than a remittance payment. It is more commonly associated with drug trafficking than with financing terrorism.

Regardless of the name, those who participate in the IVTS are "money transmitters," as defined by the USA Patriot Act (Sec. 359). Accordingly, they must register with FinCEN as money service businesses, have state licenses, and file income tax returns.

The IVTS systems were originally used for trade finance because of the dangers of traveling with gold and other forms of payment. The IVTS serves as an alternative for traditional financial institutions for a variety of reasons including political instability, lack of easy access to financial institutions, efficiency, security and anonymity. Equally important, many emerging economies do not have modern financial systems that can handle international funds transfers for individuals living in rural areas or areas that are not serviced

---

[1] For further details about ARSs, see Financial Action Task Force, "Money Laundering & Terrorist Financing Typologies, 2004-2005," June 10, 2005. Additional sources include:
FinCEN Advisory, Informal Value Transfer Systems, Issue 33, March 2003. Also see, Jost, Patrick M., and Jarjit Singh Sandhu, "The Hawala Alternative Remittance System and Its Role in Money Laundering." Interpol General Secretariat, Lyon, France, January 2000. http://www.interpol.int; El-Qorchi, Mohammed, "Hawala," Finance and Development, International Monetary Fund, Vol. 39, Number 4, December 2002; Passas (2003); Passas, Nikos, "Informal Value Transfer Systems and Criminal Organizations: A study Into So-Called Underground Banking Networks," The Hague, Ministry of Justice (The Netherlands), 1999; The Black Market Peso Exchange (BMPE) is discussed in Chapter 3.

by financial institutions. Finally, IVTS are low cost and reliable. Some argue that it is lower cost and more reliable than banks. A key feature of the *informal* value transfer systems is that they are informal. They depend on *trust* based on family or other ties. They are not based on contractual agreements.

For thousands of years it has been used for legitimate purposes. Today, the principal use is by members of expatriate communities who migrated to Europe, the Persian Gulf region, and North America to send legitimate remittances to their relatives in India, East Asia, Africa, Eastern Europe, and Asia. In addition, drug traffickers, terrorist organizations, tax evaders, and other criminals also use IVTS to transfer funds.

The IVTS systems usually involve international transactions where individuals in both countries use "broker/dealers" to serve as intermediaries. Individuals are not the only users of IVTS. Some Non-profit organizations (NPO) use IVTS to send funds overseas. In one case, law enforcement authorities discovered that an NPO headquarters was located in the same office as an IVTS that was linked with money laundering operations.[2]

Finally, some IVTS transactions, especially those in South Asia, involve gold.[3] This is because gold is important for religious and cultural reasons. Equally important is the distrust in the value of the local currencies. Thus, gold is used to preserve and protect wealth.

Although no one knows the dollar value of funds being transmitted through IVTS, estimates range from tens of billions of dollars to $200 billion.[4]

IMMIGRATION

Before examining how IVTS works, it is important to recognize that it is used primarily by immigrants. They also use other forms of exchange. In Mexico, for example, remittances, consisting mainly of electronic transfers and money orders, are the second largest source of foreign exchange after maquiladoras and ahead of tourism and foreign direct investment.[5] Remittances were estimated to be about $20 billion in 2005, up from $84 million in 1960. The growth in remittances reflects the growth in Mexican workers who came to the U.S. to earn higher wages. Stated otherwise, one consequence of globalization is that it is relatively easy for individuals to emigrate from one country to another. The data presented in Table 3-1 shows the percentage of foreign born populations in selected countries in 1992 and 2002.

According to the Organization for Economic Co-Operation and Development (OECD) foreign born populations range from a high of 38 percent in Luxembourg to a low of 1.5% in Japan. In North America, both Canada and the United States have relatively porous borders,

---

2 Financial Action Task Force on Money Laundering, "Report on Money Laundering Typologies, 2002-2003," February 14, 2003, p. 9.

3 Financial Action Task Force on Money Laundering, "1998-1999 Report on Money Laundering Typologies," February 10, 1999, p. 10; For a discussion of IVTS in Asia, see: Carroll, Lisa C., "Alternative Remittance Systems Distinguishing Sub-systems of Ethnic Money Laundering in Interpol Member Countries on the Asian Continent," Interpol, December 2, 2002 (last modification).

4 U.S. General Accounting Office, Terrorist Financing: U.S. Agencies Should Systematically Assess Terrorists' Use of Alternative Financing Mechanisms," GAO-04-163, November, 2003, p. 24.

5 Cañas, Jesus, Roberto Coronado, and Robert W. Gilmer, "U.S., Mexico Deepen Economic Ties," SouthwestEconomy, Federal Reserve Bank of Dallas, January/February 2006, pp. 11-3, 16; Coronado, Roberto, "Workers' Remittances to Mexico," El Paso BusinessFrontier, Federal Reserve Bank of Dallas, Issue 1, 2004.

and the percentages of foreign born in 2002 were 18.2% and 11.5% respectively. If illegal immigrants were included, the percentages would no doubt be higher.

Finally, Table 3-1 reveals that with the exception of France, the percentages of foreign born populations in the other countries increased during the 1992-2002 period.

Origins

A logical question is where do the immigrants come from? The answers for the United States are presented in Table 3-2. Mexico accounts for 21% of the legal immigrants. The U.S./Mexican border is virtually wide-open; therefore the 21% from Mexico and 7% from Central America are understated.

Table 3-1. Demographics of Selected Countries

Country	Population (millions) 2003	Foreign born % of total population 2002	Foreign born % of total population 1992
Australia	19.9 million	27.1%	23.0%
Canada	31.6	18.2	16.1
France	59.7	5.6 (1999)	6.3 (1990)
Germany	82.5	8.9	8.0
Japan	127.6	1.5	1.0
Luxembourg	0.5	38.1	31.0
New Zealand	4.0	19.5 (1999)	not available
Switzerland	7.3	19.9	17.6
United Kingdom	60.5	4.5	3.5
United States	291.0	11.5	8.7

Source: OECD in Figures: Statistics on Member States, 2004 Edition, OECD Observer, 2004/Supplement 1, Paris, France, July 2004.

Table 3-2. Percent of U.S. Immigrants by Region/Country of Birth 2002

Europe	16%
Asia	33%
India	7%
China	6%
Philippines	5%
Africa	6%
North America	38%
Mexico	21%
Central America	7%
South America	7%
Total	100%

Source: Statistical Abstract of the United States, 2004-2005, Washington, D.C., U.S. Census Bureau, 2005, Table 8, p. 10 (population).

Asia accounts for the next largest group of immigrants. The percentages are almost evenly split between India, China, and the Philippines.

Table 3-3 shows the extent to which foreign languages are spoken at home in the U.S. On average, a foreign language is spoken in 17.9% of U.S. homes. A foreign language is spoken in more than 30% of the homes in California, New Mexico, and Texas. A good guess is that Spanish is the dominant foreign language in these states that border Mexico. Arizona, the other state on the Mexican border recorded 25.9% of the homes speaking a foreign language.

At the bottom of the scale, West Virginia had only 2.7% of the homes speaking a foreign language.

Additional insights are gained by looking at the foreign languages spoken at home in the largest cities in the United States. As shown in Table 3-4, many of the cities, such as El Paso, San Diego, and Los Angeles are located on or near the Mexican border. However, Chicago, Boston, and New York are in the Northern part of country. Foreign languages spoken in such cities probably reflect immigrants from other parts of the world as well as Spanish.

Against this background, we examine how the informal value transfer systems work. It should be noted that survey data revealed that about 12% of Mexican immigrants in the U.S. use informal value transfer systems.[6] It should be reiterated that most of the use of IVTS is legitimate.

Table 3-3. Languages Other than English Spoken at Home in Selected States in 2000

State	Percent of Population, 5-years and over
U.S. Average	17.9
Arizona	25.9%
California	39.5
Florida	23.1
Hawaii	26.6
Nevada	23.1
New Jersey	25.5
New Mexico	36.5
New York	28.0
Texas	31.2
----	---
----	----
Alabama, Arkansas, Kentucky,	3.9
Mississippi	3.6
West Virginia	2.7

Source: Statistical Abstract of the United States, 2004-2005, Washington, D.C., U.S. Census Bureau, 2005, Table 49, p. 47.

6 Amuedo-Dorantes, Catalina, Cynthia Bansak, and Susan Pozo, 'On the Remitting Patterns of Immigrants: Evidence from Mexican Survey Data," *Economic Review*, Federal Reserve Bank of Atlanta, First Quarter, 2005, 37-58.

Table 3-4. Languages Other than English Spoken at Home in Large Cities in 2000

Large Cities	Percent of Population, 5-years and over
Boston, MA	33.4.%
Chicago, IL	35.5
Dallas, TX	37.1
El Paso, TX	71.3
Houston, TX	41.3
Los Angeles, CA	57.8
New York, NY	47.6
Phoenix, AZ	32.2
San Antonio, TX	46.7
San Diego, CA	37.4
San Francisco, CA	45.7
San Jose, CA	51.2

Source: Statistical Abstract of the United States, 2004-2005, Washington, D.C., U.S. Census Bureau, 2005, Table 50, p. 47.

It is worthwhile noting the close correlation between the cities listed in Table 3-4 and the High Intensity Financial Crime Areas (HIFCA) and High Intensity Drug Traffic Areas (HIDTAs) that were mentioned in the previous chapter.[7] These are areas where money laundering and financial crimes tend to be concentrated.

- New York/ New Jersey
- San Juan, Puerto Rico
- Los Angeles
- Miami
- The Southwestern border including Arizona and Texas
- The Northern District of Illinois (Chicago)
- The Northern District of California (San Francisco).

The World Council of Credit Unions (WOCCU) has an International Remittance Network (IRnet) that allows people to remit funds from a credit union in the U.S. to one overseas as well as to selected Money Service Businesses (MSBs) (Travelex and Vigo). The IRnet wants to provide low cost service to capture some of the IVTS market and to compete with Western Union and other MSBs. The WOCCU web site listed the following market potential for Latin American countries and the Caribbean:[8]

- Over 40 million Latinos in the US in 2004, 14% of the US population;
- About 18 million of the Latinos are foreign-born, 6.2% of US population;
- About 10 million Latinos are undocumented;

[7] U.S. General Accounting Office, Combating Money Laundering: Opportunities Exist to Improve the National Strategy, GAO-03-813, September 2003; Motivans (2004); For further discussion of HIFCAs, see FinCEN. Also see P.L. 105-310. http://www.FinCEN.gov/le_hifcadesign.html.

[8] World Council of Credit Unions, "International Remittance Network (IRnet)," https://www.woccu.org/prod_serv/irnet/index.php; https://www.woccu.org/prod_serv/irnet/faq.php

- Latinos make up 13% of the US labor force;
- Over $45 billion was sent to Latin American Countries and the Caribbean in 2004, of which $16.6 billion went to Mexico alone;
- Nearly 50% of Latinos are unbanked;
- FDIC projects that Latinos will account for more than half of US retail banking growth in the coming decade and that Latino households with checking accounts will increase by 57% and those with savings accounts by 76% in the next two years.

INFORMAL VALUE TRANSFER SYSTEMS

Compensating Balances

Consider the following simplified example of an IVTS using compensating balances.[9]

Business A in the U.S. owes $1 million (or the peso equivalent) to Business B in Colombia.

Business B in Colombia owes $1 million (of the peso equivalent) to Business C in the U.S.

The businesses find financial brokers/ IVTS operators who specialize in such transactions for a fee. The IVTS operators also may make money on the differences in exchange rates. As shown in Table 3-5, the international debts are settled by using offsetting transactions, and the funds do not leave the country. Business A in the U.S. settles its debts with B in Colombia by paying B's debt to C in the U.S. Alternatively, the *accounts can be settled* in currencies, or commodities such as gold and gems that can be traded, smuggled, or sold, and by manipulating invoices of traded goods and commodities. When businesses are involved, the invoices can be overpriced or under-priced to meet the needs of the participants. For example, a container of goods worth $50,000 may be invoiced for $100,000 thus allowing $50,000 to be laundered.

One problem that the participants in IVTS may encounter is that large bank deposits from domestic or foreign sources, and without economic justification, are red flags for money laundering. Conversely, small transactions are less likely to attract attention.

Table 3-5. IVTS Using Compensating Balances

	United States	Colombia
1	Business A owes $1 million to Business B (in Colombia)	Business B owes $1 million to Business C (in the U.S.)
2		B sends a message through a broker to A to pay C $1 million, less brokerage fees.
3	Business A pays Business C $1 million less fees	

[9] Blum, Jack A., Michael Levi, R. Thomas Naylor, and Phil Williams, "Financial Havens, Banking Secrecy and Money Laundering," New York, United Nations Office for Drug Control and Crime Prevention, 1999. p. 15.

Hawala

Hawala is a traditional IVTS which requires four participants: the sender of funds in one country, the receiver in another, and IVTS operators in both countries facilitate the transfer or remittance.[10] IVTS operators are also called hawaladars. The hawaladars in different countries are connected by family ties, ethnicity, or gang alliances where *trust is* established. Hawala can be defined as "transfer" or "wire" in Arabic, or "money transfer without money movement."[11] Equally, important, there is no paper trail.

In the following example, Amar in the U.S. wants to send $50,000 to Rahman in Pakistan. If he goes to a bank to transfer the funds, the bank would want him to open an account, charge fees for the international transfer, and for differences in the exchange rates. Equally important, dealing with a bank would leave a "paper trail." Instead, as shown in Table 3-6, (1) Amar gives $50,000 to Yasmeen, a local hawaladar named Yasmeen. (2) The Yasmeen gives Amar a code, or a means of communication. (3) Yasmeen contacts Ghulam, his counterpart in Pakistan with payment instructions and the code. The international contacts are made by phone, fax, or e-mail. (4) Amar contacts Rahman, and gives the code to him. Finally, Rahman contacts the Ghulam and gives him the code for the settlement. Rahman then receives the local equivalent of $50,000 less fess charged by the operators and differences in exchange rates, and the settlement process is complete. The payments usually take place within a day.

Table 3-6. Hawala

	United States	Pakistan
1	Amar gives $50,000 to local IVTS operator (hawaladar)	
2	U.S., hawaladar gives code to Amar	
3	U.S. hawaladar contacts IVTS operator in Pakistan, with payment instructions and code	Afghan hawaladar receives payment instructions and code.
4	Amar contacts Rahman and provides code.	Rahman receives code from Amar.
5		Rahman contacts the Afghan hawaladar, gives him the code, and receives the Afgan equivalent of $50,000 less fees.
	Direct Transfer	
1	Amar gives funds to Yasmeen	
	Yasmeen contacts Ghulam	Ghulam receives instructions
		Ghulam pays Rahman

Alternatively, Yasmeen could provide Ghulam with the details of the transaction and skip the codes. The method depends used depends on the degree of trust between the two hawaladars, and the need to obscure the transactions.

---

[10] The example is based on one that appears in FinCEN Advisory, Informal Value Transfer Systems, Issue 33, March 2003, p. 4.

[11] Jost and Sandhu (2000); El-Qorchi (2002).

No funds were transferred between the two countries when Amar paid Raham. Like in the previous case, commodities and invoices may be used to settle accounts.

Contemporary IVTS

The basic process is similar to the one just described. However, in this case, funds are transferred. The owners of cash intensive businesses may accept money from "clients" to transfer overseas. Examples of cash intensive businesses include grocery stores, import/export businesses, restaurants, phone-card stores, and used car dealers. The funds are included with funds from the business and deposited in a local bank. When sufficient funds are accumulated, they are wire transferred to accounts in the United Arab Emirates (U.A.E), London, New York, or Hong Kong. These are considered IVTS hub regions. Dubai, in the U.A.E. is widely used because it has a large population of expatriate workers from India and Pakistan who use hawalas to send money home. In addition, Dubai has a large gold market.

From these hub regions, funds are wire transferred again to IVTS operators overseas where the funds can be withdrawn. Account settlements are the same as those described in connection with compensating balances.

The process can be made obscure to outside observers by using multiple accounts, nominee accounts, false names, smurfs, and couriers to carry out some of the steps.

Box 3-1
Unlicensed Money Remitters

An indictment in U.S. District Court in Brooklyn charged 14 defendants for operating an unlicensed money remitting business and smuggling more than $5 million to Yemen. Yemeni expatriates collected funds from other Yemeni expatriates for shipment to known money remitters in their home country. The expatriates who collected the funds gave the cash to two attorneys (ages 67 and 68) licensed to practice in New York, and a real estate broker (age 81). The attorneys and real estate broker wrote checks for the same amounts from their professional checking accounts. The expatriates who originally collected the funds arranged for couriers traveling to Yemen to smuggle the checks worth more than $5 million out of the country without filing currency transaction reports.

Source: U.S. Immigration and Customs Enforcement, News Release, "ICE Arrests 14 Charged with Operating an Unlicensed Money Remitting Business and Extortionate Loan Scheme, More than $5 million Smuggled to Yemen," March 28, 2006. Additional charges for using an extortionate loan scheme are not discussed here.

Hawalas have been linked directly to several cases of terrorism in India.[12] In one case, terrorists who killed an important politician, used hawala transfer the proceeds from the sale of narcotics to arms dealers to buy weapons. In another, a major bomb blast was financed through hawala. Funds used to buy the explosives and pay the bombers were handled by hawala operators in the United Kingdom, U.A.E., and India.

---

[12] Jost and Sandhu (2000), 15; Also see Passas (2003) for cases involving India (cases 27-29).

Similarly, in 2003, a New York City diamond dealer and money transmitter was indicted for operating an unlicensed money transmitting business.[13] It was alleged that the IVTS system was used to provide funds needed to buy 50 shoulder-fired missiles that terrorists were going to use to shoot down American commercial airliners.

Manipulation of Trade

A Washington D.C. cab driver was a hawaladar for Pakistani immigrants there, in New York City, and other U.S. cities. He conducted his business from his apartment and his cab.[14] The immigrants would give him funds to be sent back to Pakistan, he deposited the funds in several bank accounts at different financial institutions. Some of the accounts were opened using fraudulent identification. The deposits were always less than $10,000 in order to avoid suspicion. Instructions were faxed to his contacts in Pakistan.

Settlement was made by manipulating the prices of goods exported from Pakistan. Pakistan gives exporters a rebate on their Value Added Tax. Therefore some exporters overstate the value of their exports and the tax. In this case, the exporters of surgical goods explained to the U.S. importers that the goods were overvalued, but someone (the hawaladar) would give them the difference the invoice price and the actual price.

The hawaladar in Washington, D.C. gave the funds collected in the U.S. to the importers. When the funds were received by the exporter in Pakistan, the exporter paid the local hawaladar, and then rupees were given to the beneficiaries.

Similarly, the value of goods can be understated. A hawaladar in the United States could buy $100,000 worth of goods that a hawaladar in Pakistan wants to acquire. The goods could be shipped to Pakistan with an invoice for $300,000. This allows the hawaladar in Pakistan to acquire the goods and move $200,000 to the U.S.[15]

Finally, several hawaladars might settle debts between themselves. For example, if hawaladar A owes money to hawaladar B, and B owes money to C, then B may ask A to settle with C.

Regulating Hawalas

Hawalas in the United States must register with FinCEN, and establish anti-money laundering programs that include record keeping and reporting requirements. Several countries, including the United Arab Emirates and Saudi Arabia regulate hawala transactions. Hawalas have been banned in India and Pakistan.[16] Nevertheless, as noted in connection with the "manipulation of trade," hawalas are still being used in Pakistan.

---

13 U.S. Department of Justice, Federal Bureau of Investigation, Press Release, August 13, 2003.

14 Financial Action Task Force, "Money Laundering and Terrorist Financing Typologies, 2004-2005," June 10, 2005, p.24.

15 Jost, Patrick, Testimony before the U.S. Senate Committee on Banking, Housing, and Urban Affairs, Subcommittee on International Trade and Finance, Hearing on "Hawala and Underground Terrorist Financing Mechanisms," November 14, 2001.

16 U.S. Department of Justice and U.S. Department of Treasury, 2003 National Money Laundering Strategy, 2003, p. 78.

Box 3-2
Being Realistic About Regulating Hawalas

According to Tarik Yousef, "... we should be realistic about the limits of what can be achieved in the short-term within our national borders to bring the *Hawala* institution into the modern world. So long as their remains a divergence between the US and other countries in financial development, banking efficiency, taxation levels and laws pertaining to foreign exchange transfers, there will exist a demand for the *Hawala* and other means of moving money across the globe. More importantly, difference in regulation and supervision standards across countries will create loopholes to be exploited by *Hawala* operators and other informal practices"

Source: Yousef, Tarik M, Testimony before the U.S. Senate Committee on Banking, Housing, and Urban Affairs, Subcommittee on International Trade and Finance, Hearing on "Hawala and Underground Terrorist Financing Mechanisms," November 14, 2001.

BLACK MARKET PESO EXCHANGE (BMPE)

The BMPE is a trade-based system. It is the largest and most efficient money laundering system in the Western Hemisphere that has been around for since the 1950s. It was originally used by as a parallel financial system to support both legitimate trade and smuggling between North and South America. Over time, Colombian drug cartels took advantage of the BMPE, and expanded its use to Australia, Canada, Europe, and the United Kingdom.[17]

In 1997, it was estimated that illegal drug sales in the United States were $57.3 billion annually, and a large part of the proceeds of those sales went to Colombian drug cartels.[18] In 2000, American spent an estimated $35 billion on cocaine, $10 billion on methamphetamine, $11 billion on marijuana, $10 on heroin, and $2.4 billion on controlled substances (see Table 3-6).[19] Although the dollar amount spent on drugs is substantial, it is down sharply from previous periods. As shown in Table 3-6, in 1988, total expenditures on drugs were estimated to be $154 billion. By 1995, they were down to $75 billion. Despite the fact that estimates of drug use derived from different sources vary widely, the data suggests that the government's anti-drug efforts are having a positive impact on reducing drug use.

---

[17] Tischler, Bonni, Assistant Commissioner, U.S. Customs Service, "The Colombian Back Market Peso Exchange," Testimony Before the Senate Caucus on International Narcotics Control," June 21, 1999; Financial Action Task Force on Money Laundering, "1999-2000 Report on Money Laundering Typologies," February 3, 2000, p.5..

[18] FinCEN Advisory, "Colombian Black Market Peso Exchange," Issue 9, November 1997; FinCEN Advisory, "Black Market Peso Exchange Update," Issue 12, June 1999; U.S. Immigration and Customs Enforcement, News Release, "ICE Undercover Investigation Dismantles International Drug Money Laundering Organization,", October 15, 2004; U.S. Department of Treasury, "Treasury Announces Signing of Multilateral Recommendations for Combating the Black Market Peso Exchange, System," Press Release, PO-2001, March 14, 2002; U.S. Customs Service, "Black Market Peso Exchange: A Trade Based Money Laundering System," June 1999.

[19] State of Iowa, Iowa Department of Pubic Safety, Intelligence Bureau "Money Laundering Threat Assessment," January 2004. The data are from the Office of National Drug Control Policy, Executive Office of the President, August 2002, (http://www.whitehousedrugpolicy.gov/); Office of National Drug Control Policy, Executive Office of the President, "What America's Users Spend on Illegal Drugs, 1988-2000," December 2001, Table 1, http://www.whitehousedrugpolicy.gov/publications/pdf/american_users_spend_2002.pdf

In 2002, the BMPE is believed to launder $3 billion to $6 billion per year. The BMPE is used to swap "dirty" dollars earned from the sale of cocaine and heroin by Colombian drug cartels in the United States for "clean" pesos in Colombia. It is part of the Informal Value Transfer System (IVTS) which refers to any non-bank system where someone receives money for the purpose of making those funds, or an equivalent value, available to someone else in a different geographic location.[20]

In 2005, the Drug Enforcement Agency announced the results of Operation Mallorca in which it shattered a Colombian drug and money laundering ring.[21] Four Colombian-based money brokers used the BMPE to process the proceeds from drug sales. The operation resulted in the arrest of 36 individual in Colombia and the U.S., and seizure of $7.2 million, 947 kilograms of cocaine, and almost 22,000 pounds of marijuana.

Table 3-6. Total U.S. Expenditures on Illicit Drugs, 1988-2000 ($ in billions, 2000 dollar equivalents)

	1988	1989	1990	1991	1992	1993	1994	1995	1996	1997	1998	1999	2000
Cocaine	107.0	88.4	69.9	57.1	49.9	45.0	42.8	40.0	39.2	43.7	43.9	35.6	35.3
Heroin	26.1	24.3	22.5	20.3	17.2	13.8	13.2	13.2	12.8	11.4	11.1	10.1	10.0
Metha-mphetamines	5.8	5.8	5.7	3.7	4.8	5.1	7.6	9.2	10.1	9.3	8.0	5.8	5.4
Marijuana	12.1	11.0	15.0	14.0	14.6	12.0	12.2	10.2	9.5	10.5	10.8	10.6	10.5
Other Drugs	3.3	2.8	2.2	1.5	1.5	2.6	2.6	2.7	2.7	2.5	2.3	2.6	2.4
Total	154	132	115	97	88	78	78	75	74	68	67	65	64

Column may not add due to rounding. Estimates for 2000 are projections.
Source: Office of National Drug Control Policy, Executive Office of the President, "What America's Users Spend on Illegal Drugs, 1988-2000," December 2001, Table 1.

Generally speaking, the BMPE is a trade-based money laundering system that works in the following manner. A Colombian drug cartel has a "contract" with a black market peso broker in Colombia who has contacts in the United States, such as a money service business (MSB). Alternatively, the peso broker in Colombia may have accounts in the United States. For example, a Colombian national who operated an independent foreign currency exchange business in Bogotá, Colombia, also had accounts at the Miami, Florida branch of Delta National Bank and Trust Company.[22] His foreign exchange transactions were $5 - $10 million.

Illegal narcotics from Colombian drug cartels are sold in the United States for dollars. The cartel contacts a Colombian peso broker to help them launder the funds. The cartel sells the dollars earned from the sale of cocaine and heroin to the peso broker's U.S. contacts (e.g., an MSB).

[20] FinCEN Advisory, Informal Value Transfer Systems, Issue 33, March 2003.

[21] U.S. Department of Justice, Drug Enforcement Agency, News Release, "Colombian Drug and Money Laundering Ring Shattered, Black Market Peso Exchange Used Illegally to Funnel Drug Money," June 14, 2005.

[22] U.S. Immigration and Customs Enforcement, News Release, "Delta National Bank & Trust Company Pleads Guilty After ICE Investigation," October 1, 2003; Also see: U.S. Department of Treasury, "Treasury Under

When the Cartel sells the dollars to the MSB, the funds are "structured" to avoid the BSA's $10,000 currency reporting requirements. The MSB may deposit the funds into a series of bank accounts under various names, but that are controlled by the MSB. The funds can be wired to other accounts in the United States, Colombia, Costa Rica, and China. In addition, the funds earned from the sale cocaine may be added to the receipts of an established business that has a relationship with the Cartel.

Ultimately, the funds are transferred to the peso broker in Colombia which then credit's the Cartel's account with an equivalent amount of pesos. At this point, the funds have been laundered and the Cartel is out of the picture. The peso broker earned fees for the laundering, and now has U.S. dollars that it will sell to Colombian importers.

The dollars are sold to Colombian importers who used them to buy goods may be shipped to the Caribbean, South America, Europe or Asia to avoid detection. The goods include consumer electronics, cigarettes, household appliances, used auto parts, and so on. They are smuggled into Colombia to avoid paying import and exchange tariffs.

In 1999, an Organized Crime Drug Enforcement Taskforce undercover "Operation Juno" involved millions of dollars being laundered.[23] Drug proceeds ranging from $100,000 to $500,000 picked up by undercover agents in Dallas, Houston, New York, Newark, Providence, Chicago, Madrid (Spain), and Rome (Italy), and were subsequently wire transferred to a bank in Atlanta. Then they were distributed to various accounts around the world, and laundered through the BMPE. Thus the BMPE is a global system for money laundering.

The payment methods may provide "red flags" for the BMPE. For example, payments for outstanding invoices that are paid in cash, wire transfers, checks or drafts by third party entities that have no connection with the underlying transaction.

Mexican Bank Drafts and Third Party Checks

Mexican bank drafts are checks or drafts that a Mexican bank draws on a correspondent bank in the U.S. Most of these drafts are legitimate, but some aren't.[24] The illegal part usually involves a customer presenting a large amount of smuggled U.S. cash to a Mexican bank purchase a check or draft denominated in U.S. dollars. The Mexican bank accepts the cash and gives the customer a check drawn on its correspondent bank in the U.S. The check can be carried across the border, and the carrier does not have to file a Currency or Monetary Instruments Report (CIMR) with U.S. Customs, unless the check has been endorsed without restriction. Alternatively, the check could be endorsed and sent to a third party in the U.S. who could deposit it.

Endorsed/third party checks are sometimes used in the BMPE. An endorsed/third party check is a check payable to somebody other than the drawer, who transfers the check to

Secretary for Enforcement James E. Johnson Fore the Senate Caucus on International Narcotics Control," Press Release, RR-3214, June 21, 1999.

[23] Warren (2001).

[24] The Bank Secrecy Act/Anti-Money Laundering Comptroller's Handbook, Washington, D.C., Office of the Comptroller of the Currency, Consumer Compliance Examination, September 2000, Revised for Web Publication, December, 2000. p. 38.

someone else by endorsing the check and writing "pay to the order of" another party.[25] The new check holder can endorse it and exchange it for cash at a financial institution.

Third party checks are widely used in currency black markets in the Middle East, Africa, and the Americas, where there is a high demand for U.S. dollars. Institutions accepting endorsed/third party checks may charge a commission of 3-5 percent to cover the risk of nonpayment. In addition, the check may be accepted for collection only, which delays the payment of the check to the payee, but protects the institution from a loss.

Large third party checks for different jurisdictions, and payable to payees with no local connection are grounds for submitting a suspicious activity report.

INTERNATIONAL REMITTANCES

Although the focus of this chapter is on informal value transfer systems, it is important to recognize the global importance of legitimate remittances including hawalas. According to the World Bank, in 2005, the total value of worldwide remittances for about 175 million migrants exceeded US$230 billion.[26] In some countries, remittances account for about one third of their Gross Domestic Product (GDP), and about one third of the global external finance.

In 2003, remittances from the United States were estimated to be $28.2 -$30.6 billion.[27] Interestingly, Saudi Arabia was the second largest source of remittances with about $10 billion. Most of the remittances from the U.S. flow into Latin America, which includes Mexico, Central America, South America, and the Caribbean. Mexico received almost $9 billion. Large amounts of remittances also went to Asia, where the Philippines were the largest recipient.

---

[25] FinCEN, "The SAR Activity Review: Trends, Tips & Issues, Issue 7, August, 2004. p. 12.

[26] The World Bank, "General Principals for International Remittance Services, Committee on Payment and Settlement Systems," Consultative Report, March 2006, p. 1.

[27] U.S. General Accountability Office, International Remittances: Different Estimation Methodologies Produce Different Results, GAO-06-210.

Chapter 4

BSA/AML VIOLATIONS AND RELATED CRIMES

The Bank Secrecy Act of 1970 (BSA) and subsequent laws requires financial institutions to have monetary record and reporting requirements. These include Currency Transaction Reports (CTRs) on currency transactions of more than $10,000, (Currency or Other Monetary Instrument Reports) for the transportation of $10,000 or more in currency into or out of the U.S., and Suspicious Activity Reports (SAR) where there is suspicion that a law has been broken. These reports play a crucial role in alerting regulators and law enforcement authorities about actual and potential violations of the law. In addition, the BSA/AML laws have requirements dealing with customer identification programs, correspondent banking, internal compliance reviews, training, etc. Violations of the BSA/AML laws are treated seriously.

Table 4-1 lists only those enforcement actions reported by the Federal Reserve Board which covers institutions over which they have statutory authority. This includes state member banks, bank holding companies, nonbank subsidiaries of bank holding companies, Edge and agreement corporations, branches and agencies of foreign banking organizations operating in the United States and their parent banks. It does not include enforcement actions of other government agencies involving other financial institutions covered by the BSA/AML laws (see Box 4-1). As noted in Chapter 1, *Financial institutions*, in the context of BSA/AML, also includes savings and loan associations, credit unions, federally regulated securities brokers, currency exchange houses, funds transmitters, check-cashing businesses, persons subject to supervision by state or federal bank supervisory authority, casinos, card clubs, futures commission merchants, introducing brokers, commodity pool operators, and commodity trading advisors. Also included in the definition of financial institutions are any individuals or groups engaged in conducting, controlling, directing or owning informal value transfer systems (IVTS) in the United States. Finally insurance companies offering selected products were added to the list of financial institutions in 2006.

Some of the enforcement actions listed in Table 4-1 involve multiple agencies. For example, the enforcement action against ABN AMRO Bank, N.V. involved the Federal Reserve, FinCEN, Office of Foreign Asset Control (OFAC), New York State Banking Department, and the Illinois Department of Financial and Profession Regulation. The enforcement actions referred to in the Table may include Civil Money Penalties (CMP), Cease and Desist Orders, and Written Agreements to make certain changes in policies and practices.

Box 4-1
Securities Broker-Dealer Fined $2.8, and Banco Popular De Puerto Rico enters Deferred Prosecution Agreement

1. Oppenheimer and Company, a securities broker-dealer based in New York was assessed a $2.8 million Civil Money Penalty for violations of the Bank Secrecy Act. Oppenheimer failed to establish and implement an adequate AML program in violation of the BSA. It also failed to identify and report suspicious transactions as required by BSA. The penalty was assessed concurrently by FinCEN and the New York Stock Exchange.
2. Banco Popular de Puerto Rico entered into a deferred prosecution agreement with the U.S. Department of Justice and it will forfeit $21.6 million dollars as part of that agreement for failure to report suspicious activities as required under the Bank Secrecy Act. Millions of dollars of drug proceeds were laundered through this bank. According to U.S. Customs Commissioner Robert C. Bonner, "In some cases, gym bags full of cash were literally brought into the bank for deposit by money launderers. Despite its legal obligation to report these suspicious transactions to the government in a timely manner, Banco Popular, in some cases, chose not to report these transactions until years after the fact- and do so only after learning about the U.S. Customs/IRS investigation into the Bank."

Sources: FinCENnews, "FinCEN Accesses $2.8 Million Penalty Against Oppenheimer and Co., Inc.," December 29, 2005; U.S. Department of Justice, "Banco Popular de Puerto Rico Enters into Deferred Prosecution Agreement with U.S. Department of Justice," January 16, 2003.

Table 4-1, lists 17 enforcement actions during the 2004-2005 period. The list reveals that the BSA/AML laws and reports apply to both large and small domestic and foreign financial institutions. Details about several of these cases are discussed in this and other chapters.[1]

Ten Fundamental Laws of Money Laundering

The United Nations Office on Drugs and Crime published "The Ten Fundamental Laws of Money Laundering," that reveal the difficulties in detecting money laundering activities.[2]

1. The more successful a money laundering apparatus is in imitating the patterns of legitimate businesses, the less the likelihood that it will be exposed.

---

[1] The Enforcement actions for each institution listed in Table 3-1 are available at the Federal Reserve's website for enforcement actions: http://www.federalreserve.gov/boarddocs/enforcement/search.cfm
Enforcement actions for FDIC, Office of the Comptroller of the Currency (OCC), the National Credit Union Administration (NCUA), and the Office of Thrift Supervision (OTS) are available on the Federal Financial Institutions (FFEIC) website: http://www.ffiec.gov/enforcement.htm.

[2] United Nations Office on Drugs and Crime, "The Ten Fundamental Laws of Money Laundering," April 4, 2005.

Table 4. 1. Board of Governors of the Federal Reserve System Enforcement Actions, 2004-2005

Press Release Date	Name of Institution and Location
12/19/05	ABN AMRO Bank N.V., New York, N.Y., and Chicago, IL.
10/15/05	Deutsche Bank Trust Company Americas, New York, N.Y.
2/2/05	Banco de Chile, Miami Fl.
1/28/05	Asian Bank, Philadelphia, PA.
1/27/05	Riggs National Corporation, Washington, D.C.
10/29/04	Country Bank, Merced, CA.
10/19/05	Union Bank of California International, New York, N.Y.
10/12/04	AmSouth Bank, Birmingham, AL.
10/8/04	Standard Chartered Bank London, U.K., New York, N.Y.
7/26/04	ABN AMRO Bank N.V., The Netherlands,
7/12/04	First Midwest Bank, Itasca, IL.
5/14/04	Riggs National Corporation, Washington, D.C., Riggs International Banking Corporation, Miami, FL.
5/10/04	UBS, AG, Zurich Switzerland
3/24/04	Planters Bank and Trust Company, Staunton, VA
3/24/04	Virginia Heartland Bank, Fredericksburg, VA.
3/4/04	Cowboy State Bancorp, Inc., Ranchester, WY.
2/24/04	Custar State Bank, Custar, OH.

Source: Board of Governors of the Federal Reserve System, "List of Enforcement Actions" as of 12/31/05; http://www.federalreserve.gov/boarddocs/enforcement/search.cfm

2. The more deeply embedded illegal activities are within the legal economy, and the less their institutional and legal separation, the more difficult it is to detect money laundering.
3. The smaller the ratio of illegal to legal financial flows through a business, the more difficult it is to detect money laundering.
4. The higher the ratio of legal "services" to physical goods production in any economy, the easier it is to conduct money laundering.
5. The more the structure of businesses is dominated by small independent firms and self-employed individuals, the more difficult it is to distinguish legal from illegal transactions.
6. The more checks, credit cards, and other non-cash instruments are used for effecting illegal financial transactions, the more difficult it is to detect money laundering.
7. The greater the degree of financial deregulation for legitimate transactions, the more difficult it is to detect money laundering.
8. The lower the ratio of illegally to legally earned income entering an economy from the outside, the harder the job of separating criminal from legal money.
9. The greater the progress towards financial supermarkets in which all manner of financial services can be satisfied in one multi-division institution, the more difficult it will be to detect money laundering.
10. The greater the contradiction between global operation and national regulation of financial markets, the more difficult the detection of money laundering.

Collectively, these "Fundamental Laws," or observations, suggest that in a complex society and economy, such as the U.S., it can be a daunting task to detect money laundering. Nevertheless, the law says that money laundering is illegal, and there are stiff penalties for those domestic and foreign financial institutions that break the law.

The process of detecting money laundering starts with the bank tellers or others who have contact with the customers. They are in the best position to determine if deposit transactions are consistent with that customer, or do they raise questions. But the system is not foolproof. Two of the hijackers (Khalid al Midhar and Nawaaf al Hazmi) in the September 11, 2001 terrorist attacks were members of al Qaeda, and had bank accounts where they received funds for their training.[3] But the banks had no reason to suspect what they were doing involved terrorist acts.

In addition, data mining and other software is available to examine anomalies in financial transactions. However, as financial institutions have become more vigilant and improve their ability to detect illicit activities, money launderers try other methods to avoid detection.

SELECTED CASE STUDIES OF BSA/AML VIOLATIONS

UBS, AG

The Federal Reserve Board issued a $100 million Civil Money Penalty against UBS, AG, Zurich Switzerland, a foreign bank. The CMP was issued in connection with "U.S. dollar banknote transactions with counterparties in jurisdictions subject to sanctions under U.S. law, specifically Cuba, Libya, Iran, and Yugoslavia."[4] At a U.S. House hearing on UBS, Representative Luis V. Gutierrez said "While this fine of $100 million seems very large, it is merely, I believe, a drop in a bucket of a $1 trillion institution."[5] This was the second largest Civil Money Penalty ever assessed a bank by the Federal Reserve. The largest was a $200 million penalty against BCCI in 1992.

By way of background, the U.S. dollar is widely used throughout the world. It is estimated that two thirds of our currency, about $400 billion, circulates outside the United States. In order to sustain the quantity and quality of the paper currency in circulation overseas, and to deter counterfeiting, the Federal Reserve and Treasury initiated the Extended Custodial Inventory (ECI) program in 1996 to facilitate the introduction of the newly designed $100 banknote. The Federal Reserve contracts with large international banks in Frankfurt, Hong Kong, London, Singapore, and Zurich to hold U.S. dollar currency (i.e., Federal Reserve banknotes), in their vaults, and to distribute the funds as needed. UBS was an ECI contractor in Zurich, Switzerland. The ECI contract required the banks to abide by U.S. laws concerning money laundering and U.S.-Embargo provisions.

---

[3] National Commission on Terrorist Attacks Upon the United States, Staff Monograph on Terrorist Financing, 2004, p. 56.

[4] Board of Governors of the Federal Reserve System, Federal Reserve Press Release: May 10, 2004, (Order of Assessment of a Civil Money Penalty Against UBS).

[5] U.S. House of Representatives, Subcommittee on Oversight and Investigations, Committee on Financial Services, "Risk Management and Regulatory Failures at Riggs and UBS: Lessons Learned," June 2, 2004, p. 3.; ECI and UBS are discussed in the hearings, and in the prepared testimony ofpáhomas C. Baxter, Jr., Executive Vice President and General Counsel for the Federal Reserve Bank of New York.

On April 20, 2003, *The New York Times* reported that the U.S. military in Baghdad, Iraq, discovered approximately $650 million of freshly printed U.S. banknotes issued, in part, by the Federal Reserve Bank of New York. This led to an investigation that revealed that UBS had engaged in U.S. dollar banknote transactions with Iran and Cuba. Both are jurisdictions that are subject to sanctions by the Office of Foreign Asset Control (OFAC) of the Department of Treasury (Libya, and Yugoslavia are two additional jurisdictions subject to sanctions). Simply stated, under the terms of their ECI contract, they were not allowed to provide currencies to countries on the OFAC list because it is against U.S. laws to do so. To make matters worse, some UBS officers and employees intentionally hid facts from the Federal Reserve that they were providing currency to countries on the OFAC list. Their deception included, but was not limited to falsification of monthly reports to the Federal Reserve. The Federal Reserve terminated the ECI contract with UBS on October 28, 2003 for its failure to comply with OFAC obligations. It was later revealed that UBS also had currency dealings with Yugoslavia (the Republics of Serbia and Montenegro) and Libya.

The Swiss Federal Banking Commission reprimanded UBS for the failure of its internal controls. UBS planned to discontinue its banknote trading business, and they were forbidden to restart it without the Swiss Federal Banking Commission's permission. During the 1999-2003 period, banknote trading had produced net profits of about $87 million.

ABN AMRO Bank N.V

Bank regulators fined ABN AMRO $80 million and required it to improve its risk management systems and to fully comply with U.S. BSA/AML laws and regulations in connection with violations of those and other laws at its branches in New York City and Chicago.[6] ABN AMRO is the 20th largest bank in the world, and it has more than 3,000 branches in more than 60 countries. Several of their violations include the following:

For about a decade prior to August 1, 2004, the branches processed wire transfers and letters of credit originated by the Bank Meli, Iran, an institution owned or controlled by the Government of Iran. The payment instructions were disguised by the Dubai branch of ABN AMRO to hide any reference to that bank. Dubai is located in the United Arab Emirates. They also dealt in letters of credit for Arab Bank for Investment and Foreign Trade that was owned by the Government of Libya. Both countries were on the Office of Foreign Assets Control (OFAC) list of sanctioned countries that supported terrorism. Sanctions against Libya were relaxed in 2004.

6 Board of Governors of the Federal Reserve System, Joint Press Release, "Agencies release supervisory and penalty actions against ABN AMRO Bank N.V." December 19, 2005; United States of America Before the Board of Governors of the Federal Reserve System, Washington, D.C., Office of Foreign Asset Control, U.S. Department of The Treasury, State of Illinois Department of Financial and Professional Regulation, New York State Banking Department, New York, New York, In the Matter of ABN AMRO BANK N.V., Amsterdam, The Netherlands, ... New York Branch, and Chicago Branch, FRB Dkt No. 05-35-CMP-FB, Order of Assessment of Civil Money Penalty...., December 19, 2005; United States of America, Department of The Treasury, Financial Crimes Enforcement Network, In the Matter of the New York Branch, ABN AMRO BANK N.V., New York, New York, Number 2005-5, December 19, 2005; Simson, Glen R., "ABN AMRO to Pay $80 Million Fine Over Iran, Libya," The Wall Street Journal, December 20, 2005, A3, A6. Simson, Glen R., "How Top Dutch Bank Plunged Into World of Shadowy Money," The Wall Street Journal, December 30, 2005, A1, A7.

In addition, the New York branch operated as the North American Regional Clearing Center for the ABN AMRO network. In 2000, about 35 financial institutions in Russia opened correspondent accounts with the New York branch which processed about 30,000 funds transfers per day. Unfortunately, the New York branch was not adequately staffed to coordinate and monitor compliance with the BSA anti-money laundering compliance programs. For example, they failed to incorporate publicly available information about "shell companies" into their monitoring systems. Shell companies do not have a physical presence, and they are typically limited liability companies. From August 2002 until September 2003, they processed 20,000 funds transfers worth about $3.2 billion that involved "shell companies" in the U.S. and Russia and the former Soviet Union that served as originators or beneficiaries in the transactions.

ABN AMRO's Chairman of the Managing Board, Rijkman Groenink, said that in the past, our compliance in certain areas did not meet the highest standards. He went on to say that improving compliance is the highest priority of the bank.[7] To recognize the fact that the Managing Board accepted full responsibility for their past shortcomings in compliance, Chairman Rijkman Groenink and Chief Financial Officer Tom de Swaan, and four others paid back €1 million collectively of the bonuses they received in 2004. To put these fines in perspective, Groenink's base pay in 2004 was €889,000, and his bonus was € 805,000. He repaid 40% of his bonus. T de Swan's base pay and bonus was €635,000 and €575,000 respectively. He repaid 30% of the bonus.[8] The other four members repaid 20% of their bonuses.

ABN AMRO Mortgage Group, Inc. (AAMG) had a $41 million settlement with the U.S. Department of Housing and Urban Affairs in 2006.[9] This settlement involved AAMG falsifying tens of thousands of documents for loans insured by the Federal Housing Administration (FHA). ABN AMRO agreed to pay the government $16.85 million, and that it would not submit insurance claims on 783 loans, which saves the FHA insurance fund about $24.35 million in potential losses. Finally, the Comptroller of the Currency imposed a $6.25 million Civil Money Penalty on the AAMG as part of the $16.85 million settlement.[10]

The Bank of New York (BONY) and its illicit dealings with certain Russians is discussed in Chapter 5. Despite the legal and regulatory problems that arose from dealing with these clients, ABN AMRO wanted to serve them too.[11]

Although neither the mortgage group nor its dealings with the BONY's former Russian clients has anything to do with BSA/AML laws, it shows a pattern of risky behavior by the bank.

---

7 ABN AMRO, Press Room, "ABN AMRO Announcement Regarding Regulatory Directive," Amsterdam, December 19, 2005.

8 ABN AMRO, Annual Report, 2004, p. 152.

9 U.S. Department of Housing and Urban Development, News Release, "HUD Announces Landmark $41 million Settlement Against ABN AMRO," January 4, 2006.

10 Comptroller of the Currency, News Release, "OCC Issues Civil Money Penalty Against National Bank Subsidiary," January 4, 2006.

11 Simson, Glen R., "How Top Dutch Bank Plunged Into World of Shadowy Money," The Wall Street Journal, December 30, 2005, A1, A7.

Beach Bank, Miami Beach, Florida[12]

While UBS and ABN AMRO are among the largest banks in world, Beach Bank is at the other end of the size spectrum. Beach Bank was an insured state nonmember bank with $117 million in assets in September 2005. It opened for business in 2000, and their web site states that it is "100% Local/Directors, Staff, Involvement."[13] The early history of this bank showed that the Board was not doing its job.

The FDIC Order to Cease and Desist issued in 2004 stated that Beach Bank operated without an effective Board of Directors oversight and executive management supervision to prevent unsafe and unsound practices and violations of the Bank Secrecy Act. In addition, it did not have effective "Know Your Customer policies and procedures. It had inadequate internal controls and systems with regard to Money Service Businesses, inadequate audit procedures, and other problems.

Beach Bank highlights a major problem that new and small banks have in attracting *competent outside directors who understand the operating and legal complexities of banking.* In very general terms, new and small banks seek outside directors who are well known in their communities and who can help the bank grow by attracting depositors and borrowers. Doctors, successful local business owners, football coaches, lawyers, and accountants are examples of such people. In fact, Beach Bank's web site states that "Beach Bank is especially fortunate to have a Board comprised of members with deep roots in the community, who bring the highest standards of integrity, as well as business acumen to their positions on the Board." The 2004 FDIC Order to Cease and Desist suggests that in the past, the directors were not doing their job. One can only hope that this bank and other small banks strive to correct such deficiencies.

Arab Bank

Arab Bank was founded in Jerusalem in 1930. Its' founder, Abdul Hameed Shoman, had close ties with the Palestine Liberation Organization (PLO). Arab Bank and the Arab Bank Group are controlled by the Shoman family. Abdel Hamid A.M. Showman is the Deputy Chairman and Chief Executive Officer of Arab Bank and Arab Bank Group. In one of the Complaints, it states that the CEO met with the Popular Committee in Support of the Infitada and discussed ways to distribute donations to the martyrs' families and the injured of the infitada.[14] At a meeting of the Arab League in 2000, it was agreed that a financing network, including Arab Bank, was needed to fund the means to achieve Palestinian political and nationalistic goals. One of those means is terrorism. Shortly after that meeting, the Saudi Committee in Support of the Infitada Al Quds was established as a private charity in Saudi Arabia.

---

[12] FDIC, Order to Cease and Desist, In the Matter of Beach Bank, Miami Beach, Florida, FDIC-04-233b, May 11, 2004.

[13] Beach Bank, Miami Beach Florida, website http://beachbank.com, 12/22/05. Beach Bank's FDIC Certificate Number is 35051. "Total Assets" of $117 million are listed in Beach Bank's Consolidated Report of Condition for September 30, 2005.

[14] Arab Bank, First Amended Complaint, Case No. CV 04-5449 (NG)(ASG), U.S. District Court, Eastern District of New York, January 21, 2005.

Donations to Arab Bank for the Saudi Committee were called for by advertisements, telethons, and radio programs throughout the Middle East. It was widely understood that funds raised through the Arab Bank were to support terrorist attacks. The Saudi Committee would pay the families of Palestinian suicide bombers a cash payment of $5,316.06, and some also received smaller monthly payments. The Saudi Committee provided millions of dollars in death benefits and dismemberment benefits to the families of suicide bombers and others. The funds were administered and distributed through Arab Bank.

The Complaint also alleges that Arab Bank provided banking services for the Hamas terrorist organization trough various bank accounts in Beirut.

Arab Bank is now headquartered in Amman, Jordon. It has assets in excess of $32 billion, and offices in 30 countries. It is the largest bank operating in the Palestinian territories. Arab Bank's Federal Branch in New York had $425 million in assets, where it had been in operation since the early 1980s. The Federal Branch was designated as a wholesale bank and it provided clearing and correspondent banking services for banks affiliated with the Arab Bank Group and other foreign banks. The Federal Branch made extensive use of wire transfers for charities and other banks wanting to send funds to the Middle East. The Holy Land Foundation for Relief and Development, and the Global Relief Foundation are two examples. Some of the funds were first channeled through several global banks such as Citibank. The OCC Consent Order noted that the Federal Branch of Arab bank had internal control weaknesses in international funds transfers.

One law suit filed in New York alleges that the Federal Branch transferred more than $100 million collected from a Saudi charity to make payments to the families of Palestinian terrorist suicide bombers who killed 15 people in Jerusalem in 2001.[15]

Between September 2000 and January 2005, it is alleged that various Palestinian terrorists have attempted about 21,000 attacks which resulted in more than 800 civilian deaths and over 6,000 injuries. The deaths include at least 30 U.S. civilians.

In this connection, it is alleged that Arab Bank had funneled billions of dollars to various terrorist organizations including the Al-Aqsa Martyrs Brigade, Hamas, Palestinian Islamic Jihad, the Popular Front for the Liberation of Palestine, and others.[16] Another law suit charges that under the Antiterrorism and Effective Death Penalty Act of 1996, Arab Bank knowingly and willfully provided and administered the distribution of funds to terrorists or their families as rewards or to encourage them.[17] Accordingly, they aided, abetted and conspired to commit acts of international terrorism that resulted in deaths and maiming U.S. citizens. The bank denies knowingly funding terrorists or their associates.

In February 2005, the OCC announced that the Federal Branch of Arab Bank PLC, New York, New York, consented to be converted into an agency office because of BSA/AML

[15] "Arab Bank Helped Saudi Charity Pay Bomber Families, Suit Says," Bloomberg.com, January 27, 2005; Simson, Glen R., "Arab Bank's Link to Terrorism Poses Dilemma for U.S. Policy," The Wall Street Journal, April 20, 2005, A1, A8.

[16] Mowbray, Joel, "The Case Against Arab Bank," The Washington Times, Washingtontimes.com, December 30, 2004.

[17] Arab Bank, First Amended Complaint, Case No. CV 04-5449 (NG)(ASG), U.S. District Court, Eastern District of New York, January 21, 2005.

violations.[18] In addition, it was fined a $24 million civil money penalty for its failure to comply with the BSA/AML procedures.

Because of the allegations, the OCC Consent Order, and the lawsuits brought by families of those lost in terrorist bombings, Arab Bank closed most of their U.S. operations.[19] It will continue to finance trade (e.g. issue letters of credit), but not engage in deposit taking and only limited wire transfers.

Failure to Get a Money Transmission License and Register with Fincen

"A federal judge sentenced a Herndon, Va., man to 10 years in prison for illegally sending more than $6 million to Pakistan and other countries. Mohammad Bajwa, a 40-year-old Pakistani national, was sentenced to prison for 10 years and ordered to give up his home in Herndon, Virginia and $3.5 million.

Mohammad Bajwa was convicted by a federal grand jury in October pursuant to the U.S. Patriot Act that requires money transmitters to obtain the required state license and register with FinCEN, an agency of the US Treasury, before engaging in the money transmission business. Testimony showed that Mohammad Bajwa operated a money transmission business in Virginia before and after March 2002 when the Virginia Bureau of Financial Institutions denied the money transmission application of Hashim Enterprises, Inc., a company owned and managed by Bajwa. The prosecution produced evidence connecting Bajwa to six million dollars he helped people wire to Pakistan and other countries from Virginia residents. He was also convicted of wire fraud connected to a refinancing application he filed on a mortgage.

Prosecutors said Bajwa collected money from people in Virginia and then wired it to overseas banks. His brother in Pakistan then collected the money and distributed it to its recipients. Prosecutors said Bajwa also illegally wired money to several other countries, including the United Arab Emirates, Japan, India, China, Taiwan, and Holland."[20] In addition, Bajwa was convicted of immigration fraud and sentenced to two years in prison.

Western Union and Bandco Check Cashing Services

The New York State Banking Department fined Western Union Financial Services, Inc. $8 million for allegedly deficiencies in complying with anti-money laundering laws.[21]

---

[18] Comptroller of the Currency, Consent Order, The Federal Branch of Arab Bank PLC, New York, New York, AA-EC-05-12, #2005-14, February 24, 2005; Comptroller of the Currency, News Release, "OCC Issues Order Against the Federal Branch Of Arab Bank PLC," NR 2005-11, February, 25, 2005.Comptroller of the Currency, New Release, "FinCEN and OCC Assess $24 Million Penalty Against Arab Bank Branch," NR2005-80, August 17, 2005.

[19] Simson, Glen R., and John R. Wilke, "Arab Bank to Close Operations In U.S. Amid Inquiry, Lawsuits," The Wall Street Journal, February 9, 2005, A2.

[20] Money Transmitter Regulators Association (MTRA), "Ten Year Sentence for Money Laundering and Operating without a Virginia Money Transmission License," November 29, 2005, http://mtraweb.org/news .shtm#ten_year. For additional discussion of MSBs, see: FinCEN, "The SAR Activity Review: Trend, Tips, & Issues, Issue 10, May 2006.

[21] State of New York Banking Department, Regulatory Action, "Banking Department Fines Western Union $8 Million for Violating Bank Secrecy, USA Patriot, New York Banking Laws," December 20, 2002: State of

Similarly, the New York State Banking department fined Bandco Check Cashing Services Inc. $50,000 for violations involving currency transaction reports and other money laundering laws.

Polish and Slavic Federal Credit Union

The former management and directors of the Polish and Slavic Federal Credit Union improperly exempted a customer from filing CTRs.[22] The customer was the former chairman of the credit union's board of directors, and the owner of a travel agency and money remittance business. During the 1989-1997 period, the remitter made more than 1,000 currency deposits in excess of $10,000, and no CTRs were filed. Beginning in 1997, the credit union took a series of enforcement actions to comply with the BSA. In 2000, FinCEN assessed them with a $185,000 civil money penalty.

Broadway National Bank, New York, New York[23]

In 1998, various accounts at Broadway National Bank were being used to structure transactions, or they were receiving large amounts of cash with wire transfers to countries that were known as money laundering and drug centers. About $4 million was seized by law enforcement authorities, and a dozen individuals were arrested. In 2002, the bank pled guilty to a three count felony that charged it with failure to maintain an AML program, failure to report approximately $123 million in suspicious bulk cash and structured deposits, and aiding and assisting customers to structure about $76 million in order to avoid CTR requirements. The $76 million in cash was placed in more than 100 accounts at Broadway.

Alfred Dauber was the largest single launderer. He laundered narcotics proceeds for a Colombian drug cartel. He, or his runner, would drop on an average of $178,000 in cash on a single day. The largest cash deposit on a single day was $660,645. The cash was in duffle bags filled with small bills wrapped in rubber bands. The tellers had to work over their lunch hours to count the money. The branch mangers would authorize the wiring most of the funds to Colombia, Panama, and Miami, Florida. Dauber liked this bank because they did not ask questions, or file CTR or SAR reports.

The bank paid a $4 million criminal fine.

New York Banking Department, Regulatory Action, "Bandco Check Cashing Services, Inc., a licensed casher of checks, has entered into a Settlement Agreement with the Superintendent of Banks which includes the payment of a $50,000 fine," April 12, 2004.

[22] D'Agostino, Davi M., (2004).

[23] This case appears in Stipano (2004); Also see U.S. Customs Service, Press Release, "Manhattan Bank Pleads Guilty to U.S. Criminal Charges for Failure to Report $123 Million in Suspicious Cash Deposits," November 27, 2002. Hawke, John D. Jr., Comptroller of the Currency, Testimony before the U.S. Senate Committee on Banking, Housing, and Urban Affairs, June 3, 2004.

Operation Casablanca

Operation Casablanca was the largest money laundering case to date in 1998. It was a law enforcement undercover operation that resulted in money laundering convictions of drug traffickers, bankers, and two Mexican banks operating in the U.S.

During this three-year undercover operation, U.S. Customs agents posed as employees of the CasaBlanca hotel in Mesquite, were they served as middlemen for the cartel brokers and bankers involved in the BMPE scheme. It resulted in the arrest of about 200 individuals including Mexican bankers and executives, and the seizure of over $100 million from 14 banks.[24] In addition, more than two tons of cocaine and four tons of marijuana were seized.

According to the indictments, officials from 12 of Mexico's 19 largest banks were involved in money laundering activities involving the Colombian Cali cartel and the Mexican Juarez cartel. Funds from drug sales were being laundered in Mexican banks along the U.S. border. Nearly 100 U.S. bank accounts were involved in the money laundering activities.

Two foreign banks with operations in the U.S., Bancomer S.A (Mexico City, Mexico) and Banca Serfin S.A. (Lomas de Sante Fe, Mexico) plead guilty to criminal charges. Each paid $500,000 in criminal fines and forfeited $9.4 million and $4.2 million respectively. Charges against Confia were dropped because most of its assets were sold to Citibank. Confia forfeited $12.1 million.

Bank of China, New York Federal Branch[25]

In 2000, there was serious misconduct on the part of the branch and its former officials and potential fraud and money laundering. The misconduct included facilitation of a fraudulent letter of credit scheme that resulted in losses. As a result of enforcement actions, fines of $20 million were imposed, and a Cease and Desist Order was issued which, among other things, required changed procedures for dealing with high-risk customers.

Banco De Estado Do Parana, Federal Branch, New York, N.Y. (Banestado)[26]

In 1997, OCC examiners found significant and unusually large numbers of monetary instruments being shipped via courier into the Federal Branch from Brazil and other South American countries. In addition, there was wire transfer activity that suggested the layering of the shipped deposits through various accounts where there was no apparent business

---

[24] Tischler, (1999); "Three Guilty, Three Innocent of Laundering Money for Drug Cartel," Las Vegas Review-Journal, June 12, 1999; U.S. Department of Treasury, "U.S. Customs Service Takes Down Major Drug Traffickers, Corrupt Banks and Bankers in Largest Drug Money Laundering Case Ever," Press Release, PR2452, May 18, 1998; Bonner, Robert C., Commissioner, U.S. Customs, Speech to the Egmont Group of Financial Intelligence Units Tracking Terrorist Financing, Washington, D.C., October 31, 2001; Board of Governors of the Federal Reserve System, Federal Reserve Press Release: December 12, 2000, Operation Casablanca Enforcement Actions..

[25] This case appears in Stipano, Daniel P., Deputy Counsel, OCC, Testimony Before the Subcommittee on Oversight and Investigations of the Committee on Financial Services, U.S. House of Representatives, June 2, 2004.

[26] This case appears in Stipano (2004).

justification for the transfers. Cease and Desist Orders were issued, and the branch paid and a CMP of $75,000.

Khalil Kharfan Organization.[27]

The Khalil Kharfan Organization operated in Colombia, Puerto Rico, Florida, and the New York Tri-State area. They had laundered more than $100 million in narcotics proceeds. The organization used several types of communications devices to facilitate the transfer of funds worldwide. The Colombian cell had staff stationed in Puerto Rico, Florida, New York, and New Jersey. They used "members" to open fictitious businesses accounts in international businesses and banks in Panama, Israel, Switzerland, and Colombia where funds could be deposited and transferred.

Jefferson National Bank, Watertown, New York[28]

In 1993, several bank customers were making large deposits that did not appear to be supported by their underlying businesses, and the funds were being wired offshore. The funds were derived from smuggling about $687 million worth of cigarettes and liquor through the Akwesasne Indian Reservation in Northern New York into Canada between 1991 and 1997. The case resulted in 21 indictments and the recovery of $557 million. R.J. Reynolds tobacco company paid a $15 million criminal fine. Seven bank officers and directors were convicted of crimes, and other fines and penalties were assessed.

Advanced Fee Frauds, Suspicious E-Mails, and Faxs

The U.S. Secret Service seized over $4.3 million from a Miami bank account in connection with money that was laundered as part of a well organized, large scale, advanced fee fraud scheme.[29] These schemes usually involve the solicitation of funds via fax or over the internet. The criminals claim to have millions of dollars available for wire transfer from Nigeria to the victim. And they need to use the victim's bank account to transfer the funds. The victim is promised a share of the proceeds for the use of the account. The perpetrators prepare legal looking documents and bank statements, and they request that the victim send a processing fee of several thousand dollars to them at an account outside the United States (e.g. Nigeria, England). Additional fees may be requested to payoff corrupt bank and government officials. Needless to say, the victim never receives the promised funds.

The common denominator in all of these schemes is an urgent need for the target to pay up-front fees in order to receive a promised amount of funds, say $10 million or more, in the future. The letters or e-mails appear to come from Nigerian government officials, Nigeria

[27] 2002 National Money Laundering Strategy, 2002, A-15.

[28] This case appears in Stipano (2004).

[29] 2002 National Money Laundering Strategy, 2002, A-14;See http://www.scamorama.com for examples of such frauds.

National Petroleum Corporation, or some other source. Presumably the fees are used to pay for licenses, taxes, legal fees, transaction fees, etc. The promised transactions may involve payoffs from awards, beneficiaries of a will, currency conversion, oil ventures, real estate, or other transactions. The victims are almost always asked to travel to Nigeria to complete the transaction. Advance fee fraud correspondence also may originate in other countries.

Box 4-2, a letter from the Nigeria National Petroleum Corporation, is an example of advance fee fraud. The Nigerian advanced fee fraud also is referred to as a 4-1-9 fraud, after the section of the Nigerian penal code that outlaws this type of activity. Financial Institutions should not file a suspicious activity report for this type of fraud scheme unless a money loss is involved or there are other indicators of illegal activity.[30]

Box 4- 2
Example of a Nigerian Advance Fee Fraud

NIGERIA NATIONAL PETROLEUM CORPORATION.
FROM THE DESk OF: ENGR MATHEW ALFRED.
MANAGER 11, BUDGET AND PLANNING
THE MANAGING DIRECTOR / CEO
PLEASE REPLY ME WITH THIS EMAIL ADDRESS mathewalfred@tsamail.co.za mathewalfred@outgun.com Tel-234-1-7212079

DEAR SIR,

WE ARE SENDING THIS LETTER TO YOU BASED ON INFORMATION GATHERED FROM THE FOREIGN TRADE OFFICE OF THE NIGERIA CHAMBER OF COMMERCE AND INDUSTRY.

WE BELIVE THAT YOU WOULD BE IN A POSITION TO HELP US IN OUR BID TO TRANSFER THE SUM OF FORTY ONE MILLION, FIVE HUNDRED THOUSAND DOLLARS ($41.5M USD) INTO A FOREIGN ACCOUNT.

WE ARE MEMBERS OF THE SPECIAL COMMITTEE FOR BUDGET AND PLANNING OF THE MINISTRY OF PETROLEUM. THIS COMMITTEE IS PRINCIPALLY CONCERNED WITH CONTRACT APPRAISALS AND APPROVAL OF CONTRACTS IN ORDER OF PRIOITIES AS REGARDS CAPITAL PROJECT OF THE FEDERAL GOVERNMENT OF NIGERIA. WITH OUR POSITIONS, WE HAVE SUCCESSFULLY SECURED FOR OURSELVES THE SUM OF FORTY ONE MILLION, FIVE HUNDRED THOUSAND UNITED STATED DOLLARS (US$41.5M). THIS AMOUNT WAS ACCUMULATED THROUGH UNDECLARED WINFALL FROM SALES OF CRUDE OIL DURING THE GULF WAR.

---

30 FinCEN, "The SAR Activity Review: Trends, Tips & Issues, Issue 7, August, 2004. p 47; For additional information about Advance Fee Frauds, see: U.S. Secret Service, "Public Awareness Advisory Regarding '4-1-9' or 'Advance Fee Fraud' Schemes, No date, http://www.secretservice.gov/alert419.shtml

WHAT WE NEED FROM YOU IS TO PROVIDE A SAFE ACCOUNT INTO WHICH THE FUNDS WILL BE TRANSFERRED SINCE GOVERNMENT OFFICIALS ARE NOT ALLOWED BY OUR LAWS TO OPERATE FOREIGN ACCOUNT. IT HAS BEEN AGREED THAT THE OWNER OF THE ACCOUNT WILL BE COMPENSATED WITH US$8.3MILLION OF THE REMITTED FUNDS WE KEEP US$31.125MILLION WHILE US$2.075 MILLION WILL BE SET ASIDE TO OFFSET EXPENSES AND PAY THE NECESSARY TAXES IT MAY INTERST YOU TO KNOW THAT TWO YEARS AGO A SIMILAR TRANSACTION WAS CARRIED OUT WITH ONE MR.PATRICE MILLER, THE PRESIDENT OF CRAINE INTERNATIONAL TRADING CORPORATION AT NUMBER 135, EAST 57TH STREET,28TH FLOOR, NEW YORK 10022 WITH TELEPHONE (212)308-7788 AND TELEX NUMBER 6731689, AFTER THE AGREEMENT BETWEEN BOTH PARTNERS IN WHICH HE WAS TO TAKE 5% THE MONEY WAS DULY TRANSFERRED INTO HIS ACCOUNT ONLY TO BE DISAPPOINTED ON OUR ARRIVAL IN! N! EW YORK AS WE WERE RELIABLY INFORMED THAT MR. PATRICE MILLER WAS NO LONGER ON THAT ADDRESS WHILE HIS TELEPHONE AND TELEX NUMBERS HAVE REALLOCAT! ED TO SOMEBODY ELSE THAT IS HOW WE LOST US$27.5M TO MR. PATRICE MILLER.

THIS TIME AROUND WE NEED A MORE RELIABLE AND TRUSTWORTHY PERSON OR A REPUTABLE COMPANY TO DO BUSINESS WITH HENCE THIS LETTER TO YOU, SO IF YOU CAN PROVE YOURSELF TO BE TRUSTED AND INTERESTED IN THIS DEAL THEN WE ARE PREPARED TO DO BUSINESS WITH YOU. WHAT WE WANT FROM YOU IS THE ASSURANCE THAT YOU WILL LET US HAVE OUR SHARE WHEN THIS AMOUNT OF US$41.5M IS TRANSFERRED INTO YOUR ACCOUNT. IF THIS PROPOSAL SATISFIES YOU, PLEASE REPLY ME THROUGH MY E-MAIL ADDRESS, ONLY YOUR RESPONSE SO WE CAN ADVICE YOU ON THE MODALITIES OF THE TRASACTION.

ALL MODALITIES OF THE TRANSFER HAVE BEEN WORKED OUT AND ONCE STARTED WILL NOT TAKE MORE THAN 14 WORKING DAYS WITH THE ABSOLUTE SUPPORT OF ALL CONCERNED THIS TRANSACTION IS 100% SAFE. PLEASE TREAT AS URGENT AND VERY CONFIDENTIAL. GOD BE WITH YOU AS I LOOK FORWARD TO YOUR REPLY.

BEST REGARDS

ENGR MATHEW ALFRED.

Source: e-mail sent to Benton E. Gup

Box 4-3 is an example of a highly suspicious e-mail message. The address given on the website listed in the e-mail for Europe Watches Ltd. is Riga, Latvia.

Latvia established its independence in 1991 following the breakup of the Soviet Union. It joined both the North Atlantic Treaty Organization (NATO) and the European Union (EU) in 2004.

Europe Watches advertises Tag Heuer, Rolex, Omega, and other brands. The web site also states that they are not authorized dealers of the watches that they sell. The web site also states that "We appreciate that some people still find purchasing via the internet a risky and unpleasant experience. We have taken many steps to help alleviate these concerns

a) being granted a used traders license, meaning we have checked by the police,

b) having all our watches checked by a Professional Watchmaker,

c) 100% satisfaction is our aim. If you are not completely satisfied with your purchase you may return it within 3 working days, at your own cost, in the same condition, for a refund of the purchase price (less our shipping cost)"

Box 4-3
Suspicious E-Mail Message

Hello,
My name is Antony Matvienko, a manager of a new perspective company Europe Watches Ltd. I found your resume on www.careerbuilder.com website and want to offer you a job opportunity.

Europe Watches Ltd. is a reseller specialized on expensive watches and jewelry. The company is registered in east Europe however we aim to take place in a broad American market. We are determined to hire a number of American representatives. The representatives will receive the money from our clients and transfer the funds on company's bank accounts. This action is absolutely legal, it is very perspective and will definitely play its part in international business.

In order to be our representative you have to:

-be 21 years old
-have a US checking bank account
-internet access from a place of living
-phone (optional)

Your duties will include recieving bank transfers on your account by wire transfer and transfering the money further on company's bank accounts after the money was accepted. You will recieve 5% from every transfer, 6-7 transfers a week 800-9000$ each. Transfer fees are paid by the company. For example: you receive a transfer of 1000$ you have to subtract your percent (5%) and trasnfer fees and then transfer the money on a given account. You have to do it as fast as possible, prefferably the same business day. We stress on the speed and quality of work performed because otherwise we will not be able to deliever the goods to the clients and lose money. You'll earn approximately 800-900$ weekly. Feel free to ask any questions.

Sincerely,
Antony Matvienko, Manager
Europe Watches Ltd.; http://www.europe-watches.com

Source: e-mail sent to Benton Gup

Fax Frauds

Even financial institutions get hit with fraudulent messages. The FDIC issued the following "Special Alert" to financial institutions. [31] "Faxed messages to foreign institutions and citizens fraudulently claim to be from the FDIC. These messages falsely claim that the FDIC is soliciting mandatory customer information as part of money laundering and anti-terrorism measures. These messages may include a fraudulent form (Form F 91-11.01, "Report of Foreign Bank and Securities Accounts"). The FDIC does not solicit customer information from foreign institutions and citizens." The FDIC warned the recipients of the fraudulent faxes that they should NOT, under any circumstance, provide account information to unknown sources.

Bank Robbery and Bookmakers

About $1.9 million was taken in two armed robberies.[32] During the investigation, police found that another individual had been placing a large number of bets with a large number of bookmakers. He always followed the same pattern of betting on "favorites," who were likely to win. This meant that he only received a relatively small amount when he won – and he had a 7% net loss over time. He never received his winning personally, but had checks made out to 14 different bank accounts in the names of 10 third parties. This ensured that the receipt of money would not raise suspicions in the banks. However, suspicions were raised when several of the checks were issued in the names of the armed robbers and their families. The link between the money launderer and the robbers was established. He had laundered about $3.3 million in total.

Trade-Based Money Laundering

Several jewelers in New York were converting the proceeds from narcotics into an equivalent dollar amount of gold.[33] The gold was then molded into various commodities, such as tools, nuts and bolts, and trailer hitches. The disguised gold was shipped to Colombia where it was sold for cash.

---

[31] FDIC, Special Alert, SA-192-2005: Fraudulent Information Request, December 21, 2005.

[32] "Report on Money Laundering Typologies, 2001-2002," (2002), 24.

[33] Forman, Marcy M. Deputy Assistant Director, Financial Investigations, Immigration and Customs Enforcement, Department of Homeland Security, Statement before the House Government Reform Committee Subcommittee on Criminal Justice, Drug Policy and Human Resources, "Terrorist Financing and Money Laundering Investigations: Who Investigates and How Effective Are They?" May 11, 2004. This incident was referred to as "Operation Meltdown."

RELATED CRIMES

Operation Cheque Mate

An organization based in the United Kingdom defrauded U.S. based securities firms.[34] Two operatives in the U.S. used stolen or false identification papers to establish on-line trading relationships with securities firms. The operatives obtained legitimate cashiers checks from banks issued in nominal amounts. Then they altered the value and other aspects of the cashiers checks so that the new values ranged from $61,000 to $600,000. Then they used the U.S. Mail to submit fraudulent new account applications and altered cashiers to selected securities firms. They preferred small securities firms that did not require the account holder to wait 10 days until the checks cleared. As soon as the accounts were opened, the U.K. based organization began trading. Before the fraudulent checks had cleared, the U.K. based organization also requested that funds from their account be wire transferred to foreign bank accounts in the U.K., Spain, and Argentina. More than 50 securities firms were involved in this scheme. The basic lesson to be learned here is clear checks before providing funds.

It should be noted that securities firms (brokers-dealers) are required to report suspicious transactions involving $5,000 or more if 1) there is reason to believe that the funds were derived from illegal activity, or the transactions are being used to hide illegal activities, 2) if the funds were structured to avoid or evade BSA reporting requirements, 3) if there is no reasonable explanation for the funds and/or they are not consistent with the customer's behavior, and 4) the transactions involve using the securities firm to facilitate criminal activities.[35]

---

[34] FinCEN, "The SAR Activity Review: Trends, Tips & Issues," Issue 9, October 2005, pp.31-32.

[35] Ibid., pp 48-49. There are exceptions for certain violations an Õtransactions that have been reported to the SEC, Self-Regulatory Organizations, and law enforcement authorities.

Chapter 5

CORRESPONDENT, OFFSHORE, AND PRIVATE BANKING

CORRESPONDENT BANKING

Correspondent banking is one bank (the *correspondent bank*) providing services to another bank (the *respondent bank*) for a fee. The services include, but are not limited to moving funds or exchanging currencies. For example, foreign banks have *correspondent accounts* with domestic banks, which means that they have a formal relationship established to provide regular services, dealings, and other financial transactions.[1] Many U.S. banks provide correspondent services for any foreign respondent bank that has a valid banking license as proof of its good standing. However, some U.S. banks have failed to conduct due diligence and monitor the respondent bank's anti-money laundering policies, the regulatory environment in which it operates, and their customers that used the correspondent services, all of which opened the door for money laundering. For example, in one case an offshore bank allowed at least a half dozen other offshore banks to use its account with a U.S. correspondent bank.[2] Another example is that a U.S. correspondent bank discovered that a high risk foreign bank that it would not have accepted as a client was using another bank's correspondent account.

Correspondent banking allows banks to provide services for their customers in cities or countries where they have no physical presence. It is used to expand a bank's market and income. While this is a good thing, correspondent banking has been used for money laundering because the money launderers want a quick, anonymous way to transfer funds across international borders.

Correspondent banks are typically used in the "layering" and "integration" stages where the launderer tries to hide the nature and origin of the underlying funds after they have been "placed" in the financial system. According to Mary Lee Warren (2001), Deputy Assistant Attorney General, "Determining the true beneficial owner of funds being transferred through

---

[1] For additional details about correspondent accounts, see 31 CFR 103.175(d) and 103.177 and 103.185.

[2] United States Senate, Permanent Subcommittee on Investigations, Committee on Governmental Affairs, "Minority Staff of the Permanent Subcommittee on Investigations Report on Correspondent Banking: A Gateway for Money Laundering," February 5, 2001, p. 3.

a correspondent account can be a very difficult challenge for investigators in the second and third stages of money laundering."[3]

A Congressional "Report on Correspondent Banking: A Gateway for Money Laundering (2001, p.1) said that "U.S. banks, through correspondent accounts they provide to foreign banks, have become conduits for dirty money flowing into the American financial system and have, as a result, facilitated illicit enterprises including drug trafficking and financial frauds."[4] Of particular concern are correspondent relationships with "high risk" foreign banks. The high risk category includes:

1. *shell banks* - banks with no physical presence in any country,
2. *offshore banks* - banks with licenses limited to transacting business with persons outside of the country where the bank is licensed, or banks that are barred from transacting business using the local currency where the bank is licensed.[5] The term also is used to mean any bank in a foreign country that takes deposits or manages accounts for someone legally domiciled elsewhere.[6]
3. banks that are licensed or regulated by countries with weak anti-money laundering laws and controls, or countries that do not cooperate with international anti-money laundering efforts.

The USA Patriot Act prohibits "covered financial institutions" from providing "correspondent accounts" in the United States to foreign shell banks, and to take reasonable steps to assure that correspondent accounts of foreign banks are not being used to provide services to foreign shell banks.[7] Covered financial institutions in the U.S. include banks, securities brokers-dealers, futures-commission merchants and introducing brokers in commodities, and mutual funds.[8] It also applies to various foreign financial institutions including money transmitters or currency exchanges organized under foreign laws.

Some of the high-risk institutions may have clients engaged in criminal activities, or because of weak controls, may not even know if their clients are engaged in criminal activities.

The Congressional report went to say that the norm today is for U.S. banks to have dozens or even thousands of correspondent relationships, including some with high risk foreign banks. Two large foreign banks had 12,000 and 7,500 correspondent bank accounts worldwide. A large U.S. bank processed about 1 million wire transfers per day, and the

---

[3] Warren, Mary Lee, Deputy Assistant Attorney General, Criminal Division, United States Department of Justice, Testimony before the Permanent Subcommittee on Investigations of the Committee on Governmental Affairs of the United States Senate, March 6, 2001.

[4] "Report on Correspondent Banking: A Gateway for Money Laundering," Minority Staff of the Permanent Subcommittee on Investigations, U.S. Senate Committee on Governmental Affairs, February 5, 2001. p.1

[5] It is estimated that there are about 60 offshore jurisdictions around the world. About 44% are in the Caribbean and Latin America, 29% in Europe, 19% Asia and Pacific, and 10% in Africa and the Middle East.

[6] Blum, Jack A., Michael Levi, R. Thomas Naylor, and Phil Williams, "Financial Havens, Banking Secrecy and Money Laundering, New York, United Nations Office for Drug Control and Crime Prevention, 1999. 28.

[7] 31 U.S.C. 5318; 31 CFR 103.177 (a)(1)(ii).

[8] FinCEN Fact Sheet, Section 312 of the USA PATRIOT Act, Final Regulation and Notice of Proposed Rulemaking, December, 2005. This section deals with the due diligence obligations of covered financial institutions in connection with correspondent banking and private banking...

largest amount of money processed by a U.S. bank was over $1 trillion per day. In other words, correspondent banking is big business.

Box 5-1

VEF Banca (VEF), Lativa

According to FinCEN, VEF Banca (VEF), Latvia is a financial institution of primary money laundering concern. VEF, one of the smallest banks in Latvia, had $80 million in assets, and 34 correspondent accounts worldwide, and at least one in the U.S. VEF offers "confidential banking services" for non Latvian customers. About 75% of its fee income was generated by payment cards and money transfers to and from correspondent banks. VEF had over 300 wire transfers, involving countries such as the United Arab Emirates, Kuwait, Russia, India, and China, totaling more than $26 million for a single shell corporation. And it transferred over $200 million for two corporate customers – which was highly suspect. Several of their customers repeatedly engaged in a pattern of activity indicative of money laundering, and some are linked to international crime organizations. Some of these individuals made payments using digital currency services such as e-Gold and Web money that were discussed in Chapter 1. Special measures were proposed that would prohibit U.S. correspondent banks from maintaining direct correspondent relationships with VEF, and take reasonable steps to prevent indirect correspondent relationships with VEF through intermediary financial institutions.

Source: U.S. Department of Treasury, "Financial Crimes Enforcement Network; Amendment to the Bank Secrecy Act Regulations- Imposition of Special Measures Against VEF Banka," Federal Register, Vol. 70, No. 79, April 26, 2005, pp. 21369-21376.

The Report cited two due diligence failures on the part of U.S. banks. The first was the failure of U.S. banks to determine the extent to which their foreign bank clients were allowing other foreign banks to use their U.S. accounts. For example, an offshore bank was allowing dozens of shell banks to use its U.S. accounts. The shell banks were *nested correspondents* - foreign or shell banks that use their correspondent's bank accounts in the U.S., without the U.S. bank's knowledge or consent. Nested correspondents should not be confused with payable through accounts (PTAs) that are also known as "pass-through" or "pass-by." In a PTA, the foreign bank provides its customers with checks that allows them to draw funds from the foreign institution's account at the U.S. bank. PTAs may be high risk if the banks do not provide the same due diligence as they do for their own customers.

The second failure is that U.S. banks do not apply their due diligence procedures to foreign banks that have few assets and no credit relationship. They may be providing fee based services such as wire transfers or check clearing for such banks. As a result of these due diligence failures, the report cited numerous cases of foreign banks laundering money through their U.S bank accounts (see table 5-1). Thus, correspondent banks face having to deal with the conflicting goals of expanding their markets and incomes while at the same time complying with BSA/AML programs.

Table 5-1. High Risk Foreign Banks Examined by Permanent Subcommittee on Investigation in the Minority Staff Report

Bank Name	License and Operation	U.S. Correspondents	Money Laundering Concerns
American International Bank (AIB)	Licensed in Antigua/Barbuda Offshore, Physical Presence in Antigua	BAC of Florida Bank of America Barnett Bank Chase Manhattan Bank Toronto Dominion Union Bank of Jamaica	Financial fraud money, Nested correspondents, Internet gambling
British Bank of Latin America	Licensed in Bahamas, Offshore, Physical presence in Bahamas and Colombia, Owned by Lloyds TSB Bank	Bank of New York	Drug money from Black Market Peso Exchange
British Trade and Commerce Bank	Licensed in Dominica, Offshore, Physical presence in Dominica	Banco Industrial de Venezuela (Miami), First Union National Bank, Security Bank, NA	Financial Fraud money, High yield investments, Nested correspondents, Internet gambling
Caribbean American Bank	Licensed by Antigua/Barbuda, Offshore, No physical presence	U.S. correspondents of AIB	Financial fraud, Nested correspondents, Shell bank
European Bank	Licensed by Vanuatu, Onshore, Physical presence in Vanuatu	ANZ Bank (New York), Citibank	Credit card fraud money
Federal Bank	Licensed by Bahamas, Offshore, Physical presence in Cayman Islands	Bank of New York	Bribe money, Shell bank
Guardian Bank and Trust (Cayman) Ltd.	Licensed by Cayman Islands, Offshore, Physical presence in Cayman Islands	Bank of New York	Financial fraud, Tax evasion
Hanover Bank	Licensed by Antigua/Barbuda, Offshore, No physical presence	Standard Bank (Jersey) Ltd's U.S. correspondent, Harris Bank International (New York)	Financial fraud money, Nested correspondents, Shell bank
M.A. Bank	Licensed by Cayman Islands, Offshore, No physical presence	Citibank Union Bank of Switzerland (New York)	Drug money, Shell bank
Overseas Development Bank and Trust	Licensed by Dominica, Offshore, Physical presence in Dominica, formerly in Antigua	U.S. Correspondents of AIB, AmTrade International (Florida), Bank One	Financial fraud money, Nested correspondents
Swiss American Bank	Licensed by Antigua/Barbuda, Offshore, Physical presence in Antigua	Bank of America Chase Manhattan Bank	Financial fraud money, Internet gambling, Drug and illegal arms sales money
Swiss American National Bank	Licensed in Antigua/Barbuda, Onshore, Physical presence in Antigua	Bank of New York Chase Manhattan Bank	Financial fraud money, Drug and illegal arms sales money

Source: "Report on Correspondent Banking: A Gateway for Money Laundering," Minority Staff of the Permanent Subcommittee on Investigations, U.S. Senate Committee on Governmental Affairs, February 5, 2001. pp 6-7.

FINANCIAL HAVENS

A United Nations study by Blum, et. al., on "Financial Havens, Banking Secrecy, and Money Laundering" (1999) argues that criminal organizations make extensive use of offshore banks that offer facilities that shield foreign investors from disclosing the origin of their assets. Table 5-2 lists jurisdictions with largest number of offshore banks.

Under the International Business Corporations Act of 1982 (IBCs) or shell companies do not disclose of shareholders or beneficial owners.[9] "The IBC Act provides criminal penalties for any disclosure of the business affairs of customers regarding banking or trust matters. The only exception for the disclosure of information relates to sound evidence regarding an alleged criminal offense that is triable in Antigua (or which would have been triable if it had been committed in Antigua)."[10] The bottom line according to the U.N. study by Blum, et. al., (p. 93) is that IBCs are at the heart of virtually all money laundering schemes to hide the ownership of assets.

Similarly, *private investment companies/corporations* are shell companies incorporated in financial secrecy jurisdictions that are used for various tax or trust related purposes. FinCEN defines shell corporations as companies with no independent assets or operations of their own, which are used by their owners to conduct business dealings or maintain control of their companies.[11] The shell corporation is registered or licensed in the state or country in which it is incorporated or established, but is not traded on securities exchanges and does not operate on its own. It exits only on paper.

Table 5-2. Number of Offshore Banks in Selected Jurisdictions

Rank	Jurisdictions	Number of Offshore Banks
1	Cayman Islands	570
2	Switzerland	500
3	Nauru	400
4	Luxembourg	200
5	Singapore	83
6	Guernsey	71
7	Barbados	55
8	Vanuatu	55
9	Labuan (Malaysia)	54
10	Bahrain	48

Source: "Money Laundering and Financial Crimes," U.S. Department of State, No date, www.state.gov/documents/organization/8703.pdf, 13-17.

When used in combination with "trust" accounts, IBCs are very effective in shielding the identity of the owners and their assets. Asset protection trusts (APT), for example, protects

[9] Blum, Jack A., Michael Levi, R. Thomas Naylor, and Phil Williams, "Financial Havens, Banking Secrecy and Money Laundering," New York, United Nations Office for Drug Control and Crime Prevention, 1999.

[10] Antigua and Barbuda, Finance and Investments, Offshore Financial Sector, http://www.antigua-barbuda.com/finance_investment/offshore_sector.asp. Also see: http://www.antiguabarbuda.gov.ag/business/economy.htm

[11] FinCEN, "The SAR Activity Review: Trends, Tips & Issues, Issue 7, August, 2004, p.4.

the assets of individuals from civil judgments in their home country.[12] Some APTs have "flee-clauses" that provide for the trust funds to be transferred to another offshore center if the APT is threatened by an inquiry.

The problems of dealing with banks in financial havens are compounded by technology – banking over the internet. By way of illustration, European Union Bank was founded in 1994 in Antigua and Barbuda.[13] It was founded by two Russians, Alexandr Konanykhine and Mikhail Khodorosvky, who represented themselves as officers of the Menatep Bank of Moscow. Konanykhine was alleged to have absconded from Moscow after embezzling $8.1 million from another bank.

In 1995, European Union Bank of Antigua launched its website and became an internet bank. Lord Mancroft, the bank's chairman and the British House of Lords, admitted that the benefits of dealing with his bank included tax evasion, numbered accounts so the clients' name is not used, and privacy. It is alleged that the bank was used to launder illicit proceeds of Russian organized crime.

The internet bank was operated on a license from the government of Antigua, the computer server was located in Washington, D.C., and both were operated by a man in Canada. Some of the bank assets were "stolen." However, under Antiguan law, the theft of the bank assets was not illegal. The problems are: Where was the crime committed? Who committed it? Who is going to investigate it? And finally, will anyone be punished?

European Union Bank was closed in 1997 The State of Idaho Department of Finance issued a Cease and Desist Order against European Union Bank because it is unlawful in that State for any person to engage in banking by soliciting deposits unless that person has a bank charter issued by the State Department of Finance or a federal bank regulator.[14]

True Confessions – How an Offshore Bank Laundered Money

John Mathewson was the former majority owner and chief executive officer of Guardian Bank and Trust Ltd., an offshore bank that was licensed in the Cayman Islands. In 1997, Mathewson, a U.S. citizen, pled guilty to multiple counts of money laundering, aiding and abetting tax evasion, and conspiracy to commit wire fraud. The following is based on information that he provided to the Senate Minority Staff investigation.[15]

Guardian Bank operated in the Cayman Islands from 1984-1995. During that period it had over 1,000 clients, and about $300 million - $500 million was passed through correspondent bank accounts on their behalf. Ninety five percent of the bank's clients were from the United States. Guardian Bank was licensed in the Cayman Islands because of their strict laws limiting government and bank disclosure of bank records and customer

[12] U.S. Department of State, "Money Laundering and Financial Crimes," No date, www.state.gov/documents/organization/8703.pdf, 9.

[13] Blum, et. al. (1999), 58-62.

[14] Idaho Department of Finance, "State Orders Another Offshore Uninsured Bank to Stop Soliciting Deposits on the Internet," Press Release, November 4, 1997; Idaho Department of Finance, Cease and Desist Order, 97-03-01, Re European Union Bank of Antigua, West Indies, May, 29, 1997.

[15] "Report on Correspondent Banking: A Gateway for Money Laundering," (2001). pp 43-58.

information. In addition, tax evasion is not a crime or considered money laundering in the Caymans. Guardian Bank specialized in income tax evasion.

The Guardian name was selected because there are at least 11 other banks around the world with "Guardian" in their title. Since small offshore banks conduct most of their business through the international payments system, having a common name helped to minimize detection.

Guardian Bank provided shell corporations to their clients for a fee. Shell corporations are usually chartered offshore to hide their identity, and they may exist on paper only. They can be used to transfer funds in what may or may not be legitimate transactions. Some of the shell corporations that Guardian Bank provided to its clients were several years old so the clients could back-date invoices or create fictitious records of past operations. Almost all of the bank's clients used such shell corporations whose ownership was not reported in public records. A Guardian Bank subsidiary (Guardian Directors Ltd.) provided nominee shareholders and directors to further shield their clients. In this way, a U.S. client (beneficial owner) could do business anywhere in the world with complete anonymity. Finally, the clients account statements were kept in the Caymans to preserve their secrecy.

Along this line, when clients made deposits by check, they were instructed to make the deposit to one of the subsidiaries of Guardian Bank (Fulcrum Ltd., Sentinel Ltd., or Tower Ltd.), or to the client's shell corporation. The clients were told to wrap the check in a plain piece of paper with their Guardian Bank account number on the sheet. In this way the deposit was not directly tied to the client. Alternatively, the checks could be deposited at a correspondent bank for credit to Guardian Bank. A Guardian account number was given, but no reference was made to the fact that Guardian Bank was in the Cayman Islands. When U.S. checks were sent to Guardian Bank, the bank would accumulate 50 or 100 of them, and then deliver them by international courier to a U.S. correspondent bank for deposit into a Guardian account. Guardian Bank would then apportion the funds to the client's accounts.

In order to have access to the check and wire clearing capabilities of the Fedwire and Chips, Guardian Bank opened about 15 correspondent bank accounts in the U.S., Canada, Caymans, and Guernsey. Guardian Bank's major correspondents were Bank of New York, First Union in Miami, and Credit Suisse in Guernsey. It also had a correspondent relationship with Popular Bank of Florida. The island of Guernsey is located in the English Channel, northwest of France. It is ruled by the British Crown. By using correspondent banks, Guardian offered its clients almost any service that was offered by U.S. banks.

Clients could wire transferred funds to Guardian Bank's non-U.S. correspondents such as Credit Suisse in Guernsey or the Bank of Butterfield in the Caymans to minimize documentation in the U.S. Before the wire transfers were made, the clients alerted Guardian and indicated which accounts should be credited.

Clients who wanted to withdraw funds could use credit cards, checks, or wire transfers. Visa Gold credit cards were issued in the name of the client's shell corporation. The clients were instructed to sign the back of the card using a signature that was reproducible, but hard to read. The cards were issued and managed by a Miami firm, Credomatic.

Credomatic is owned by the same individuals that own Popular Bank. Some financial institutions that used Credomatic established escrow accounts at Popular Bank that used the escrow account list to market its correspondent banking services. Guardian Bank and AIB Bank (listed in Table 5-1) used Popular Bank's correspondent banking services for several years until their accounts were closed. Credomatic did not do background checks on Guardian

Bank because Guardian provided a letter of credit backing its credit card account. Although there was no credit risk, the risk of money laundering was present.

Some clients withdrew funds by using checks drawn on Guardian's U.S. correspondent accounts. The correspondent banks provided Guardian with a checkbook that could be used to withdraw funds from its correspondent accounts. One of the checkbooks provided by the Bank of New York only said "Guardian Bank" at the top, with no information about its location in the Caymans, and the identifier number at the bottom. Checks with such minimum information about the issuer are common in Europe, Asia, and offshore jurisdictions. Guardian Bank had no problems using them.

Sometimes the checks were used to transact business for the clients. For example, it might send multiple checks of less than $10,000 each to a car dealer amounting to $40,000 in order to avoid currency transaction reports.

Guardian Bank offered two additional services that facilitated evading U.S. taxes. The first service involved invoicing. A typical transaction involved a client's Cayman corporation buying a product from abroad, and selling it the client's U.S. corporation, with a 30% mark-up. Guardian provided the invoice. The client's Cayman corporation could deposit the difference in the clients account at Guardian. There are no corporate taxes in the Caymans, and the client may choose not to pay U.S. taxes on it. In addition, the client's U.S. corporations could claim higher costs and less revenue, thereby have a lower U.S. tax liability.

Finally, Guardian helped U.S. clients establish Dutch corporations in connection with fake loans and large tax deductions. The shares of the Dutch corporation were owned by the client's Cayman shell corporation. The Dutch corporation would loan the U.S. client funds, using the client's deposit at Guardian. The loan plus interest was repaid to the Dutch corporation's bank account that was set up with ANB AMRO Bank in Rotterdam in the Netherlands. The Dutch corporation would forward the loan payments to the client's Guardian account by using one of Guardian's correspondent accounts. Basically, this was a closed loop where the client transferred and received his own funds, but giving the appearance of loan payments plus interest. For example, if the loan was a mortgage, the client could deduct interest payments from his or her U.S. taxes.

BANK OF NEW YORK

The Bank of New York (BONY) was founded in 1784 by Alexander Hamilton. Thomas A. Renyi, Chairman and CEO of BONY, testifying before a U.S. House Banking and Financial Services Committee, said that BONY had been doing business with Russia since 1922.[16] However, in the 1990s, there was a flight of capital from Russia. The Russian Central Bank attempted to stem the flight of capital but individuals and financial institutions found both legal and illegal ways to get money out of the country. Russia did not have

[16] Thomas A. Renyi, Chairman of the Board and CEO of the Bank of New York, Testimony in Panel III of a Hearing of the House Banking and Financial Services Committee Subject: Russian Corruption and Money Laundering, U.S. House of Representatives, September 22, 1999.

comprehensive anti-money laundering laws and regulations, and those laws that they did have were not effectively enforced.[17]

Against this background, Renyi said that Peter Berlin, a Russian national who became a U.S. citizen in 1996, represented himself as operating small businesses. He opened about nine commercial accounts for shell businesses (e.g. Benex International Co. Inc., Becs International LLC, and Lowland Inc.) at BONY, but only three or four were active at any one time.[18]

Russian banks (Depositarno-Kliringovy Bank, and Commercial Bank Flamingo) deposited more than $7 billion in funds in correspondent bank accounts, and then transferred them again into the commercial accounts of the shell businesses. Well over half of the Russian funds were wired through Nauru, a tiny island in the South Pacific. Nauru's banking system is characterized by draconian secrecy laws and minimal regulation. According to the State Department in 1999, Nauru extended "an open invitation to financial crime and money laundering."[19]

Mr. Berlin's wife, Ludmila Edwards was a BONY account executive. Over time, bank employees noticed an increased volume of transactions, and questions were raised about Berlin and his customers. However, nothing was done about it since he was married to Lucy Edwards, a respected bank officer. Renyi said that Berlin moved $7.5 billion in funds from 1996-1999. That is an average of about $6 million per day. Berlin's shell corporations completed 160,000 wire transfers of funds between February 1996 and August 1999.[20] Many shell corporations cited in SAR reports are located in Eastern European countries.[21]

Renyi also pointed out that the BONY deals with about 160 Russian correspondent banks, and that, on average, they move about $3.7 billion per day through the BONY. That represents about one half of a percent of the $600 billion in correspondent accounts that BONY clears each day. Renyi made it clear that no one at the management level was aware of the Russian money being laundered through the BONY.

In 2000, BONY and the Federal Reserve Bank of New York reached an agreement that the bank would take steps necessary to improve its AML policies including its customer due diligence practices.[22] *The Wall Street Journal* reported that BONY negotiated with federal prosecutors to avert a potential criminal indictment for failure to report a suspicious activity.[23]

Berlin and Edwards pled guilty to conspiracy, money laundering, operating an unlawful banking and money transmitting business in the U.S., and aiding and abetting Russian banks in conducting unlawful and unlicensed banking activities. Seizure warrants were executed

---

[17] Phillip L. Robinson, and Ethan S. Burger, "The Regulatory Framework and Potential Implications of the Bank of New York Money-Laundering Scandal for Russia and the United States," Ludwig & Robinson, P.L.L.C., Washington, D.C. (approx. date 2000).

[18] See Renyi (1999) for additional details; 2002 National Money Laundering Strategy, U.S. Department of Treasury and U.S. Department of Justice, July 2002, Appendix 7.

[19] James A. Leach, Chairman, Committee on Banking and Financial Services, U.S. House of Representatives, Statement before the Financial Academy, Moscow, Russia, April 25, 2000.

[20] *Money Laundering: A Bankers Guide to Avoiding Problems* (2002), 26.

[21] FinCEN, "The SAR Activity Review: Trends, Tips & Issues, Issue 7, August, 2004, p.5. Eastern European countries with shell companies that were listed in the SAR reports included: Armenia, Belarus, Bulgaria, Croatia, Cyprus, Czech Republic, Estonia, Georgia, Greece, Kazakhstan, Latvia, Lithuania, Moldova, Poland, Romania, Russia, Slovenia, Turkey, Turkmenistan, Ukraine, Uzbekistan, and Yougoslavia.

[22] Federal Reserve Press Release, February 8, 2000, Enforcement Actions (Bank of New York).

[23] Simpson (2004).

against BONY accounts and other Berlin accounts, a correspondent account for a Russian bank at BONY, and a total of $21.6 million was seized from 11 different accounts.[24] Berlin and his wife agreed to criminal forfeitures of about $8.1 million and they were awaiting sentencing.

In an unrelated incident, BONY disclosed that it did not know that one of its respondent banks, British Bank of Latin America (BBLA), an offshore bank that operated in Colombia and the Bahamas, had moved $2.7 million in drug money though its correspondent account despite numerous warnings and seizure orders about that bank.[25] This is an example of weak due-diligence and inadequate BSA/AML controls.

Finally Glen Simson, in a Wall Street Journal Article stated that despite BONY's problem with the Russian clients, ABN AMRO solicited them and others for their business.[26]

Security Bank, N.A. provides another example of weak due-diligence and inadequate controls. Security Bank was a small bank with about $90 million in assets.[27] Its Miami Florida office was in the same building as First Equity Corporation of Florida (FECF). Rodolfo Requina, was the President of BTC Financial Services, a U.S. bank holding company that owned FECF. In addition, he was the Chief Executive Officer of British Trade and Commerce Bank (BTCB), a high-risk offshore bank licensed in Dominica, a Caribbean island nation known for weak anti-money laundering programs.

BTCB opened a correspondent account at Security Bank. BTCB was a big foreign account for the small Security Bank.

Security Bank stated that because it only had one account with BTCB, it was not cost effective to visit that bank as part of their due diligence. The account was used for deposits and wire transfers; no credit relationship was involved. It is common practice for correspondent banks to have on-site visits of their foreign banks prior to opening an account and annually thereafter.

A representative from Security Bank had an ongoing dialog with BTCB's president, but he could not explain that bank's major activities which included high-yield investments promising extravagant returns. Some CDs offered returns of 46% to 79%!

A related problem was that BTCB's accounting firm refused to provide information about the bank's 1998 unaudited financial statements. It contained unusual entries, such as a $400 million in "securities held for investment and financing" that listed three unusual securities that accounted for most of that total. One was $130 million in "Government of Grenada Guarantees," that could not be verified. Another was $76 million in Bolivian Municipal Bonds, which have a very thin market, and $140 million in "Russian Government Guarantees." The statements also claimed that BTCB had $9 million in retained earnings after being in business only nine months, and that it earned $10 million from financing Venezuelan government bonds. Venezuela was experiencing economic hardships at that time. Simply stated, many items on the unedited financial statements did not make sense. Weak accounting practices add to the problems of evaluating banks. It is a red flag.

---

24 2002 National Money Laundering Strategy, 2002, A-15.

25 "Report on Correspondent Banking: A Gateway for Money Laundering," 2001, p. 27.

26 Simson, Glen R., "How Top Dutch Bank Plunged Into World of Shadowy Money," The Wall Street Journal, December 30, 2005, A1, A7.

27 "Report on Correspondent Banking: A Gateway for Money Laundering," 2001, various chapters and appendix.

After two years of dealing with BTCB, Security Bank had never reviewed for suspicious activity wire transfers involving more than $50 million that went into and out of that bank's correspondent account. The funds were associated with money laundering, financial fraud, and internet gambling. Some of the frauds were committed by William H. Koop who swindled millions of dollars from over 200 of U.S. citizens. Koop offered fictitious financial instruments, "prime bank notes," that promised returns as high as 489%. Other frauds were committed by Benjamin Franklin Cook who bilked over 300 investors out of more than $40 million by selling unregistered "prime bank" securities to religious and charitable groups and individuals for retirement funds. Finally, Gold Chance International Ltd. had been fraudulently induced to deposit $3 million as collateral for a loan. The funds were deposited in an attorney trust account in Canada, and then secretly transferred offshore to BTCB. No loan was made. These three cases illustrate how criminals can use offshore banks to facilitate their crimes and launder money.

Security Bank admitted that BTCB had engaged in suspicious activities and ultimately closed their account when it discovered BTCB was involving Security Bank in internet gambling which is against the law in the U.S.

RED FLAGS FOR SHELL CORPORATIONS AND SHELL BANKS

The following red flags are based on SARs, and are taken directly from FinCEN's "The SAR Activity Review " (August, 2004, pp 7-8).

- "An unusually high volume of wire transfers activity with multiple transfers totaling hundreds or thousands and with dollar amounts in the thousands or millions. These wires frequently involve originators located in high-risk regions considered vulnerable to money laundering.
- Payment originators with addresses in the United States but who originate the payments from accounts held at foreign banks.
- Inability to identify a location in the United States, corporate officers and/or directors or the nature of the business.
- Suspected shell companies based in foreign countries, which are customers of foreign banks that maintain correspondent accounts with United States-based banks. The shell companies, through the correspondent accounts, wire funds to offshore jurisdictions.
- Foreign-owned corporations based in the United States as originators or beneficiaries (or both) of dollar denominated wire transfers.
- Numerous wire transfers from a particular originator to a particular beneficiary, with one of the parties being a registered corporation in the United States for which no physical location can be identified, the other party is located offshore.
- Individual wire transactions conducted within a short period of time (i.e. daily basis, two times daily or every other day).
- Unusually large numbers of wire transfers involving offshore correspondent account holders for domestic companies that do not appear to maintain an operating business

in the state of incorporation and for which there is no indication of legitimate business activity."

PRIVATE BANKING

Private banking is aimed at wealthy clients. The USA Patriot Act defines a private banking account as established for the benefit of one or more persons with minimum aggregate value of $1 million or more, and is assigned to a bank employee who acts as liaison between the bank and the non-U.S. person.[28] Private banking offers personalized financial services to meet the client's needs. The private banking activities can be carried out in the U.S., or offshore.[29] Offshore private banking includes 1) private banking activities carried out by banks operating in the U.S. that involve financial secrecy jurisdictions, such as the Cayman Islands and the Channel Islands. 2) Private banking activities conducted by foreign branches of U.S. banks located in such jurisdictions.

Banks like private banking and wealth management because it provides fee income and does not require regulatory capital. The number of households in the U.S. valued at more than $10 million has more than doubled since 1989, and is estimated to exceed 430,000.[30] These are prime targets for private banks, wealth management and trust accounts.

Private banks also deal with politically exposed persons (PEPs) such as former Chilean dictator Augusto Pinochet who will be discussed shortly. PEPs include heads of state, high level politicians and government officials, party officials, and others. The others include the immediate family and close associates including personal advisors and consultants.[31]

PEPs that come from countries where corruption is widely accepted present the greatest risk. They may try to launder funds from bribes, kickbacks, and from the theft of state funds. This is why the Know Your Customer due diligence is so important. KYC includes verifying the customer's personal and business backgrounds: verifying their identity, character, credit, determining the source of wealth, and understanding the types of transactions to be conducted.

Beginning in 2006, the USA Patriot Act required enhanced due diligence requirements for Senior Foreign Political Figures (i.e. PEPs), their families, and associates.[32]

---

28 FinCEN Fact Sheet, Section 312 of the USA PATRIOT Act, Final Regulation and Notice of Proposed Rulemaking, December, 2005.

29 U.S. General Accounting Office, Money Laundering: Observations on Private Banking and Related Oversight of Selected Offshore Jurisdictions, Statement for the Record of Thomas J. McCool, Director, Financial Institutions and Markets Issues, General Government Division, Before the Permanent Subcommittee on Investigations, Committee of Government Affairs, U.S. Senate, GAO/TGGD-00-32, November 9, 1999.

30 Frank, Robert, "Have $50 million? Come On In," The Wall Street Journal, February 1, 2005, C1, C6.

31 Comptroller of the Currency, OCC Bulletin, Guidance on Foreign Official Corruption, OCC 2001-9, February 20, 2001. This bulletin discusses the Know Your Customer aspects of dealing with PEPs.

32 FinCEN Fact Sheet, Section 312 of the USA PATRIOT Act, Final Regulation and Notice of Proposed Rulemaking, December, 2005.

Box 5-2
Comments of Senator Carl Levin on Private Banking[33]
The Quintessential Shell Game

"Private bankers are marketers and promoters who are expected to attract wealthy clients to the bank. Once a person becomes a client of a private bank, the bank's primary goal is to service that client, and servicing a client almost always means using services that are also the tools of money laundering—secret trust, offshore accounts, secret name accounts, and shell companies called private investment corporations.

These private investment corporations or PICs are designed for the purpose of holding—and hiding—one person's assets. ....The nominal officers, trustees, and shareholders of these shell corporations are, in turn often shell corporations controlled by the private bank. The PIC then becomes the owner of various bank and investment accounts, and the ownership of the private bank's client is buried in the records of so-called secrecy jurisdictions, such as the Cayman Islands. Private banks keep pre-packaged PICs 'on-the-shelf,' awaiting activation when a private bank client wants one."..... Citibank's private banking brochure advertised "PIC assets are registered in the name of the PIC and your ownership of the PIC need not appear in any public registry."

"No one is suggesting that private banking is an improper banking activity or that banks should not be making a profit on the services they offer their clients. As several of Citibank's top managers said to us, the question is how you conduct private banking in an 'honorable' way."

Riggs Bank N.A. [34]

In 2004, Riggs Bank was fined a civil money penalty of $25 million for violations of the BSA/AML compliance. In addition, Cease and Desist (C&D) Orders were issued to correct certain deficiencies in connection with the BSA/AML compliance. The most notable violations were in their Embassy and International Private Chile, Equatorial Guinea and Saudi Arabia.

---

[33] United States Senate, Permanent Subcommittee on Investigations, Committee on Governmental Affairs, "Private Banking and Money Laundering: A Case Study of Opportunities and Vulnerabilities," S. Hrg. 106-428, November 9, 10, 1999. p. 25, 26, 27.

[34] Stipano, Daniel P., Deputy Counsel, OCC, Testimony Before the Subcommittee on Oversight and Investigations of the Committee on Financial Services, U.S. House of Representatives, June 2, 2004; Comptroller of the Currency, New Release 2004-34 (2004); U.S. Senate, Permanent Subcommittee on Investigations, Committee on Homeland Security and Governmental Affairs, "Money Laundering and Foreign Corruption: Enforcement and Effectiveness of the Patriot Act, Supplemental Staff Report on U.S. Accounts by Augusto Pinochet," March 16, 2005;Also see O'Hara, Terence, "In Cultivating International Clients, Riggs Went down a Perilous Path," Washingtonpost.com, March 21, 2005, E01. Although not discussed here, in 2003, the OCC had serious concerns about BSA policies, systems and controls in connection with Saudi Arabian Embassy accounts at Riggs. As of April 2005, no penalties or fines were assessed in connection with those accounts.

Pinochet

In January 2005, Riggs Bank pleaded guilty to failing to report suspicious transactions in accounts held by former Chilean dictator Augusto Jose Ramon Pinochet Ugarte (a.k.a. Augusto Pinochet) who ruled that country from 1973-1990, and served as Commander and Chief of their military until 1998. After that he became a “Senator for Life.”

In 1998, Pinochet was arrested in London and the courts ordered his accounts to be frozen. However, Riggs helped him move funds from England to the United States, and did not alert the courts or law enforcement authorities.[35]

Pinochet had been accused of arms sales, assassinations, corruption, death squads, drug trafficking, human rights abuses, and torture.[36] But, because Pinochet was unavailable, unfit, or immune to prosecution, he was not convicted in a court of law. That changed in August 2004 when the Chilean Supreme Court held that Pinochet was not immune to prosecution in the “Operation Condor” case involving the disappearance of political figures in the 1970s. In December 2004, he was found fit for trial in that case.

Riggs had been dealing with Pinochet and his family for from 1979-2004 and actively solicited those accounts and those of the Chilean military. Pinochet had 28 accounts and CDs at Riggs under disguised and fictitious names as well as the names of other military officers. In 2002, the average balance of all of the Chilean accounts at Riggs exceeded $100 million.[37]

Senator Norman Coleman, Chairman of the Permanent Subcommittee on Investigations said …"it does not take a Ph.D. or a degree in finance or accounting for some red lights to go on and for somebody to think, hey, you know something? There is something amiss here. I think we have an obligation to affirmatively do something about it. It appears from everything that we have seen, that doing something about it (at Riggs Bank) was really slow in coming.”[38]

Citigroup

Citigroup’s relationship with the Pinochet family in the United States extended over 24 years. Pinochet and his immediate family had 63 accounts and CDs at Citibank under various names at the bank’s operations in New York and Miami. For example, Pinochet had opened accounts using the names J. Ramone Urgarte, Jose Ramone Urgarte, Jose P. Urgarte, and others.[39] As previously noted, his complete name is Augusto Jose Ramon Pinochet Ugarte. Similarly, the accounts of his wife and daughters disguised their names to hide the true ownership of their accounts.

---

35 U. S. Senate, Permanent Subcommittee on Investigations, Committee on Governmental Affairs, “Money Laundering and Foreign Corruption: Enforcement and Effectiveness of the Patriot Act, Senate Hearing 108-633, July 15, 2004, p. 21.

36 U.S. Senate, Permanent Subcommittee on Investigations, Committee on Homeland Security and Governmental Affairs, “Money Laundering and Foreign Corruption: Enforcement and Effectiveness of the Patriot Act, Supplemental Staff Report on U.S. Accounts by Augusto Pinochet,” March 16, 2005.

37 Ibid.

38 U. S. Senate, Permanent Subcommittee on Investigations, Committee on Governmental Affairs, “Money Laundering and Foreign Corruption: Enforcement and Effectiveness of the Patriot Act, Senate Hearing 108-633, July 15, 2004, p. 45.

The 2005 Senate Report on Pinochet stated that "Over the past 10 years, despite having excellent anti-money laundering policies and procedures on paper, Citibank Private Bank has undergone repeated criticism for poor due diligence practices, lax implementation of its AML controls, and failure to close accounts for foreign public figures who appear to be depositing the proceeds of foreign corruption into their private banking accounts….. In 2004, however, in an indication of ongoing AML deficiencies within the Private Bank, the Financial Services Agency of Japan determined that, due to poor AML practices and other misconduct, Citibank Private Bank had engaged in improper transactions and harmed customers, and ordered it to leave the Country. In response, Citigroup closed down its Japanese private banking operations, apologized to Japan, and fired the head of Citibank Private Bank."[40] More will be said about Citigroup's Private Bank shortly.

Other Banks

Other U.S. based banks that had accounts with Pinochet et. al. include, but are not limited to, Banco de Chile-United States(where Pinochet et. al. had 24 accounts and CDs), Espirito Santo Bank in Florida – a subsidiary of a Portuguese bank (6 accounts and CDs), Banco Atlantico, Bank of America, Coutts and Co. (USA) International, Ocean Bank in Miami, and PineBank N.A. in Miami.[41] It was estimated that Pinochet had a total of about 125 accounts and CDs in the United States.

Some of the Pinochet accounts at these banks were opened in the name of offshore entities, such as Trilateral International Trading, to hide their identity and make it difficult for U.S. banks to do due diligence on international wire transfers. Espirioto Santo Bank officials stated that it was common practice for people from South America to use disguised names "to protect their privacy and foil attempts at kidnapping, theft, or other misconduct," and for other purposes.[42] In January 1991, $1.5 million was wire transferred from Pinochet and his wife's account at Riggs bank in Miami to the Bank of Bahamas for credit to Deloitte and Touche. Deloitte and Touche had an agreement with Riggs to provide various services, including the management of Riggs Bank and Trust Co. (Bahamas), which was a shell bank at that time. In October 1991, Deloitte and Touche wire transferred $1.19 million to Espirito Santo bank for deposit in the newly opened account of Trilateral International Trading.

Pinochet and his family also had accounts in Argentina, the Bahamas, Cayman Islands, Chile, Gibraltar, Spain, Switzerland, and the United Kingdom that were used on a regular basis to move funds and transact business.

Riggs agreed to a $16 million fine for a felony count. This was in addition to the $25 million regulatory fine, $8 million to settle a Spanish criminal action that was related to Pinochet, and $2.7 million to settle a shareholder lawsuit. Former Chairman and CEO Joe Allbritton and his son Joe Allbritton, also a former Chairman, agreed to pay $1 million in the

---

[39] Ibid; O'Hara, Terence, "6 U.S. Banks Held Pinochet's Accounts," Washington Post.com, March 16, 2005, E03.

[40] U.S. Senate, Permanent Subcommittee on Investigations, Committee on Homeland Security and Governmental Affairs, "Money Laundering and Foreign Corruption: Enforcement and Effectiveness of the Patriot Act, Supplemental Staff Report on U.S. Accounts by Augusto Pinochet," March 16, 2005, p. 38-39; p. 67.

[41] Ibid. Coutts & Co. (USA) International is an Edge Act corporation that was part of the international private banking part of The Royal Bank of Scotland Group.

[42] Ibid. p. 64.

Spanish Settlement.[43] In 2004, Riggs spent more than $100 million on fines, lawyers, consultants, and auditors in connection with resolving its improper and illegal activities.

Equatorial Guinea

Riggs Bank relationships with the Republic of Equatorial Guinea involved its dealings with President Brig. Gen. (Ret.) Teodoro Obiang Nguema Mbasogo (a.k.a. President Obiang). Riggs opened 60 accounts and certificates of deposit, and held about $750 million worth of accounts associated with Equatorial Guinea.[44] That made Equatorial Guinea the single largest customer at Riggs Bank.

By way of background, The Republic of Equatorial Guinea is a small West African country with large oil reserves that contributed to its growth in recent years. It is a major oil and gas supplier to the U.S. The Central Intelligence Agency estimates that the population was 535,881 in April 2005.[45] A U.S State Department report in 2000 about Equatorial Guinea reported that "The investment and other uses of oil revenues lacked transparency…Poor fiscal management and lack of public accounting transparency ….Little evidence that the country's oil wealth is being devoted to the pubic good….The government's human rights record remained poor and continued to commit serious abuses…"[46] In addition, President Obiang was depicted in the popular press as "one of the world's 10 worst dictators." Therefore, it is not surprising that such government officials might dip into the rich pools of oil for their own benefit. However, Riggs bank seemed oblivious to it --- they "turned a blind eye" to the possibility that their largest customer may be doing something illegal.

Riggs helped President Obiang establish Otong S.A., and offshore shell corporation, incorporated in the Bahamas. Between April 2000 and April 2002, he placed $11 million in cash in that account. Some of the cash deposits weighed 60 pounds. However, Riggs failed to file the required SAR reports. In addition Riggs failed to file SAR reports on 16 wire transfers amounting to $26.4 million from an account at Riggs that held Equatorial Guinea oil royalty payments to an account in Spain.[47] Some of those accounts were believe to be owned by President Obiang.

The Kingdom of Saudi Arabia was of concern because of the increased risks of money laundering and terrorism financing after 2001. Riggs failed to monitor and to report as suspicious transactions "tens of millions of dollars of cash withdrawals from accounts related to the Embassy of Saudi Arabia; dozens of sequentially-numbered international drafts that totaled millions of dollars that were drawn from accounts related to officials of Saudi Arabia,

---

43 O'Hara, Terence, "Judge Backs Rigg's $16 million Plea Deal," Washington Post.com, March 30, 2005, E02.

44 U. S. Senate, Permanent Subcommittee on Investigations, Committee on Governmental Affairs, "Money Laundering and Foreign Corruption: Enforcement and Effectiveness of the Patriot Act, Senate Hearing 108-633, July 15, 2004, p. 18, 23.

45 Central Intelligence Agency, The World Fact Book, 2005, www.cia.gov.

46 U. S. Senate, Permanent Subcommittee on Investigations, Committee on Governmental Affairs, "Money Laundering and Foreign Corruption: Enforcement and Effectiveness of the Patriot Act, Senate Hearing 108-633, July 15, 2004, p. 28, 54.

47 U.S. Department of Justice, Press Release, "Riggs Bank Sentenced to Pay $16 Million for Criminal Violation of the Bank Secrecy Act," March 29, 2005; . U. S. Senate, Permanent Subcommittee on Investigations, Committee on Governmental Affairs, "Money Laundering and Foreign Corruption: Enforcement and Effectiveness of the Patriot Act, Senate Hearing 108-633, July 15, 2004, p. 30.

and that were returned to the bank; and dozens of sequentially-numbered cashier's checks that were drawn from accounts related to officials at Saudi Arabia made payable to the account holder."[48]

A U.S. Senate Report said that "The corporate culture at Riggs failed to communicate the importance of the bank's anti-money laundering program....Even more telling is the fact that Riggs' Board failed over a five year period to ensure that regulators' directives to improve the bank's AML program were implemented.....Riggs 'willfully violated' the requirements of the U.S. anti-money laundering laws."[49] One of the key findings of the report was that Riggs management "turned a blind eye to evidence suggesting the bank was handling the proceeds of foreign corruption...." Michael Jensen (1993. p. 852) said that "By nature, organizations abhor control systems, and ineffective governance is a major part of the problem with internal control mechanisms. They seldom respond in the absence of a crisis."

The Riggs case also highlights the problems of dealing with politically exposed persons (PEPs) such as former Chilean dictator Augusto Pinochet. It also raises red flags when dealing with foreign governments and embassies.

Banco De Chile, New York and Miami Branches

The story of former Chilean dictator Augusto Pinochet did not end with Riggs bank. In February 2005, administrative actions by the OCC and Federal Reserve were taken against the Banco de Chile's New York and Miami branches. The New York branch was set up under the OCC and the Miami branch under the Federal Reserve. The OCC found that branch former personnel had concealed accounts for Augusto Pinochet under the names of nominees and others acting under his direction. An attorney, Oscar Aitken is one example. The OCC News Release stated that "The OCC discovered that the branch opened accounts without determining the source of the funds and failed to scrutinize the purpose of the transactions. Former representatives of the branch allowed millions of dollars in deposits and credits from internal and external transfers to accounts controlled by persons acting under Pinochet's direction or authorization. These often included circular transactions with no disclosed or apparent legitimate business purpose and without suspicious activity reporting by the branch."[50] More will be said about reporting suspicious activity shortly.

---

48 Stipano (2004), p. 18.

49 U.S. Senate, 2004, Permanent Subcommittee on Investigations, Committee on Governmental Affairs, "Money Laundering and Foreign Corruption: Enforcement and Effectiveness of the Patriot Act, Case Study Involving Riggs Bank," Report prepared by the Minority Staff of the Permanent Subcommittee, July 15. (July 15, 2004), pp. 7, 71.

50 Comptroller of the Currency, New Release, "OCC Issues Cease and Desist Order Against New York Branch of Banco de Chile," NR 2005-11, February 2, 2005; Press Release, "Cease and Desist Order Against Banco de Chile," Board of Governors of the Federal Reserve System, Enforcement Action, February 2, 2005; Gordon, Marcy, "Banco de Chile to Close Pinochet Accounts," Seattle Post-Intelligencer, February 2, 2005. www.seattlepi.com

Citigroup – Salinas, Bongo, and Abacha Sons: Examples of a Lack of Due Diligence, Secrecy, and Anti-Money Laundering Controls

Raul Salinas

Raul Salinas de Gotari (a.k.a. Raul Salinas) is the older brother of Carlos Salinas de Gotairi, the former President of Mexico (1988-1994). Raul Salinas served as an aide to the President, and as a government food distribution officer. In 1995 Raul Salinas was arrested for murdering Pepe Ruiz Massieu, his former ex-brother-in-law. He was also charged with money laundering. In 1999, he was convicted of murder and was sentenced to 27.5 years in jail.

Between 1992-1994 Raul Salinas transferred between $90 to $100 million using Citibank private banking relationships in Mexico, New York, London, and Switzerland.[51] Some of the funds are believed to have come from the Colombian Medellin and Cali drug cartels, to facilitate their shipments of cocaine through Mexico to the United States.[52]

In 1992, Raul Salinas set up a private banking relationship with the Mexican Division of Citibank with an initial deposit of $2 million. Although his salary was never more than $190,000 per year, his private banker in Mexico knew that he came from a wealthy family, he had funds returned from an incomplete business venture, he had sold his construction company, the Mexican stock market was doing well, and his new wife had received a large divorce settlement from her previous husband.[53] She had no reason at that time to suspect that he was doing anything wrong.

To hide his private banking relationships, Raul also set up an offshore private investment company (PIC) named Trocca, to hold his assets through Cititrust, a Citigroup affiliate located in the Cayman Islands (see Figure 1).[54]

Establishing PICs is standard practice in the international private banking industry to someone's assets.[55] The assets can be real estate, art, money, or other valuables. The nominal

---

[51] U.S. General Accounting Office, Private Banking: Raul Salinas, Citibank, and Alleged Money Laundering, Statement for the Record of Robert H. Hast, Acting Assistant Comptroller General for Investigations, Office of Special Investigations, Testimony Before the Permanent Subcommittee on Investigations, Committee on Governmental Affairs, U.S. Senate, GAO/T-OSI-003, November 9, 1999: U.S. General Accounting Office, Private Banking: Raul Salinas, Citibank, and Alleged Money Laundering, Statement for the Record of Robert H. Hast, Acting Assistant Comptroller General for Investigations, Report to the Ranking Minority Member, Permanent Subcommittee on Investigations, Committee on Governmental Affairs, U.S. Senate, GAO/OSI-99-1, October, 1998.

[52] "Frozen Millions Are Drug Proceeds, Raul Salinas Incriminated by Numerous Witnesses," Office of the Attorney General of Switzerland, Federal Office for Police Matters, Press Office, October 20, 1998.

[53] United States Senate, Permanent Subcommittee on Investigations, Committee on Governmental Affairs, "Private Banking and Money Laundering: A Case Study of Opportunities and Vulnerabilities," S. Hrg. 106-428, November 9, 10, 1999, 38.

[54] Source for Figure 1--: U.S. General Accounting Office, Private Banking: Raul Salinas, Citibank, and Alleged Money Laundering, Statement for the Record of Robert H. Hast, Acting Assistant Comptroller General for Investigations, Report to the Ranking Minority Member, Permanent Subcommittee on Investigations, Committee on Governmental Affairs, U.S. Senate, GAO/OSI-99-1, October, 1998.

officers of the PICs are often affiliated shell corporations within shell corporations that are controlled by the private bank. The accounts, and the ownership of the private bank's clients are buried in the records of secrecy jurisdictions such as the Cayman Islands. One justification for such accounts is to shield the assets of wealthy citizens in some Latin American clients from acts of violence, such as extortion, and kidnapping.

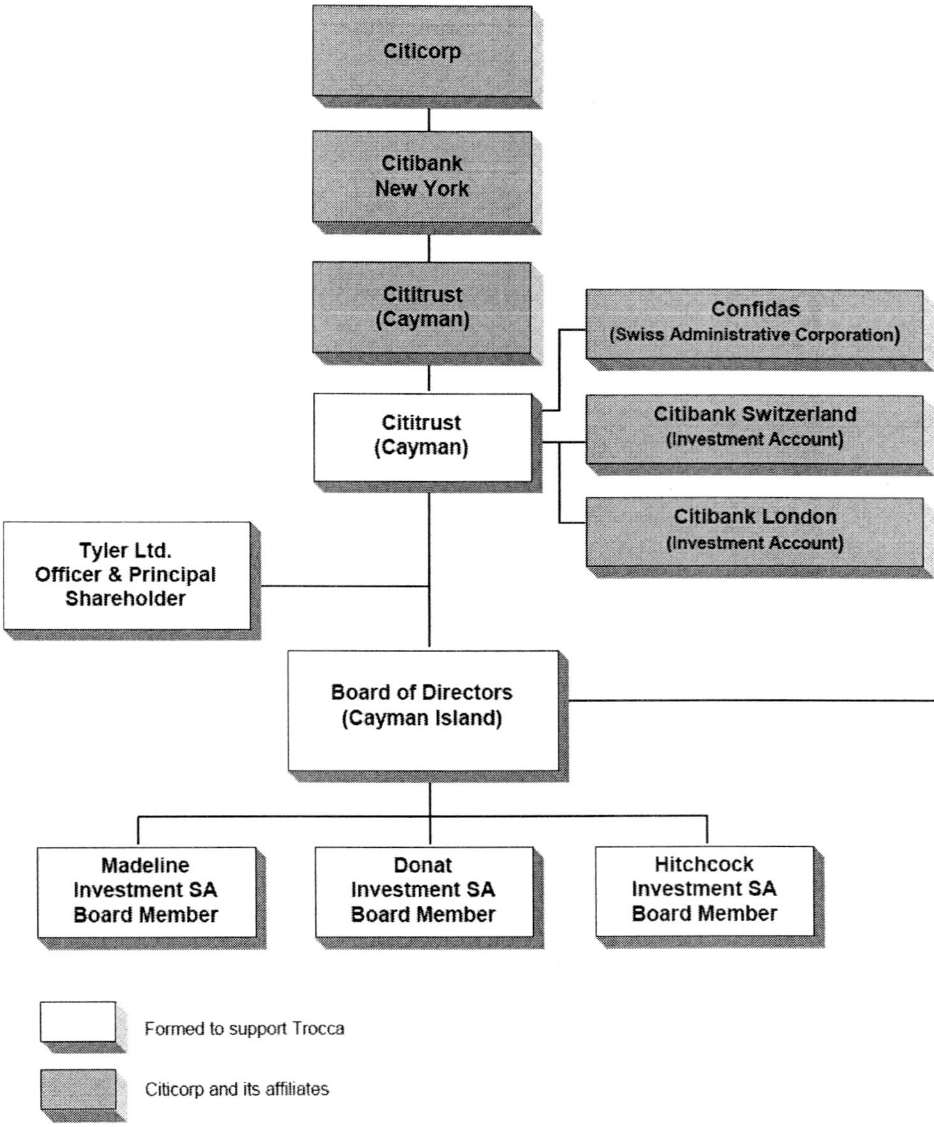

Figure 1. Trocca and Related Entities.

[55] Opening statement of Senator Carl Levin, United States Senate, Permanent Subcommittee on Investigations, Committee on Governmental Affairs, "Private Banking and Money Laundering: A Case Study of Opportunities and Vulnerabilities," S. Hrg. 106-428, November 9, 10, 1999, p. 25.

To hide the fact that he owned Trocca, Raul used additional shell companies in the Cayman Islands (Madeline Investment SA, Donat Investment SA, and Hitchcock Investment SA) to serve as Trocca's board of directors. Trocca's principal officer and shareholder was Tyler Ltd., a Cititrust (Cayman) affiliate. Confidas, another Cititrust (Switzerland), served as Trocca's manager. Troccas also had investment accounts with Citibank London and Citibank Switzerland. In other words, Cititrust controlled the shell companies that served as the directors and officers of the PICs that it made available to Raul Salinas who was the secret beneficiary of the trust.[56] Cititrust did not use the Salinas name in any communications. He was referred to as "Confidential Client No. 2," or "CC-2." Salinas moved money out of Mexico to Trocca accounts in Switzerland and London.

Salinas used his wife (who had at least five bank accounts in Mexico), and other names (e.g. Patricia Rios) to initiate funds transfers from Citibank Mexico to a concentration account at Citibank New York. A concentration account for a business is used to commingle funds that are subsequently transferred to other accounts. In this case, the funds were transferred to Trocca's accounts in London and Switzerland.

There was no documentation in the U.S. that suggested that Raul Salinas was the beneficial owner of Trocca. Along this line, Cititrust (Cayman) did not follow Citibank's policies on Know Your Customer in their dealing with Salinas. Thus, he effectively broke the "paper trail" by hiding both the origin and the destination of the funds. It was only after he was arrested for murder in February 1995 that his fund transfers were discovered. However, the investigations were hampered by bank secrecy laws in other countries and jurisdictions.

El Hadj Omar Bongo

El Hadj Omar Bongo Ondimba has been the President of Gabon since it gained its independence from France in 1960, and Bongo was a private bank client of Citibank.[57] Gabon is located next to Equatorial Guinea on the west coast of Africa. Equatorial Guinea was discussed in connection with Riggs bank. Gabon has a population of about 1.38 million, and oil accounts for about half of its Gross Domestic Product. Timber and manganese are also important. Gabon is a relatively stable and prosperous African Country.[58]

The Bongo relationship with Citibank included consumer and private bank accounts in Gabon, London, New York, Paris, and Switzerland. The largest account was in the name of Tendin Investments, a Bahaminian PIC established by Citibank in 1985. Over a 14 year period, the account held more than $130 million, and issued President Bongo loans of more than $50 million that were secured by the deposits. The accounts were kept secret by using code names. Bongos code name was "OS." In 1997, OCC examiners wanted documentation concerning the source of Bongo's funds because of a scandal concerning bribes by Elf Aquitaine, a French oil company that paid to government officials. The funds in the Citibank accounts came from the Gabon budget. In 1995, Citibank thought that the Gabon budget authorized $111 million for Bongos use, but that was not the case. Thereafter, Citibank

---

[56] Ibid. p. 30.

[57] Ibid. 32-36,

[58] See the Central Intelligence Agency, The World Fact Book, 2005 (www.cia.gov) for additional details about Gabon.

assumed that Bongo had *carte blanche* authority over his government's funds and never bothered to double check whether this was the case. No one explained the source of the $20 million that was deposited in Bongos account in 1997. Citibank expected to close his accounts in 2000.

Sani Abacha

General Sani Abacha was the military leader of Nigeria from 1993 until he died in June 1998. He was widely condemned as being corrupt, and Nigeria was recognized as a high risk country for money laundering. He had three sons, Mohammed, Ibrahim, and Aba. Mohammed and Ibrahim opened accounts with Citibank Private Bank in 1998, in London and New York, and they used PICs to shield their identities. The Citibank account manager in New York (the same person that managed Bongos accounts) was not aware that the son's father was the military leader of Nigeria. The London accounts held as much as $60 million, and the New York accounts were under $2 million. Shortly after the General died, his wife and one of the sons were stopped at the Lagos airport. They had 38 suitcases containing over $100 million in cash that was seized by the Nigerian government. In September 1998, while the Nigerian government was still investigating the source of the funds, Abacha's sons transferred $39 million from their Citibank accounts in London to Switzerland. Citibank closed the accounts in 1999.

Box 5-3
Political Corruption

The Nicaraguan government asked for help in identifying assets in the U.S. belonging to Byron Jerez Solis, the former head of the equivalent of their Internal Revenue Service. It was believed that more than $100 million had been embezzled by Solis and others from the Nicaraguan government acting on orders from Arnoldo Aleman, the former President of the country. The funds were wired to Panamanian banks, and then to the U.S. They were used to buy Certificates of Deposit, a $3 million condominium, a $300,000 beach house, and a helicopter.

Aleman was convicted on money laundering charges, fined $17 million, and sentenced to 20 years in prison. In addition, he was required to pay twice the amount that he laundered.

As a result of the investigation in the U.S., $5.6 million in assets was recovered on behalf of the Nicaraguan government.

U.S. Department of State, "International Narcotics Control Strategy Report – 2003, Released by the Bureau for International Narcotics and Law Enforcement Affairs, March 2004.

Citibank, Japan

Citibank's private banking operation in Japan was shut down by Japan's Financial Services Agency (FSA) for money laundering and other charges.[59] "Kiochiro Kitade, a marketing whiz who headed the office, was robbing hundreds of wealthy new clients. But he had a tin ear for regulations."[60] Subsequently, FSA inspectors found that Citibank allowed transactions in an account that raised suspicions of money laundering because that account had been flagged as suspicious by Citibank branches in other countries.[61] In addition, the FSA found that a Citibank employee allegedly embezzled $16.8 million from depositors over a seven year period. Finally, Citibank employees made misleading statements in connection with the sale of structured bonds in a private placement, and they tied the handling of the private placement as a condition of granting loans for the customer's business activities in a foreign country. This is a violation of Japanese laws.[62]

Collateralized Loans[63]

If a private bank encourages its customers to establish credit facilities, a foreign customer who wants to launder, say $10 million, opens an account. Then he borrows $9 million, secured by the initial deposit, and uses those funds to establish a business in his home country. This also gives them credibility and respect in their country, and it makes the banker look good too. The bank has a $10 million and a $9 million loan. The borrower can use funds from illegal sources in his country to repay the loan.

---

[59] Mitchell Pacelle, Martin Fackler, and Andrew Morse, "For Citigroup, Scandal in Japan Shows Danger of Global Sprawl," The Wall Street Journal, December 22, 2004, A1, A10.

[60] Ibid.

[61] Morse, Andrew, and Mitchell Pacelle, "Citigroup Submits Plan to Mend Private- Banking Unit in Japan," Wall Street Journal, October 25, 2004, C3.

[62] Financial Services Agency (FSA, Japan), "Administrative Actions on Citibank, N.A., Japan Branch" (Provisional Translation), News Release, September 17, 2004.

[63] Based on the Testimony of Antonio Giraldi. Appears in United States Senate, Permanent Subcommittee on Investigations, Committee on Governmental Affairs, "Private Banking and Money Laundering: A Case Study of Opportunities and Vulnerabilities," S. Hrg. 106-428, November 9, 10, 1999. p. 98. Mr. Giraldi is a former private banker who was convicted of money laundering.

Chapter 6

SUSPICIOUS ACTIVITIES

In 1964, Justice Potter Stewart tried to explain hard core pornography, or what is obscenity, by saying "I know it when I see it..."[1] The definitions of "suspicious activities" are equally vague, and they vary from country-to-country. In the U.S., *Black's Law Dictionary* defines "suspicion" as "the imagination or apprehension of the existence of something wrong based only on slight or no evidence without definitive proof."[2] In Switzerland, a "founded suspicion" is a suspicion grounded on some factual bases, however slim.[3] In the Netherlands it is based on the "unusual" nature of transactions, while in Canada you must "have reasonable grounds to suspect a transaction is related to a money laundering or a terrorist financing offence."[4]

John Trapani, Federal Reserve Bank of Chicago, said that Suspicious Activity Reports (SAR) means "Something Ain't Right."[5] Such vague definitions of suspicious activity can be useful. According to FinCEN, "...a critical aspect of suspicious transaction reporting is that it enables law enforcement to benefit from the expertise of financial institution employees and officers in judging which transactions are suspicious in the context of the particular financial servies offered by the financial institution."[6]

U.S. financial institutions are required to file SARs within 30 days after the date of initial detection of facts that constitute suspicious activity, or face the consequences. Federal regulations require the filing of SARs with respect to:[7]

- Criminal violations involving insider abuse in any dollar amount.
- Criminal violations amounting to $5,000 or more when the suspect can be identified.

---

1 Jacobellis v. Ohio, 378 U.S. 184, 197 (1964).

2 Garner, Bryan A., Ed., *Black's Law Dictionary*, 7th ed. , St. Paul, MN, West Group, 1999, p. 1460.

3 Financial Intelligence Units: An Overview, Washington, D.C., The International Monetary Fund and The World Bank, 2004. p. 45.

4 Welcome to FINTRAC, What Must Be Reported, Suspicious Transactions, http://www.fintrac.gc.ca/publications/brochure/may-2003/pamphlet2_e.asp

5 Trapani, John, Team Leader, BSA/AML Risk Specialist Unit, Federal Reserve Bank of Chicago, "Money Laundering," Presented at the 2005 Financial Management Association Annual Meeting, Chicago, IL, October 13, 2005.

6 Federal Register/Vol. 67, No. 187, September 26, 2002, Rules and Regulations, Department of Treasury, 31 CFR Part 103. p. 60725.

7 Federal Financial Institutions Examination Council, Bank Secrecy Act/Anti-Money Laundering Examination Manual, June 2005, (FFIEC BSA/AML Examination Manual), pp. 40-41, www.ffiec.gov/pdf/bsamanual.pdf

- Criminal violations amounting to $25,000 or more even if there is no suspect.
- Attempted or actual transactions through banks or their affiliates amounting to $5,000 or more if the bank has reason to suspect money laundering or other illegal activities, or it is designed to evade BSA regulations. Finally, reporting is required for transactions that have no apparent business or lawful purpose or reasonable explanation.

Federal law provides bank directors, officers, and employees, protection from civil liability for all reports of suspicious transactions that are made to appropriate authorities.[8] This safe harbor is in connection with the reporting of any possible violation of laws or regulations.

In fiscal year 2004, there were 663,655 SAR reports filed with FinCEN, a 17% increase over the previous year.[9] About 54% of the reports were filed by financial institutions, 44% by Money Service Businesses, and the remainder were split between casinos and securities and futures industries.[10]

EXAMPLES OF SUSPICIOUS ACTIVITIES

The *Bank Secrecy Act/Anti-Money Laundering Comptroller's Handbook* (2000) provides lists of potentially suspicious activities that warrant further investigation to determine whether a SAR should be filed. Selected items adapted from the Comptroller's Handbook are presented here to illustrate such activities. This listing of suspicious activities is not all inclusive. It is only for purposes of illustration.

Activities Inconsistent with the Customer's Business

- The customer opens several accounts for the business, and transfers funds among those accounts.
- The customer's corporate account(s) deposits and/or withdrawals are primarily in cash rather than checks.
- The customer makes large dollar deposits, withdrawals, or purchases of monetary instruments without an explanation as to how they will be used in the business that generally does not deal in a large amount of cash.
- A business that has no regular, periodic activity, and that appears to be used primarily as a temporary repository for funds that are being transferred abroad.
- A retail business that deposits checks, but rarely withdraws cash for daily operations.
- Businesses that do not normally generate cash, such as a sanitation company, making numerous cash deposits.

---

[8] For additional details see 31USC 5318(g)(3).

[9] Financial Crimes Enforcement Network, "Annual Report, Fiscal 2004," Washington, D.C., 2005, Appendix A.

[10] FinCEN, "The SAR Activity Review, By the Numbers," Issue 3, December 2004.

Avoiding the Reporting or Record Keeping Requirements

- A customer that intentionally withholds part of a cash deposit or withdrawal to keep the transaction under the reporting limits.
- A customer who asks to be exempted from reporting requirements/ and or ties to coerce bank employees from filing required reports.
- Using automatic teller machines (ATMs) to make several deposits below reporting limits.
- Unusually large deposits of U.S. food stamps – that may be used to buy narcotics.

Fund (Wire) Transfers

- Wire transfers to or from offshore financial secrecy havens, such as Antigua, without an apparent business reason, or that is inconsistent with the customer's business or history.
- Large income wire transfers on behalf of a foreign client with little or no explicit reason for the transaction.
- Large, round dollar amounts of funds.
- Fund transfers in or out of an account in a short period of time.
- Deposits of amounts less than $3,000 into several accounts, then consolidated into one account, and transferred out of the country.
- Regular deposits or withdrawals of large amounts of cash, using wire transfers involving countries that are known sources of narcotics, or whose anti-money laundering laws are weak.

Insufficient or Suspicious Information by Customer

- A business establishing a new account that is reluctant to provide complete information about the purpose of the business, prior banking relationships, names of officers, directors, etc.
- A customer who wants to open an account without providing proper identification, local address, or other information required by the institution.
- The customer's home/business phone is disconnected.
- No record of past or present employment on a loan application.
- A customer's financial statements differ from those of similar businesses.

Bank Employee Activities

- A lavish lifestyle that is not consistent with the employee's earnings from the bank.
- Does not conform with bank policies, especially in private banking.
- Reluctance to take vacations.

Bank-to-Bank Transactions

- Significant changes in the pattern of currency shipments between correspondent banks.
- High turnover in large denomination bills that are not consistent with the bank's location.
- A significant increase in small denomination bills, and corresponding decrease in large denomination bills, with no corresponding filings of CTRs.
- A rapid increase in the size and frequency of cash deposits with no corresponding change in noncash deposits.

Other Suspicious Customer Activities

- Large deposits of $50 and $100 bills.
- Mailing address outside of the United States.
- Certificates of Deposit, or other investments, used as collateral for loans.
- Large loans paid down with no reasonable explanation for the source of funds.
- Frequent deposits of musty or dirty bills, and/or currency wrapped in currency straps or rubber bands that do not balance when counted.
- A professional service provider, such as a lawyer or accountant, who makes substantial cash deposits into a client's trust, escrow, or other accounts.
- Offshore companies, especially those located in bank secrecy havens, asking for loans from a U.S. bank.
- Money orders that are deposited by mail, which are numbered sequentially, or that have unusual markings.

Box 5-1

Two Best Points for Detecting Suspicious Activity

"A bank can best detect suspicious activity at one of two points. The 'front-end' of a transaction involves tellers and other individuals who may have face-to-face contact with the customer and can often determine if a specific transaction is worth a second look....The second likely point of detection occurs in the 'back office' – an analysis of financial transactions, which takes placed in a specialized unit, for example, or in particularly high-risk areas such the bank's wire transfer operations. Money-laundering analysts look at the bank's transactions to determine if they can conclude, by examining patterns of transactions, whether those patterns are suspicious."

However, the models used to detect illicit activity may not apply to terrorist financing because of the routine methods of financing that they used – cash and traveler's checks, credit and debit cards, wire transfers, etc.

Source: Source: National Commission on Terrorist Attacks Upon the United States, Staff Monograph on Terrorist Financing, 2004, p. 55, 56. http://www.9-11commission.gov

Box 5-2
Cash Deposits from a Large Handbag

A Colombian national was observed making cash deposits from a large handbag into numerous bank accounts. The total deposits amounted to $1.8 million. One of the deposit accounts was an attorney trust fund. The owner of the trust fund was a prominent attorney for drug traffickers. The Colombian was arrested for violations of U.S. money laundering laws.

Source: U.S. Department of State, "International Narcotics Control Strategy Report – 2003, Released by the Bureau for International Narcotics and Law Enforcement Affairs, March 2004.

SAR Reports

In general terms, all financial institutions are required to file SARs for *transactions* aggregating $5,000 or more in funds or other assets if the institution knows, suspects, or has reason to suspect that money laundering or other illegal activity such as financing terrorism is involved.[11] For example, the funds are derived from illegal activities, or the transaction has no apparent business reason, or it is not the sort of transaction that the customer might normally do. Similarly, Currency Transaction Reports (CTR) whenever multiple currency transactions exceed $10,000. The transactions could take the form of smaller dollar amounts aggregating to $10,000 or more over a period of time, such as 15 days. Some organizations, such as government agencies, stocks (other than banks) listed on the major stock exchanges, and domestic banks are exempted form the CTR filings.

If transactions exceed $10,000 and are suspicious, both the SAR and CTR must be filed. In a broader context, SARs must be filed anytime there is insider abuse, federal criminal violations in excess of $5,000 when the suspect can be identified, and $25, 000 regardless of the suspect.

Transactions include deposits, withdrawals, transfers between accounts, extensions of credit, buying and selling stocks, bonds, CDs, or other monetary instruments or investment securities, or any other payment or transfers made by or though or to a bank.[12]

It should be noted that while financial institutions are required to report within 30 calendar days of initial detection of suspicious activities, BSA/AML violations, and certain crimes, they are not required to investigate those violations. If no suspect can be identified in connection with the suspicious activities, the time frame for reporting is extended to 60 calendar days.

Table 3-1 lists the frequency distribution of SAR filings by type of suspicious activity over a seven year period. Although the mix varied from year-to-year, the data show that BSA/Structuring/Money laundering account for almost half of the SAR reports filed by depository institutions. The number of reports varied from 35,625 in 1997 to 88,877 in 2002.

---

[11] All financial institutions must include certain customer information in transmitting orders for funds of $3000 or more. This is called the "Travel Rule." See 31 CFR 103.33 for additional details.

[12] Federal Financial Institutions Examination Council, Bank Secrecy Act/Anti-Money Laundering Examination Manual, June 2005, (FFIEC BSA/AML Examination Manual), p. 41, www.ffiec.gov/pdf/bsamanual.pdf

Collectively, check frauds, check kiting, and counterfeit checks are the second largest group, followed by credit and debit card frauds.

Total SAR filings by all covered industries were 413,052 in fiscal year 2003, and 663,655 in fiscal year 2004.[13] To some extent, the increased number of SAR filings may reflect "defensive reporting" on the part of financial institutions that find it less costly too many reports than to be fined or criticized by regulators for not filing a report.[14]

Table 3. 1. Depository Institution's SAR Filings by Characterization of Suspicious Activity April 1, 1997 Through June 30, 2003

Violation Type	1997	1998	1999	2000	2001	2002	2003
BSA/Structuring/Money Laundering	35,625	47,223	60,983	90,606	108,925	154,000	72,462
Bribery/Gratuity	109	92	101	150	201	411	261
Check Fraud	13,245	13,767	16,232	19,637	26,012	32,954	16,803
Check Kiting	4,294	4,032	4,058	6,163	7,350	9,561	5,333
Commercial Loan Fraud	960	905	1,080	1,320	1348	1,879	934
Computer Intrusion[1]	0	0	0	65	419	2,484	3,605
Consumer Loan Fraud	2,048	2,183	2,548	3,432	4,143	4,435	2,271
Counterfeit Check	4,226	5,897	7,392	9,033	10,139	12,575	6,445
Counterfeit Credit/Debit Card	387	182	351	664	1,100	1,246	659
Counterfeit Instrument (Other)	294	263	320	474	769	791	615
Credit Card Fraud	5,075	4,377	4,936	6,275	8,393	12,780	6,037
Debit Card Fraud	612	565	721	1,210	1,437	3,741	4,575
Defalcation/Embezzlement	5,284	5,252	5,178	6,117	6,182	6,151	2,887
False Statement	2,200	1,970	2,376	3,051	3,232	3,685	2,316
Misuse of Position or Self Dealing	1,532	1,640	2,064	2,186	2,325	2,763	1,564
Mortgage Loan Fraud	1,720	2,269	2,934	3,515	4,696	5,387	3,649
Mysterious Disappearance	1,765	1,855	1,854	2,225	2,179	2,330	1,264
Wire Transfer Fraud	509	593	771	972	1,527	4,747	4,317
Other	6,675	8,583	8,739	11,148	18,318	31,109	15,854
Unknown/Blank	2,317	2,691	6,961	6,971	11,908	7,704	2,290
Totals	88,877	104,339	129,599	175,214	220,603	300,733	154,141

[1]The violation of Computer Intrusion was added to Form TD F 90-22.47 in June 2000. Statistics date from this period.

---

[13] FinCEN, Annual Report, Fiscal Year 2004, p. 35; Data for 2004 are reported in U.S. Department of Treasury (and other U.S. Government agencies, bureaus, and offices), U.S. Money Laundering Threat Assessment, December, 2005, Table 1. However, they are not comparable with the data shown in Table 3-1.

[14] "Global Anti-Money Laundering Survey 2004: How Banks are Facing Up to the Challenge," KPMG International, 2004.

Source: U.S. Department of State, International Narcotics Control Strategy Report -2003, Released by the Bureau for International Narcotics and Law Enforcement Affairs, March 2004, http://www.state.gov/g/inl/rls/nrcrpt/2003/vol2/html/29910.htm

Finally, banking institutions are required to file SAR reports on money service businesses that have failed to register with FinCEN, or have not obtained a required state license.[15] Failure to register with FinCEN can result in both civil and criminal penalties for the MSBs. The criminal penalties carry a maximum sentence of 5 years in prison.

SELECTED CASE STUDIES

AmSouth Bancorporation

AmSouth Bancorporation agreed to pay $40 million to the United States and a $10 million Civil Money Penalty for violating the anti-money laundering program and suspicious activity reporting requirements of the Bank Secrecy Act.[16] According the Assessment of the Civil Money Penalty, AmSouth failed to file timely suspicious activity reports concerning the following activities of its customers.[17]

- "The perpetrators of a fraudulent investment scheme maintained accounts at AmSouth to handle funds contributed by individual investors. AmSouth did not perform adequate due diligence on the perpetrators, which could have revealed financial and prior regulatory problems. Further, AmSouth ignored red flags, including concerns communicated to Bank management by several employees at various AmSouth branches indicating the accounts were being used in furtherance of a Ponzi scheme. Despite such warnings, AmSouth failed to file a suspicious activity report until two years after it knew or should have known about the suspicious nature of the activity and millions had been deposited and then withdrawn from related accounts at the Bank. The perpetrators ultimately were convicted of money laundering and money laundering conspiracy.
- The Chief Financial Officer of an AmSouth corporate customer embezzled several million dollars from the corporation over three years using forged and improperly authorized checks. Although AmSouth employees noticed that the Chief Financial Officer was conducting a number of highly unusual transactions, the Bank did not file a suspicious activity report because it suffered no loss.
- A municipal official contacted the manager of a local AmSouth branch regarding the suspected misappropriation by another municipal officer of approximately $450,000 through the fraudulent endorsement of a number of city checks. Shortly thereafter,

---

15 Comptroller of the Currency, OCC Bulletin, Interagency Guidance on Providing Banking Services to Money Services Businesses Operating in the United States, OCC 2005-19, May 6, 2005, p. 8; 18 U.S.C., 1960; U.S. v Uddin, No 04-CR-80192 (E.D. Mich. April 11, 2005).

16 AmSouth Bancorporation, United States Securities and Exchange Commission, Form 8-K, October 12, 2004.

17 U.S. Department of Treasury, Financial Crimes Enforcement Network, In the matter of AmSouth Bank, Assessment of Civil Money Penalty, No. 2004-2, October 12, 2004. (Also shown in AmSouth's Form 8-K, October 2004).

the responsible party acknowledged the misappropriation in a suicide note. Nonetheless, AmSouth did not file a suspicious activity report because the suspect was dead. Another municipal employee was eventually indicted for his role in the fraud.

- Another matter involved an employee of AmSouth's broker-dealer who allegedly committed fraud in clients' accounts by, among other things, forging customers signatures on numerous documents. The broker-dealer reported his employee's misconduct to the National Association of Securities Dealers ("NASD"). The broker-dealer also had a duty to report what it knew to be suspicious activity by its own to FinCEN, and it failed to do so. AmSouth now acknowledges that a SAR should have been filed in this matter, and recently filed a SAR.
- An employee of a car dealership formed his own corporation and then opened an account at AmSouth under the name of the corporation "dba" (doing business as) the name of the car dealership. Over a year, an employee deposited several hundred thousand dollars worth of checks made payable to his employer into an AmSouth account. The employee ultimately sued AmSouth concerning these transactions. AmSouth handled the litigation without conducting a review to determine whether a SAR should have been filed.
- An individual operated a fraudulent multi-million dollar trading operation for five years before being arrested. More than $20 million in assets from investors in the program were frozen in various banks, including AmSouth. AmSouth received Securities and Exchange Commission and grand jury subpoenas seeking information on the matter. Months after the individual pleaded guilty to felony charges of securities fraud, money laundering and wire fraud, AmSouth closed the last of his accounts without ever having filed a suspicious activity report.
- A corporate customer deposited into its AmSouth account an official check for $220,000 drawn on another U.S. bank. Six days later, the customer initiated a wire transfer of $190,000 from its AmSouth account to a bank in a foreign country. All but $30,000 of the wired funds were then withdrawn from the foreign bank. Nine days after its deposit, the check was returned unprocessed to AmSouth because the amount had been altered. Although AmSouth notified local law enforcement of the incident, and fully cooperated with the government investigation, it did not file a suspicious activity report.
- A bank cashier at another bank embezzled money from his employer by wiring funds from an account maintained by his employer to deposit accounts at AmSouth held in his or his wife's name. The bank cashier then invested these funds in investment accounts at AmSouth's broker-dealer subsidiary. The employer contacted AmSouth about the bank cashier's accounts. Although AmSouth notified federal law enforcement of the incident, it never filed a suspicious activity report.
- In addition, the Federal Reserve's June 2004 examination disclosed that AmSouth had not filed suspicious activity reports on a number of instances of check kiting activity involving possible losses above $5,000, which appeared on an AmSouth internal report. In response to the examination, AmSouth has now filed suspicious activity reports on several matters identified by the Federal Reserve. Various cases

involving fraudulent activity by customers of the bankcard business unit, and matters identified by the fraud prevention unit, also were not reported."

It is worthwhile examining the previously mentioned Ponzi scheme in greater detail to understand how such schemes work, what red flags the bank missed, and the bank's actions and reactions. AmSouth refers to this incident as "The Hamric Matter." The following is taken directly from AmSouth's 2004, SEC Form 8K.[18]

1. In the spring of 2002, the United States Attorney's Office for the Southern District of Mississippi, along with a number of federal and state agencies, began an investigation of a fraudulent promissory note scheme perpetrated by Louis D. Hamric, II, a licensed attorney, Victor G. Nance, a registered investment adviser employed by Mutual of New York ("MONY"), and various other individuals. In essence, Hamric would issue a Promissory Note to each investor promising to pay a very high interest rate for one year. Hamric had little, if any, contact with the actual investors. Various "promoters" of the scheme, including Nance, would bring investors to Hamric and receive a commission for their services. Hamric told Nance that he needed a "block" of $10 million to participate in a "trading program" that would provide returns through the promissory notes of up to 25% annually. Nance, a registered investment advisor representative, convinced over 40 of his clients to invest in Hamric's program by making numerous misrepresentations to them about the nature and risk of the investment. Many of these investors were retired and had their life savings invested with Nance.[19]
2. After Nance assured Hamric that he could provide the $10 million, both Hamric and Nance approached AmSouth[20] to seek help in dealing with the large number of investors, many of whom had funds invested in individual retirement accounts ("IRAs"). Hamric and Nance misrepresented to AmSouth that the business venture involved construction of medical clinics overseas. In August 2000, after Hamric and Nance had spoken with several AmSouth officers, AmSouth agreed to perform, and performed, the following custodial services for Hamric and Nance, for a fee of $2,000 per year per account:[21]
   a) AmSouth established a custodial trust account, which could be designated as an IRA if requested, for each person for whom Hamric and Nance provided completed new account documents;[22]

---

[18] AmSouth Bancorporation, United States Securities and Exchange Commission, Form 8-K, October 12, 2004. c 2004, EDGAR Online, Inc.; The format of the presentation has been modified.

[19] Victor Nance pled guilty to a money laundering charge, 18 U.S.C. 1957, in connection with this scheme and is currently serving a 10-year sentence in the custody of the Federal Bureau of Prisons. Hamric paid Nance over $4 million in "commissions" for finding investors. Louis Hamric pled guilty to money laundering conspiracy, 18 U.S.C. 1956(h), and is awaiting sentencing.

[20] AmSouth did not perform adequate due diligence with regard to Hamric or Nance, who had been prior customers of the Bank.

[21] Hamric orally agreed to pay the fee for each custodial account established on behalf of Nance's investors.

[22] AmSouth provided blank account opening documents to Hamric and Nance and entrusted them to complete and return the documents to AmSouth for a custodial trust account to be opened. AmSouth did not question the existence or identity of any of the persons who were signing the forms.

b) Upon receipt of customer funds into each custodial trust account, AmSouth transferred all funds to an AmSouth money market account controlled by both Hamric and Nance, and accepted into each custodial trust account a Promissory Note, issued by Hamric;[23]

c) AmSouth distributed interest payments, on a monthly basis, to each custodial trust account upon receipt of a check from Hamric and a spreadsheet from Nance directing how much money should be credited to each account; and

d) AmSouth provided a copy of each custodial account holder's bank statement to both Hamric and Nance on a quarterly basis, with the knowledge or consent of custodial account holders.

3. When the customer chose to reinvest, upon the maturity of the Promissory Notes, AmSouth agreed, without the knowledge of any of the account holders, to "net" the proceeds of the old note against the new one, and send Hamric the difference.
4. Beginning in early 2001, several other "promoters" brought a second wave of investors into the Hamric scheme, and AmSouth held promissory notes promising to pay these new investors as much as 25% interest monthly. Although a note promising such interest is suspicious on its face, AmSouth did not question the terms or nature of any of these promissory notes.
5. By early 2002, Hamric had stopped sending interest payment checks to AmSouth. On March 13, 2002, AmSouth sent a letter to each investor informing them that six (6) checks sent by Hamric in January had been returned unpaid, that AmSouth had mistakenly sent interest payments to certain custodial account holders, and that AmSouth had demanded reimbursement from Hamric in the amount of $119,013.50. AmSouth stated that "it may be necessary for those account holders that received direct distributions in 2002 to refund such distributions," in the event that the money could not be recovered from Hamric. AmSouth then advised its account holders that the reason for the letter was to inform them of Hamric's delinquencies so that the account holders could take any action they deemed necessary.
6. Without AmSouth's participation through, among other things, the failure of one, or more, AmSouth mangers to properly question whether the Hamric and Nance schemes were fraudulent, Hamric and Nance would not have succeeded in their schemes pursuant to which they attracted a total of approximately $20 million in fraud proceeds, caused those proceeds to be deposited into AmSouth accounts, and transferred those proceeds, in violation of 18 U.S.C. 1956 and 1957, among and out of those accounts.
7. When Hamric failed to pay interest owed to the investors, the fraudulent promissory note scheme fell apart.....The scheme also became the subject of several investigations by state and federal authorities, including a federal grand jury investigation in the Southern District of Mississippi."

---

[23] Hamric and Nance prepared a "Direction of Investment" form, which each account holder was required to complete and sign. The purpose of the form was to instruct AmSouth how much each account holder wished to invest in a Hamric Promissory Note. AmSouth did not follow the instructions on the Direction of Investment forms for the overwhelming majority of Nance's clients. Instead, AmSouth transferred all funds deposited into each custodial trust account to the money market account controlled by both Hamric and Nance. No AmSouth employee could explain why AmSouth disregarded the instructions on the Direction of Investment forms and

8. Beginning on April 29, 2002, and concluding just prior to June 4, 2003,[24] eight federal grand jury subpoenas were issued to AmSouth. These subpoenas requested all documents relating to the Hamric and Nance promissory note scheme, including all documents for any custodial trust accounts opened by either Hamric or Nance on behalf of an account holder; all documents for any bank accounts held by Hamric or Nance and various others associated with the scheme; and all internal and external communications between any AmSouth employee and Hamric, Nance or any custodial trust account holder.
9. In responding to these grand jury subpoenas, AmSouth (i) failed to timely produce certain documents called for by these subpoenas; (ii) failed to produce certain documents in the manner they were kept in the regular course of business as required by the subpoenas; and (iii) failed to locate and produce certain documents called for by the subpoenas until AmSouth was targeted in this criminal investigation.
10. AmSouth's outside counsel[25] assumed certain responsive documents had been produced even though they had not been produced. Inside counsel overseeing the production failed to search his own files even though they contained documents responsive to the subpoenas. AmSouth's inside counsel was aware, or should have been aware, of other AmSouth employees who had documents directly responsive to one or more of the federal grand jury subpoenas, but he did not request any documents from these employees.
11. AmSouth Custody Services Department employees, who were made aware of the federal grand jury subpoenas, failed to provide all documents in their possession which were responsive to one or more federal grand jury subpoenas.
12. Through the course of the investigation and through grand jury subpoenas to other sources, certain AmSouth documents became available to federal investigators, including, but not limited to, the AmSouth account holders' bank statements, which were discovered in Hamric's office. Attorneys for the government had discussions with AmSouth's outside counsel concerning the discovery of Bank documents from other sources that had not been produced by AmSouth. AmSouth's outside counsel's responses to these concerns were misleading and inadequate given AmSouth's legal obligations with respect to the grand jury subpoenas. Even after many discussions and other communications between AmSouth's outside counsel and attorneys for the government, AmSouth still failed to produce all responsive documents in a timely manner.
13. Although AmSouth ultimately produced all of these documents after it became the subject of a criminal investigation,[26] the delays in production are legally inexcusable. Given its failures in responding to these numerous grand jury subpoenas, AmSouth

instead transferred all of the funds out of each custodial trust account and into the Hamric/Nance money market account.

[24] Hamric and Nance were indicted on June 4, 2003.

[25] All references to AmSouth's outside counsel in this document refer to the counsel it employed prior to September 24, 2003, at which time AmSouth replaced this counsel with new Mississippi counsel, and later retained Washington, DC based counsel, in connection with the criminal investigation that is the subject of the Information and Deferred Prosecution Agreement filed in conjunction with this Statement of Facts.

[26] On September 24, 2003, AmSouth employed new outside counsel who began discussions with the United States Attorney's Office for the Southern District of Mississippi concerning AmSouth's criminal exposure. AmSouth was formally advised that it was a target of a criminal investigation on November 17, 2003.

has revised its policies and procedures for responding to such subpoenas and will devote additional resources to ensure full and timely responses to all grand jury subpoenas.

International Business Creations/ Euro-American Corporate Services

The International Business Creations/Euro-American Corporate Services case study is one illustration of suspicious activities. In 1991, a native of the Republic of Georgia, who was living in the United States, formed International Business Creations (IBC) that was incorporated in Delaware.[27] IBC opened bank accounts at U.S. banks for corporations that were formed in Delaware at the request of Russian brokers. In 1996, IBC created European-American Corporate Services Inc. (Euro-American) to form Delaware corporations for Russian brokers, act as their registered agent, and open bank accounts for them. IBC/Euro-American received fees for their services. They worked with about 30 to 50 Russian brokers, and formed about 2,000 corporations. The corporations established 136 bank accounts at Citibank of New York and 100 at the Commercial Bank of San Francisco. During the 1991-January 2000 period, more than $1.4 billion in wire transfers were deposited in those accounts. Of that total, about $800 million was wired from foreign countries to the Citibank accounts. Over 70 percent of these deposits were wire-transferred to accounts in Eastern Europe.

Similarly, about half of the $600 million deposited in Commercial Bank came from abroad, and was subsequently transferred out of the U.S. to Eastern Europe. These suspicious activities raised questions about whether these accounts were used to launder money.

Banco Popular of Puerto Rico

In 2003, Banco Popular of Puerto Rico agreed to pay a civil money penalty of $20 million for failing to file SARs.[28] In this case, an individual who was later convicted of money laundering had deposited $21.6 million during the 1995-1998 period. The bank agreed to forfeit the $21.6 million to the United States to settle any claims by the government. Although some branch employees were aware of suspicious activity, the bank had not investigated it or reported it until several years after the suspicious activity began.[29] Banco Popular had $33 billion in assets.

---

[27] U.S. General Accounting Office, "Suspicious Banking Activities: Possible Money Laundering by U.S. Corporations Formed for Russian Entities," Report to the Ranking Minority Member, Permanent Subcommittee on Investigations, Committee on Governmental Affairs, United States Senate, GAO-01-120, October, 2000.

[28] Beckett, Paul, "Banco Popular to Pay Millions in U.S. Fines," The Wall Street Journal, C1, C14; Federal Reserve Press Release: March 9, 2000, Enforcement Actions (Banco Popular de Puerto Rico). .

[29] D'Agostino, Davi M., Director, Financial Markets and Community Investment, "Anti-Money Laundering: Issues Concerning Depository Institution Regulatory Oversight," Testimony Before the U.S. Senate Committee on Banking, Housing, and Urban Affairs, U.S. General Accounting Office, GAO-04-833T, June 3, 2004.

Credit Card Bust-Out Scheme[30]

FinCEN distinguishes between "proactive" and "reactive" reporting of SARs. *Proactive* refers to anticipating that something in advance. *Reactive* refers to reporting something that has already happened. The Credit Card Bust-Out Scheme is an example of proactive reporting by a financial institution that filed seven SARs. In this case, the perpetrator opened a credit card account. He or she used it to the maximum limit, and then made a fraudulent payment. Then additional charges to the limit were made before the fraudulent payment was returned as uncollectible. The credit card charges were used for airline tickets, cash advances, cigarettes, and jewelry. One individual used the credit card to pay federal income taxes.

al-Barakaat[31]

This case started when a Minneapolis bank filed a SAR report in 1996. Subsequently, hundreds of SAR reports were filed concerning the al-Barakaat network of money transmitters. al-Barakaat was founded by Ahmed Nur Ali Jumale in 1985. By 9/11/01 al-Barakaat had more than 180 offices in 40 countries existing primarily to transfer money to Somalia in East Africa. It was headquartered in Dubai, United Arab Emirates (UAE).

As a result of a civil war in Somalia in the early 1990s, a large number of immigrants came to the United States and settled in Minneapolis. They used al-Barakaat to transfer money to Somalia. Intelligence sources indicated that the terrorist group Al-Itihaad Al-Islamiya (AIAI) had a cell in Minneapolis, and that it supported radical Islamic activities against the United States. There were links between AIAI, Ahmed Nur Ali Jumale, the founder of al-Barakaat, and Osama Bin Ladin. It was alleged that Bin Ladin was a silent partner in al-Barakaat. Other reports linked al-Barakaat to the Muslim Brotherhood and Hamas.

In early 2001, the Somali community in Minneapolis was transferring more than $1 million though al-Barakaat. Most of those in that community had low level skills and wages. The SAR reports indicated that the large amount of funds being transferred by al-Barakaat to a single account in the UAE was not consistent with normal banking activity.

On November 7, 2001, federal agents raided and closed al-Barakaat offices in Minneapolis, Columbus, Ohio, Alexandria, Virginia, Seattle, Washington, and Boston Massachusetts. The Treasury estimated that the raids disrupted about $65 million in annual remittances from the U.S.

The al-Barakaat case highlights some of the problems between intelligence and law enforcement units. Although there was intelligence information linking al-Barakaat to terrorist organizations, the Federal Bureau of Investigation (FBI) could not substantiate the links. The only criminal charge filed in Minneapolis in connection with this case involved one customer who committed welfare fraud. Nevertheless, the banks did what they were supposed to do – report suspicious activity.

---

[30] FinCEN, "The SAR Activity Review: Trends, Tips & Issues, Issue 8, April 2005, p. 11.

[31] National Commission on Terrorist Attacks Upon the United States, Monograph on Terrorist Financing, Staff Report by John Roth, Douglas Greenburg, and Serena Wille, 2004, Chapter 5, Ahmed Nur Ali Jumale is the

Identity Theft

Identity theft means that someone is using your personal information (e.g., name, Social Security number, credit history, etc.) without your permission to commit frauds and other crimes. The crimes include, but are not limited to insurance and real estate frauds that will be discussed next.

A 2003 survey by the Federal Trade Commission estimated that about 4.6% of the U.S. population over 18 years of age - about 9 million people - has been victims of identity theft.[32] The total losses to businesses and individuals amounted to about $53 billion.

In 2004, the FBI announced that Philip J. Cummings, former Telecommunications Data, Inc., technical support representative, pled guilty in U.S. District Court, Southern District of New York, to various counts of fraud, including identity theft. He participated "in a massive scheme to steal the identities of individuals which defrauded financial institutions of more than $11 million. It was alleged that Cummings stole the passwords and access codes of Ford Motor Credit and other financial companies, to access Equifax, Trans Union, and Experian credit report records and downloaded credit report information on 30,000 individuals. These credit reports were allegedly sold to a group of co-conspirators. To date, this is the largest identity theft case."[33]

Insurance Sector

Although the insurance sector was not included in the listing to financial institutions that were subject to the BSA/AML laws in 2005, the International Association of Insurance Supervisors (IAIS) provided a "Guidance Paper on Anti-Money Laundering and Combating the Financing of Terrorism" (CFT).[34] The *insurance sector* includes insurers, reinsurance companies, their agents, brokers, and mediators who operate on their behalf. The Guidance explains that the vulnerability to such acts depends on the complexity and terms of the contract, how payments are made (cash or bank transfer), and contract law. Single premium life insurance polices that store cash value, and fixed and variable annuities are examples of such insurance policies. When a life insurance policy matures, or is surrendered before maturity, the premiums and funds become available to the policy holder or other beneficiaries. In the case of "Bearer policies," the contract requires that the insurer pay the funds to the person(s) holding the document. The policy is a financial instrument that can be exchanged from person to person, without the endorsees being identified. It is only when the benefits are claimed that the bearer must be identified by the insurer.

spelling used in the National Commission Report. Shaykh Ahmed Nur Jimale is the name that appears in the U.S. Department of Treasury, "Statement of John B. Taylor," Press Release, PO-771, November 7, 2001.

32 For additional information, see: Federal Trade Commission web based resource about identity theft. http://www.consumer.gov/idtheft/#; FDIC, Financial Institutions Letters: "Identity Theft Study on "Account-Hijacking" Identity Theft and Suggestions for Reducing Online Fraud," FIL-132-2004. Population data are from the U.S. Census Bureau, American FactFinder, "United States 2004 American Community Survey, Data Profile Highlights," http://factfinder.census.gov

33 U.S. Department of Justice, Federal Bureau of Investigation, Press Release, "FBI Announces Operation Continued Action Targeting Financial Institution Fraud," September 17, 2004.

In the case of property and casualty insurance, there can be inflated or bogus claims. For example, a building is burned down in order to collect part of the illegitimate funds that were invested in it. Alternatively, if the building was under-insured, the criminal can claim that he/she received full compensation for the building when that was not the case. Another example is the overpayment of insurance premiums, and requesting a refund for the excess amount.

Box 5-3
Cashing /out Drug Proceeds from Life Insurance Policies

In 2002, a Federal Grand Jury indictment found that Colombian drug cartels bought life insurance policies in Europe, the United Kingdom, and the Isle of Man, to launder the proceeds of narcotics sold in the U.S. and Mexico. They bought 250 life insurance policies in the Isle of Man alone. The policies were worth as much as $1.9 million each. The policies were taken out in the names of people associated with the cartels and their families. Some of the policies were cashed out prematurely, and there was a 25 percent penalty that they viewed as a cost of doing business to launder drug proceeds.

Source: The case of U.S. v. Rodrigo Jose Murillo, Alexander Murillo, Jaime Eduardo Ry Albornoz, Arturo Delgado, Esperanza Romero, Mag. Docket No. 02 CR 21007 (S.D. FL 2002) is discussed in 31 CFR Part 103, RIN 1506-AA36, Financial Crimes Enforcement Network: Amendment to the Bank Secrecy Act Regulations – Requirement that Insurance Companies Report Suspicious Activity. FinCEN Final Rule.

The Guidance states that if an insurer suspects that funds it receives are the proceeds of criminal activities or associated with terrorist financing, it should be reported to the appropriate authorities (e.g. FinCEN). The Guidance lists the following examples of suspicious transactions.[35]

- "any unusual financial activity of the customer in the context of his own usual activities
- any unusual transaction in the course of some usual financial activity
- any unusually linked transactions
- any unusual or disadvantageous early redemption of an insurance policy
- any unusual employment of an intermediary in the course of some usual transaction or financial activity e.g. payment of claims or high commission to an unusual intermediary
- any unusual method of payment
- any involvement of any person subject to international sanction."

---

[34] International Association of Insurance Supervisors, "Guidance Paper on Anti-Money Laundering and Combating the Financing of Terrorism," Guidance Paper No. 5, October 2004.

[35] Ibid., p. 16. Additional suspicious activities and examples of money laundering can be found on the IAIS website, www.iaisweb.org

In October 2005, rules were announced that included insurance companies offering selected products to the list of financial institutions covered by the Bank Secrecy Act anti-money laundering programs and regulations.[36] The selected products include permanent life insurance policies and annuity contracts (other than group life insurance and annuities), property and casualty insurance, and health insurance, and any other insurance products with cash values or investment features.

REAL ESTATE SECTOR

Stealing Empty Homes and Mortgage Fraud

The FDIC *Consumer News* (Fall 2005) published a warning that criminals are filing fake quit claim deeds on vacant homes in order to gain control of the property and sell it.[37] Simply stated, quit claim deeds are used to remove someone from or add someone to the titles of residential real estate or other property. The crooks target nice homes that are vacant, and they file a fraudulent deed on that property at the local courthouse. After the court records show that the property has been transferred, the crooks try to sell the house and then disappear with the proceeds.

Another type of mortgage fraud involves *property flipping* - buying real estate and then selling the property quickly at artificially high prices based on false appraisals and documentation. The schemes may involve sham sales, inflating the buyer's income, kickbacks to straw buyers, investors, appraisers, and others. After three or four sham sales, the lenders may foreclose and the overvalued properties. The losses may be covered by the Federal Housing Administration (FHA), other loan insurers, or lenders.[38] *Straw buyers* are individuals who buy real estate for others by allowing them to use their names and credit history to borrow funds. The straw buyers are paid a fee for their services. Note that buying and quickly selling a house at a profit is not illegal. However, it is illegal if the sale involves artificially inflated values abetted by the appraisers. The straw buyers may be liable for any losses.

David Jackson, a reporter for the *Chicago Tribune*, wrote a series of five articles dealing with mortgage fraud in connection with Chicago's poorest residential areas.[39] Thus, real estate fraud spans both upper-income and lower-income housing. According to Jackson, low interest rates, the ease of obtaining mortgages, and the serge in identity theft contributed to

---

[36] 31 CFR Part 103, RIN 1506-AA36, Financial Crimes Enforcement Network: Amendment to the Bank Secrecy Act Regulations – Requirement that Insurance Companies Report Suspicious Activity. FinCEN Final Rule; 31 CFR Part 103, RIN 1506-AA70, Financial Crimes Enforcement Network: Amendment to the Bank Secrecy Act Regulations-Anti-Money Laundering Programs for Insurance Companies, Final Rule; FinCEN News, "Insurance Companies Required to Establish Anti-Money Laundering Programs and File Suspicious Activity Reports," October 31, 2005.

[37] FDIC, *Consumer News*, "A Special Guide for Seniors and Families: Fake Documents Used to Steal Homes," Fall 2005. Note that the FDIC did not specify the type of deeds. It should be noted that quit claim deeds do not have warranty of title.

[38] U.S. Department of Justice, Federal Bureau of Investigation, "Financial Crimes Report to the Public," May 2005.

[39] Jackson, David, "Mortgage Fraud is The Thing to Do Now," *Chicago Tribune*, November 5, 2005; Jackson David, "Scams Build Gang Empire, " *Chicago Tribune,* November 7, 2005; Jackson, David, " Even Big Boys Get Scammed," November 8, 2005; Jackson, David, "How Fraud Became the Nightmare on May St.," *Chicago Tribune*, November 9, 2005; Jackson, David, "With Mortgage Fraud, It's Catch 'em if You Can," *Chicago Tribune*, November 10, 2005.

the growth of mortgage frauds. Mortgage swindlers buy old dilapidated buildings in auctions at low cost or inflated costs, or use other techniques to gain control of a property. The other techniques include filing false quit claim deeds to transfer property. Then they apply for large mortgage loans, and disappear with the funds. A Chicago police officer describing one building said "The building is a pigsty, all busted up. You think it's only worth 30 grand, but you find that it just sold for $200,000."[40]

The swindlers include mortgage loan professionals, lending company executives, appraisers, attorneys, and scouts who look for potential victims.

Box 5-4
Appraiser and Straw Buyer Convicted

"Marcos Daniel Jiménez, United States Attorney for the Southern District of Florida, and Michael S. Clemens, Special Agent in Charge, Federal Bureau of Investigation, announced today that defendants, Juan Carlos Suarez and Rodney Way were convicted of several charges relating to "land flip" transactions that victimized federally insured banks and private lenders. Specifically, they were convicted of one (1) count of conspiracy to commit bank and mail fraud, and three (3) substantive counts of bank fraud. Additionally, Way was convicted of four (4) counts and Suarez was convicted of three (3) counts of mail fraud. Both defendants face a maximum penalty of five (5) years' imprisonment on the conspiracy count, thirty (30) years' imprisonment on each of the bank and mail fraud counts, a $2,000,000 fine, and restitution to lenders who were defrauded in the fraudulent scheme.

The evidence at trial showed that between June 30, 1998 and August 27, 1999, Suarez and Way, along with Doyle Aaron and Stuart Blum, participated in twenty-six (26) illegal land flip transactions. Doyle Aaron, who on the eve of trial pled guilty to conspiracy to commit bank and mail fraud and conspiracy to commit money laundering, held himself out as a real estate investor and targeted properties in Broward County. Aaron falsified employment and asset information in order to qualify for loans. Stuart Blum, the owner of Old Florida Mortgage and a mortgage broker, prepared and submitted fraudulent loan applications to various lenders on behalf of Doyle Aaron. Blum also pled guilty to one (1) count of conspiracy to commit bank and mail fraud in November 2004. Suarez performed the appraisals on most of the properties being purchased by Aaron. Suarez misrepresented that straw buyers were owners of properties and inflated values of properties. Way, Aaron's cousin, acted as one of the straw buyers in whose name property was transferred, then subsequently resold to Aaron. All loans went into foreclosure, causing several million dollars in losses."

Source: U.S. Department of Justice, Press Release, Marcos Daniel Jiménez, United States Attorney for the Southern District of Florida, "Appraiser and Straw Buyer Convicted," June 7, 2005.

In eighty one mortgage fraud cases in one year, $9.6 million in funds were borrowed from the Chicago central branch office of CitiFinancial, the mortgage and personal loan

[40] Ibid., Jackson, November 10, 2005.

division of Citigroup. CitiFinancial's internal investigation revealed how the swindlers took advantage of the firm's "sloppiness and misconduct."[41] Part of the lack of due diligence may have been associated with CitiFinancial's "grow at any cost" policy. However, a Citigroup official said that the actions in Chicago were "unacceptable and contrary to CitiFinancial policies."

Jackson also reported that the U.S. Department of Housing and Urban Development (HUD) sold swindlers dozens of homes at discount prices, and paid others hundreds of thousands of dollars in Section 8 rent subsidies to serve as landlords for poor people. In addition, the "Black Disciples," one of Chicago's drug dealing gangs, used mortgage frauds to gain control over certain street corners, obtain safe houses, and to launder money.

The following is an example of mortgage fraud.[42] David Evans, the branch manager of Greater Investment Mortgage Company, had his co-workers arrange for a $94,000 mortgage loan for David Shank, a mentally disabled man. Shank's mother had died leaving the family home free and clear of debt. The co-workers filed a false quit claim deed purportedly transferring the property to David Shank. The phony mortgage application said that Shank was the manager of a beauty salon. In fact, he never worked there. At the signing of the mortgage, an employee of Law Title Insurance Company, who was working with Evans, notarized the forged signature of David's deceased father. Although David Shank had no debts outstanding, the fraudulent mortgage application claimed that he owed $40,000 to firms associated with Evans.

Out of the $94,000 mortgage loan, $6,000 went to closing costs, $23,000 went to Shank, and $65,000 went to Evans and his associate "for services rendered." Shank lost his home because the mortgage went unpaid. Evans denied wrongdoing, and he was not charged with any crime in this case.

Mortgage Fraud is Widespread

Mortgage fraud is widespread across the United States. The Mortgage Asset Research Institute index of mortgage fraud ranked Georgia, South Carolina, and Florida as the three top stated during the 2001-2004 period.[43] The report also indicated that 56% of the mortgage frauds in 2004 were in connection with the applications, 33% involved tax and financial statements, and 16% involved verification of deposits. Appraisals and valuations accounted for 10%.

One of the shocking statistics about mortgage fraud is that the FBI reports that about 80 percent of the losses involve collaboration or collusion by industry insiders.[44] The FBI also reported that in 2004, there were 17,127 mortgage related SARs, and total losses of $429 million associated with those reports.

---

[41] Ibid., Jackson, November 8, 2005.

[42] Ibid., Jackson, November 5, 2005; Jackson, David, "Mortgage Fraud: The New Street Hustle," *Chicago Tribune,* Broadband, November 2005. http://www.chicagotribune.com.

[43] Matthews, William H., Merle Sharick, Erin E. Omba, Catherine B. Ontero, and D. James Croft, "Seventh Periodic Mortgage Fraud Case Report to the Mortgage Bankers Association," Mortgage Asset Research Institute, Inc., Reston, VA, May 2005.

[44] Ibid.

Laundered Funds Invested in Real Estate

Real estate transactions have been used as a cover for laundered funds. In Norway, the money launderer rents real estate from a company from an offshore location.[45] The company itself is owned by the money launderer, but his identity is hidden from officials in Norway. That way, the property cannot be confiscated if the money launderer is caught, because the government could not establish a link between the launderer and the owner of the property.

---

[45] Financial Action Task Force on Money Laundering, "1999-2000 Report on Money Laundering Typologies," February 3, 2000, p.13.

Chapter 7

OVERVIEW OF ANALYTICAL METHODS FOR MONEY LAUNDERING

***J. Michael Hardin*[1], *Billie S. Anderson*[2], *Tim Lutz*[3] *and David Stewart*[4]**

[1] Professor, The University of Alabama

[2] Ph.D. Candidate, The University of Alabama

[3] Financial Behavior Expert, SAS

[4] Program Manager, Anti-Money Laundering, SAS

INTRODUCTION

Since the terrorist attack on September 11, 2001 and Congress passing the USA PATRIOT Act, law enforcement, government, and other financial institutions have placed a distinctive emphasis on detecting the laundering of money for illegal purposes. The advances in data mining have made this task much more manageable for law enforcement. Data mining techniques have the ability to reduce law enforcement's time to detect money laundering, accurately and efficiently detect any trends that may be hidden in mounds of data, and prevent money laundering all together. Complex data mining is a requirement at larger, high-risk banks while simpler investigative reviews are more widespread at community and regional banks.

The ever-expanding 'electronic universe' of transactional data is a perfect mask for suspicious or deceptive monetary transactions. It is nearly impossible to detect a suspicious transaction given the relentless flow of data that passes through the financial system on a daily basis. Employing enough time, people, and other resources to money laundering activities can be daunting for law enforcement. Prioritizing particular transactions out of literally millions can also impede the process of detecting money laundering. Particular data mining techniques and data mining software are now available to help meet these challenges.

This chapter provides an overview of data mining and artificial intelligence-based techniques that support law enforcement and financial institutions in the detection and prevention of money laundering activities.

WHY TO WE NEED DATA MINING TECHNIQUES TO COMBAT MONEY LAUNDERING?

The goal of data mining is to identify novel, valid, useful, and understandable patterns in large databases. John Naisbett once stated, "We are drowning in data, but starving for knowledge"[1]. Due to the enormity of data that is now available, how does one explore millions of records, tens of hundreds of fields, and find patterns? Data volumes are simply becoming too large for standard data mining investigative techniques.

Some traditional techniques include drilling down into a large database with queries, online analytical processing (OLAP), and establishing particular rules to identify certain groups. As databases grow the ability to support the decision support process using traditional structured query language (SQL) becomes infeasible. Many queries of interest are difficult to state in SQL e.g. "find all structured deposits." The development of rules that need to be developed for investigators to detect an elaborate money laundering scheme may be extremely difficult to construct. Thresholds for establishing money laundering activities are not easy to set because there are few patterns money launderers employ[2]. Given the difficulties analysts face in detecting money laundering, there are emerging money laundering detection software tools that use standard data mining techniques[3]. Many larger financial institutions, businesses and government agencies have turned to software tools to help make the detection of money laundering more automated and less labor intensive.

Even with the aid of software, many of the conventional data mining techniques require the investigator to ask the correct questions and know exactly what type of suspicious activity needs to be detected. Due to the large datasets an investigator must comb through, many standard data mining techniques are time consuming and employ ineffective ways of detecting patterns. It is imperative in a post-9/11 period that institutions successfully meet the challenges posed by money launderers. Many organizations are turning to newer data mining techniques to detect suspicious behavior. Some of these are discussed below.

DATA MINING AND ARTIFICIAL INTELLIGENCE APPROACHES TO COMBAT MONEY LAUNDERING

One description of data mining is "the collection of automated tools and Artificial Intelligence (AI) techniques that facilitate searching of large data sets to discover 'hidden' or 'buried' relationships among the data, not easily identified by inspection."[4] The term artificial intelligence was developed out of computer science. Russell and Novig[5] were the first to coin the term. Artificial intelligence refers to computer algorithms that can model aspects of

---

[1] Naisbitt, J. (1995). *Global Paradox,* Avon Books.

[2] Moorman, M. (2004). "Detecting Terrorist Financing (brief article)." *American Banker* 169(185): 11.

[3] Mena, J. (2004). *Homeland Security Techniques and Technologies.* Hingham, Massachusetts, Charles River Media.

[4] Watkins, R. C., K. M. Reynolds, et al. (2003). "Tracking Dirty Proceeds: Exploring Data Mining Technologies as Tools to Investigate Money Laundering." *Police Practice and Research* 4(2): 163-178.

[5] Russell, S. and P. Norvig (1995). *Artificial Intelligence: A Modern Approach.* Upper Saddle River, NJ, Prentice-Hall.

human thought and operations. Expert systems are one such subfield of artificial intelligence that is being used to detect money laundering. Hardin[6] defines expert systems as "a computer-based system that can perform problem-solving tasks equal to the performance of human experts and, in some cases, can actually exceed the abilities of human experts." Examples of expert systems are discussed later in the chapter.

The techniques described below are some data mining techniques that could be employed to combat money laundering activities. All of the methods discussed rely heavily on statistical, data mining, and AI processes.

Linear Regression

Linear regression is one of the more simple data mining techniques. The model is designed by defining a response (dependent) variable and a number of predictor (independent) variables. The purpose of the model is to determine a functional relationship (an equation) between the response and the predictor variables that best fits the data. The model is then used for predictive purposes. This technique can be useful for discovering patterns from previously solved money laundering cases. Suppose investigators suspect certain times or places that illegal activities are taking place. Using certain variables (information) can help predict these times or places.

Benning[7] describes an example in which linear regression is used to predict "hot spots" of illegal money laundering activities. The response is the number of suspicious activity reports (SARs) per 100 million of state population. The predictors used are the number of adult drug arrests reported by local police, proximity to the Mexican and Canadian border, number of bank tellers employed in the state, urban population, sin tax, and income. The article explains in more detail the reasoning behind these particular predictor variables. Using a linear regression, a prediction for which states have a higher number of SARs can be obtained. This allows investigators to narrow down which geographical locations have a higher propensity towards more SARs. Law enforcement can concentrate more time and effort on combating money laundering in these particular locations. In this case, linear regression gives law enforcement an information advantage that money launderers would find difficult to counter.

Logistic Regression

Logistic regression is a useful predictive modeling tool and is one of the most widely used data mining technique. This method has been employed in many other contexts[8]. This model is functional because it allows the dependent (response) variable to be categorical (e.g. variables of the form yes/no or male/female). The user can examine and extract particular

[6] Hardin, J. M. (2006). Health Information Management: Concepts, Principles, and Practice, Chapter 19. *Health Information Management*. K. LaTour and S. Eichenwald-Maki. Chicago, Illinois, American Health Information Management Association.

[7] Benning, J. F. (2002). "Following the Dirty Money: Does Bank Reporting of Suspicious Activity Pose a Threat to Drug Dealers?" *Criminal Justice Policy Review* 13(4): 337-355.

[8] Hosmer, D. W. J. and S. Lemeshow (2000). *Applied Logistic Regression*. Hoboken, New Jersey, John Wiley & Sons.

financial information of all cases belonging to a certain class. Logistic regression analysis allows for easy to view graphs and a more manageable way to sort through and detect patterns or trends in large data sets. This eliminates time that an investigator would have traditionally spent searching large data sets in search of the patterns or trends looking for illegal monetary transactions. The result for investigators using this technique advances the way in which large data sets can be efficiently investigated in search of new leads on cases.

Logistic regression is used to model data in which the response variable is binary, i.e. whether the transaction is fraudulent or not. The main objective is to develop a model that relates the response variable to the predictor variables. Logistic regression estimates the probability that a response variable will have a given value e.g. what is the probability a particular transaction is suspicious. From the probabilities an analyst can select a cutoff probability that will be helpful in determining suspicious activity.

Derrig and Frances[9] give an example of using logistic regression to detect insurance fraud. The authors try to estimate fraudulent medical claims (response variable) submitted by doctors. Such variables as age, income, time since last medical exam, and type of insurance policy, etc... are used as possible predictors for false medical claims. Using a logistic model, a likelihood of fraudulency can be obtained for each submitted claim given the predictor variables information.

Cluster Analysis

Cluster analysis is a technique that categorizes data into groups with similar characteristics. The goal is to find closely related groups of objects. Cluster analysis partitions a set of observations into groups based on one or more variables e.g. amount of deposits, frequency of visiting a particular business. This technique has major advantages due to the fact that it can automate the detection of crime activity as well as detect crime activity that is only revealed in clusters. Figure 7-1 is an example graph showing several clusters in terms of two variables.

This technique might be used to identify certain suspects who carry out illegal activities in similar ways or to differentiate between suspects that belong to different crime organization networks. In financial data, clusters might reveal similar account types, individuals, or businesses. For example, similar bank deposits of a particular type of business might cluster together in comparison to other businesses. These clusters might signal to investigators that certain transactions are atypical and need closer examination to determine if the business is a “shell” within to hide a money laundering scheme[10].

Coplink is a clustering algorithm that associates different items such as persons, vehicles, and gangs in crime records[11]. For example, suppose a robbery at a convenience store occurs and the single witness only remembers that the suspect drove away in a white pickup truck. The detective needs to generate a lead from this small amount of information only using the type of crime and vehicle description. Coplink’s graphical user interface allows the detective

---

[9] Derrig, R. and L. Francis (2006). *Comparison of Methods and Software for Modeling Nonlinear Dependencies: A Fraud Application.* International Congress of Acturies, Paris, France.

[10] U.S. Congress, O. o. T. A. (1995). Information Technology for Control of Money Laundering. Washington, D.C.

[11] Hauck, R., H. Atabakhsh, et al. (2002). "Using Coplink to Analyze Criminal-Justice Data." *Computer:* 30-37.

to search on four fields: Person, Organization, Location, and Vehicle. Using the Coplink software, the detective can easily narrow the results to eight individuals related to a white pickup truck and the particular type of crime.

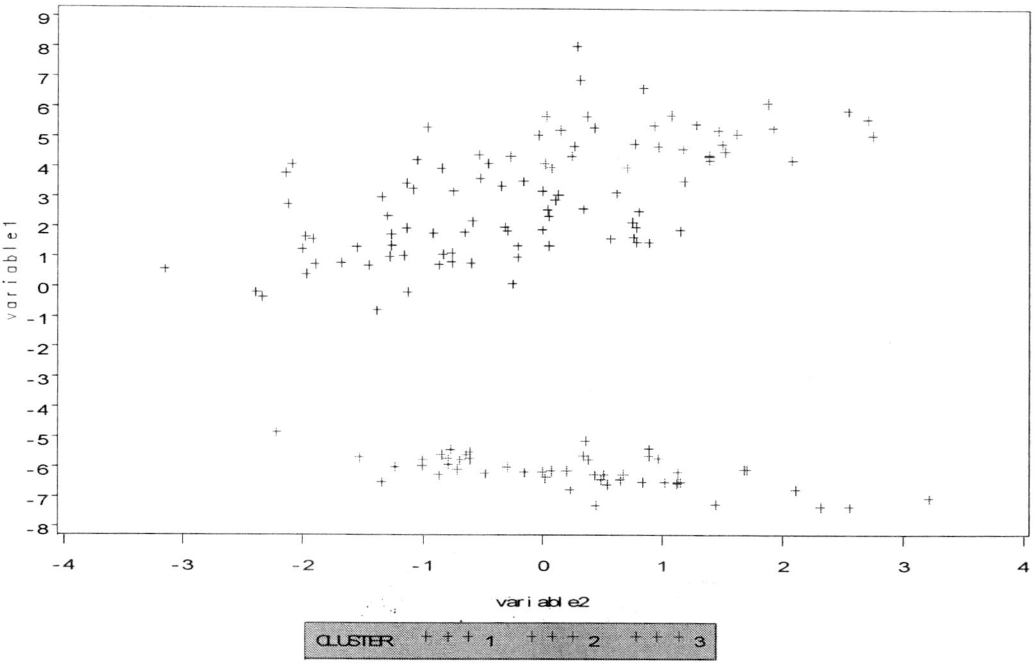

Source: Office of Technology Assessment, 1995

Figure 7.1. Example of Clustering

Inductive Algorithms

Inductive algorithms are another data mining technique to help uncover illegal money laundering activities. Inductive algorithms are sometimes referred to as link analysis. Link analysis is a technique used to investigate associations among objects of different types. In the case of money laundering, these objects might include people, businesses, bank accounts, and cash deposits. Link analysis can point to particular individuals involved in money laundering. For example, if an individual is connected to other individuals or businesses participating in money laundering activities, then link analysis can help confirm those suspicions.

Link analysis works by creating certain classifications of the financial data that occur frequently and presents the patterns as rules. The algorithm derives these rules from the transactional data. For example, the data records may contain information such as name, address, phone number, bank, bank account number, number of wire transfers in a day, business, business owner, board members, etc... The analysis involves searching these records for matching fields. Matches could indicate that two individuals wire money into the same account or are involved in the same business. These matching fields are developed into rules. An example of a rule developed from link analysis is shown in Figure 7-2. These rules are presented in the form of a decision tree which can easily be used to follow a path of possible money laundering. These paths can be used by the investigators to better understand the path of illegal activity. The paths that are created in the decision tree can be used to update old rules, create new rules, and allow investigators to explore more focused structures in money laundering activities. See Figure 7-3 for a graphical description of the results of performing link analysis.

IF	destination bank is foreign; and
	deposit amount > $10,000; and
	originator is not a business
THEN	transaction is suspicious

Figure 7.2. An Example Rule.

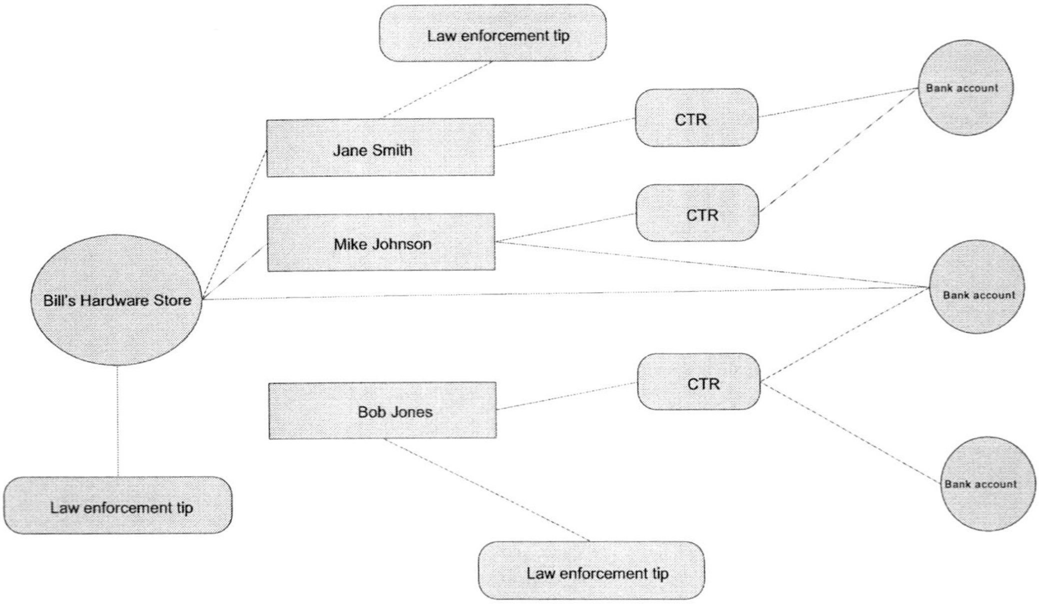

Figure 7.3. Example of Link Analysis Results; Key: CRT=cash transaction.

The Financial Crimes Enforcement Network (FinCEN) has developed one of the most sophisticated inductive algorithms, named Financial Crimes Enforcement Network AI System (FAIS)[12]. FAIS is a rule-based algorithm that pulls in relevant information from the universe of CTRs (currency transaction reports). The algorithm then connects disparate pieces of information, such as banking transactions and accounts, and this linking process reveals patterns of financial transactions are known to launder money or to perpetrate other crimes. Thus, potential suspects can be identified during the AI analysis that might have gone undetected.

12 Senator, T. E., H. G. Goldberg, et al. (1995). The Financial Crimes Enforcement Network AI System (FAIS): Identifying potential money laundering from reports of large cash transactions. *AI Magazine*. 16: 21-39.

Neural Networks

Neural networks are beginning to show potential in the detection of money laundering.[13, 14] Neural networks are a form of artificial intelligence that can be trained to recognize patterns in data. This model can accept several inputs, and then execute several mathematical operations on the inputs and generates output. A neural network operates by imitating the learning mechanisms of a human brain[15,16]. This technique resembles the learning process of the human brain because the network learns from examples of input and output and they have the ability to store knowledge through interconnection weights[17]. Neural networks use historical financial transactional data to discriminate between normal transactions from patterns of suspicious deposits and withdrawals. The interconnection weights are attached to each transaction with a higher weight signaling a risky or fraudulent transaction is occurring. The network has the ability to learn the patterns of money laundering shown to the network during training. The networks are trained through experience. This training takes place when the network is fed the past historical data. This technology can also adapt very well to changes in financial behavior. The main advantage of a neural network is they can handle both categorical and continuous variables as well as handle data that is not linear. Another advantage of neural networks is their ability to detect account behavior that deviates from typical account activity. This enables the networks to spot patterns never seen before.

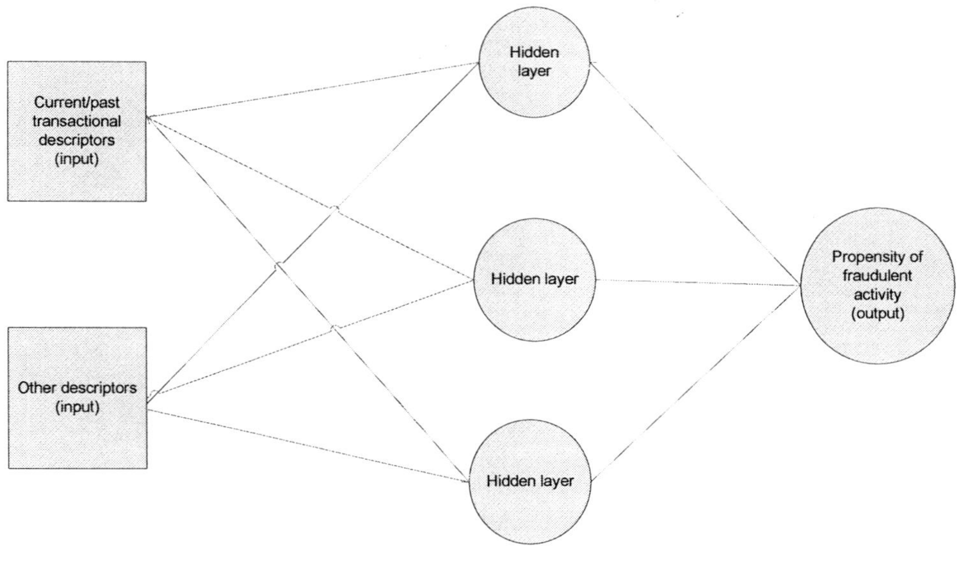

Figure 7.4. Neural Network Process Diagram.

---

13 Watkins, R. C., K. M. Reynolds, et al. (2003). "Tracking Dirty Proceeds: Exploring Data Mining Technologies as Tools to Investigate Money Laundering." *Police Practice and Research* 4(2): 163-178.

14 Vikram, A., S. Chennure, et al. (2004). *A Solution Architecture for Financial Institutions to Handle Illegal Activities: A Neural Networks Approach.* Proceedings of the 37th Hawaii International Conference on System Sciences.

15 Beale, R. and T. Jackson (1990). *Neural Computing: An Introduction,* Taylor & Francis.

16 Warner, B. and M. Misra (1996). "Understanding Neural Networks as Statistical Tools." *American Statistician* 50(4): 284-293.

17 Ripley, B. D. (1996). *Pattern Recognition and Neural Networks.* New York, Cambridge University Press.

In using a neural network to detect fraud, an investigator must first input data that is specific to the objective. For example, historical transaction descriptors, current transaction descriptors, and other descriptors the investigator deems necessary and a variable indicating whether the account is fraudulent or not. The input data is first fed into hidden layers of the neural network. Within each one of these hidden layers, the interconnection weights are estimated from the data. The output consists of the propensity of each case being fraudulent or not. If an account has a high likelihood of being fraudulent, then that particular case needs to be investigated further. A diagram of the neural network process is given in Figure 7- 4.

Fuzzy Logic

Fuzzy logic is a technique for dealing with decision making processes which involve inexact, imprecise, or ambiguous data[18]. For example, if the heights of all students in a class had to be classified as short, tall, or very tall then there are no exact measurements that define the heights into each one of these categories. Fuzzy logic deals with the grayness of particular items or objects[19]. Fuzzy logic is an algorithm that uses "if-then" rules to make decisions.

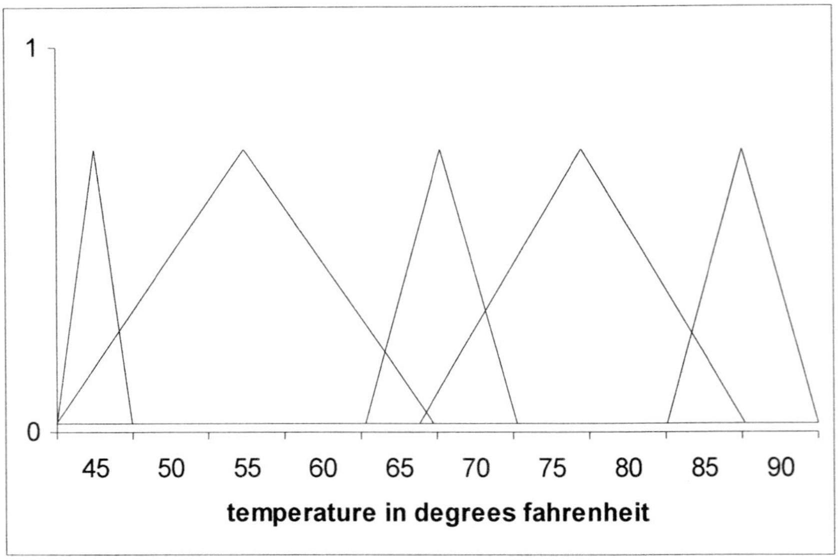

Figure 7.5. Fuzzy categories for temperature

A simple example of using a fuzzy logic method is given by an analogy using room temperature and air conditioner speed[20]. Let X be the temperature in degrees Fahrenheit. Let Y be the change in the motor speed of an air conditioner. The motor needs to speed up when the room is hot and slow down when the room is cold. First, the categories need to be

[18] Sabhnani, M. R., P. R. Rao, et al. (2001). *AI Software in Everday Life: A Survey.* Midwest AI and Cognitive Science Conference, Miami, Ohio.

[19] Kosko, B. (1993). *Fuzzy Thinking: The New Science of Fuzzy Logic.* New York, Hyperion.

[20] Kosko, B. (1993). *Fuzzy Thinking: The New Science of Fuzzy Logic.* New York, Hyperion.

specified. For temperature there are five categories, COLD, COOL, JUST RIGHT, WARM, and HOT. Motor speed has five categories, STOP, SLOW, MEDIUM, FAST, and BLAST. Figures 7- 5 and 7- 6 show the categories. The temperature degrees go from 45° to 90° and the motor speed goes from 0 to 100 r.p.m. (revolutions per minute, motor speed).

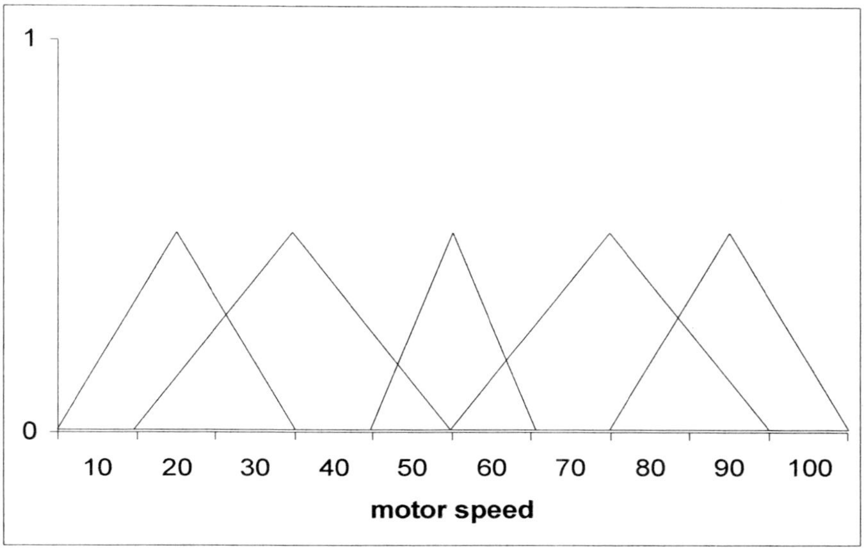

Figure 7. 6. Fuzzy categories for motor speed.

The fuzzy rules are now developed in order to associate the temperature with the motor speeds. The rules are fuzzy because “cold” and “fast” are grey categories. The air conditioner speed should adjust to keep the room temperature just right. So our first rule is: if X is COLD, then Y is STOP. Five rules can be developed using the information given:

Rule 1: If the temperature is cold, the motor speed stops.
Rule 2: If the temperature is cool, the motor speed slows
Rule 3: If the temperature is just right, the motor speed is medium
Rule 4: If the temperature is warm, the motor speed is fast
Rule 5: If the temperature is hot, the motor speed blasts

Fuzzy logic can easily be employed in money laundering cases due to the uncertainty of particular measurements. For example, it may be difficult to determine what is meant by ‘frequent’ deposits or withdrawals. This is obviously an example of an inexact measurement that is vital to the money laundering investigation process. Fuzzy logic allows investigators to take vague data and process it and produce a product that is meaningful.

Genetic Algorithms

Genetic algorithms are problem-solving algorithms used for optimization purposes[21]. The algorithms are based on the biological evolutionary idea of natural selection and evolution[22]. As populations go through many generations, poor performing individuals are eliminated and allows for better performing individuals to replicate themselves during each generation. This is analogous to individuals having many financial transactions over their lifetime.

Genetic algorithms use natural selection or "survival of the fittest" by continuously changing a set of possible solutions in order to find the optimal solution to a problem. By removing weak or "low scoring" components, the algorithm converges toward an optimal solution. The genetic algorithm is designed so that each individual represents a behavioral model. Using a genetic algorithm, the behavior of an individual's account can be monitored to detect fraud.

When it comes to choosing one of the above techniques to detect money laundering activities, the decision must be based on the needs of the investigators, resource constraints, and a commitment on the part of management in reducing the institution's exposure to money laundering risk.

SOFTWARE TOOLS

Two software company innovators in developing AML (anti-money laundering) software are Searchspace and SAS®. We discuss both companies' approaches to AML software below.

SEARCHSPACE

Searchspace, a leading supplier of AML and fraud solutions uses expert systems approach that learns about financial crimes over time[23]. Searchspace's clients include Wells Fargo, UBS, Bank of New York, and the London Stock Exchange.

Through an innovative use of neural networks, fuzzy logic, and genetic algorithms, Searchspace was able to detect insider trading for the London Stock Exchange[24].

In the past, AML software companies focused on algorithms that trained and learned how to detect criminal activity. The problem is that over time, new money laundering schemes are being developed[25]. The new age of AML software monitors transactions at the individual level. For example, the software can employ data mining techniques to determine how much cash is withdrawn from ATM's on a daily basis. In the past, fraud was alerted by examining past transactional data. But the new age of AML software is able to alert fraudulent activity

---

21 Davis, L. (1991). *Handbook of Genetic Algorithms*. New York, Van Nostrand Reinhold.

22 Wicks, T. (2001). "Intelligent Systems for Money Laundering Prevention." *Money Laundering Bulletin*.

23 Mena, J. (2004). *Homeland Security Techniques and Technologies*. Hingham, Massachusetts, Charles River Media.

24 Bolton, R. J. and D. J. Hand (2002). "Statistical Fraud Detection: A Review." *Statistical Science* 17(3): 235-255.

25 Mena, J. (2004). *Homeland Security Techniques and Technologies*. Hingham, Massachusetts, Charles River Media.

when deviations from the norm occur. This involves comparing transactions among peer groups (known as peer grouping). For example, if there are several Chinese restaurants in a downtown location within the same vicinity and one is depositing much more money than its peers, a review of their activity may be in order.

Searchspace's answer to tracking transactions at the individual level is the Intelligent Enterprise Framework®[26]. The IEF® can be viewed as a four stage process: *Monitor, Learn, Decide, and Act.* The IEF® consists of the components shown in Figure 7-7. Each one of these components is discussed below.

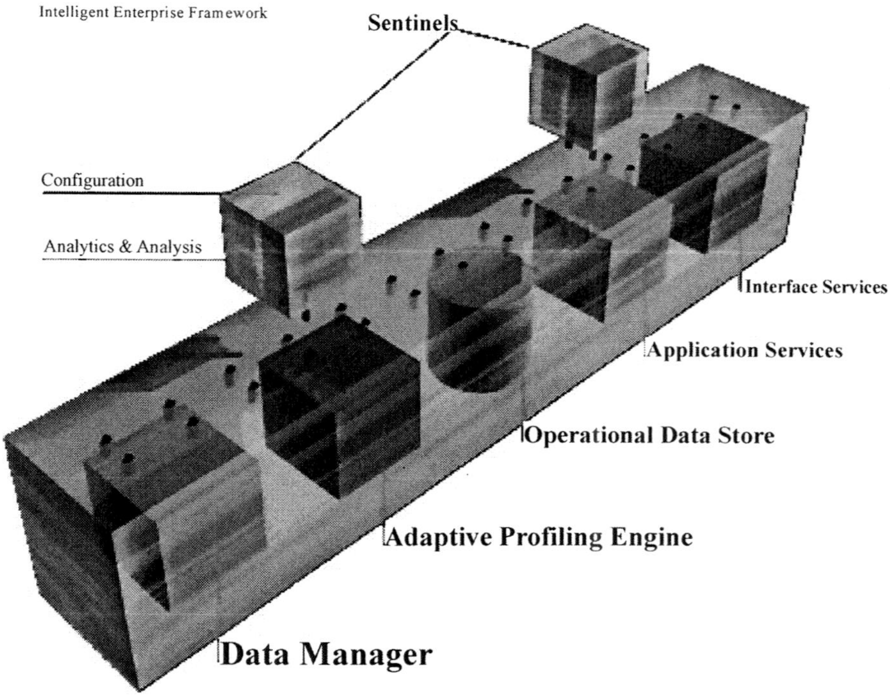

Source: www.searchspace.com; Fortent,. Used with permission.

Figure 7.7. Architecture of the IEF®.

Monitor (Data Manager)

IEF® gathers transactional data from operational systems in real-time. The data is then validated and cleaned at this stage.

Learn (Adaptive Profiling Engine and Operational Data Store)

Once the transactional data is cleansed, each entity can be accurately profiled. For each individual, information relating to their transactions can be compactly stored so that a behavioral history can be made and updated. Individuals and their financial relationships can be extremely complex. One transaction can interact and affect multiple profiles. The *Adaptive Profiling Engine* allows for continual updating of individuals profiles and behavior status.

The *Operational Data Store* has two components within it; the *Adaptive Profile Store* and the *Operational Transaction Cache*. The *Adaptive Profile Store* houses the models generated by the *Adaptive Profiling Engine* and provides the information the Sentinels need to detect fraud or money laundering. The *Operational Transaction Cache* is a temporary database that allows easy access to transactional data.

Decide (Sentinels)

The Sentinels are where the decisions are made whether or not to consider transactional activities suspicious or not. Sentinels are similar to electronic experts. It is within the sentinels that money laundering, fraud, and patterns of unusual activity can be detected. Unusual events are based on an individual's activity. This activity is then compared against account history and peer behavior. Once the suspicious activity is identified, an automated review of all account activity is conducted. Any support of unusual activity is scored and validated within the *Analytics and Analysis* component of the Sentinels. This allows law enforcement not to waste time on unwarranted leads.

Act (Application and Interface Services)

It is within these components of the IEF® that efficient and secure decision-making can be performed. The *Applications and Interface Services* allow efficient and timely information to be delivered so that action can be taken swiftly and priorities can be established. The completeness of a solution can be demonstrated through standardized audit and regulatory reports. This component also has a navigation profile that allows the user to dig deeper into a selected individuals account profile.

SAS®

Another leader in AML software is the statistical computing software company SAS®. SAS® is one of the leading companies making AML software available to smaller and mid-sized banks and financial institutions. The AML software SAS® offers can be broken into the following components: *Data Management, Alert Generation and Management, Reporting, and Administration*[27]. Each of these is described below.

---

[26] Searchspace (2006). Intelligent Enterprise Framework: Enterprise Analytics for Right-Time Decisions.

[27] Stewart, D., T. Lutz, et al. (2005). "SAS Money Laundering Detection: A dynamic, risk-based solution for identifying, investigating and reporting suspicious patterns of behavior." *SAS white paper*.

Data Management

SAS® has a complete software suite available for cleaning large amounts of data. Many types of data from many different platforms can be easily combined into a form that is ready to have data mining procedures applied to it, with the goal of detecting suspicious activities. There is also a high-quality repository which ensures the quality and integrity of reports and any decisions that stem from those reports.

Alert Generation and Management

The AML software solution SAS® offers goes beyond peer grouping or basing money laundering activity on simple "if-then" rules. There are built-in scenarios to help identify suspicious activity. The investigator can change standard templates or create new scenarios based on their own knowledge of particular information. The SAS® approach to AML software allows weights to be assigned to certain risk factors such as the tendency to deposits funds via cash or other high risk transaction types, the customer belonging to a high risk group, etc. Then potentially suspicious activity can be ranked based on the risks presented by the customer. This will allow investigators to reduce the number of false leads and immediately know why one individual represents a higher risk than another. Suspicious activity can be tracked by an individual account, customer household, or individual transaction level.

Reporting

Investigators can use the reporting tool to produce ad hoc reports to view transaction information and generate reports. Every component of the ad hoc analysis can be observed, confirmed, and audited. This component also allows the querying of data in order to drill down into large databases and dissect the data on many dimensions. One helpful feature of the Reporting tool is that it can generate correctly formatted reports for electronic submission of SAR's to the appropriate regulatory agencies. Many institutions find the transparency of the Reporting tool useful; there are no behind the scenes activities, every action is recorded in a log.

Administration

The SAS® AML software allows the regulation of which users can use the software and what privileges are admitted based on a user profile. The user can modify the software by changing certain system parameters such as scenarios and risk factors. This ensures that the software is reflecting the most current knowledge of customers and real world conditions. There are built in audit checks that follow all administrative activity and which individuals made any modifications to any records.

Risk Factors

The SAS® AML software was the first package to incorporate the use of *risk factors*. Risk factors are potential indicators of risk that are red flags of suspicious activity, but are too common to review every instance. An example of a risk factor would be use of multiple branches in a single day. Alone, this behavior is not significant enough to prompt a review, but when a review is taking place, risk factors save the investigator's time and prevent errors by identifying all high risk behaviors and characteristics of a customer.

BEYOND PEER GROUPING

All of the data mining techniques discussed and the objectives of the AML software mentioned above have presupposed one thing: that financial institutions can differentiate between suspicious and legitimate behavior, or that a set of target data exists Necessarily, this also assumes that a set of non-target data exists. Clearly, this is not the case as billions of dollars are laundered annually while only a fraction of this activity is ever detected. Most normal data mining techniques do assume that there is a reliable and complete target. This makes the classical data mining techniques of questionable validity for the detection of money laundering.

Most recently, some researchers in the development of AML software at SAS® have moved beyond these classical data mining techniques and have begun to propose AML techniques that do not require an institution to exhaustively distinguish between target and non-target activity in order to maintain their efficacy. This prevents highly skilled money launderers from training the system that their hare-to-detect money laundering techniques are normal behavior and should be ignored.

One popular monitoring technique that has been consuming the resources of financial institutions is peer grouping. Because it is extremely difficult to predict the financial life span of an individual, profiling becomes difficult. The lifespan of an individual takes on many different phases; from college student, professional life, and retirement. Within each one of these stages, different types of income and life changes come and go. For example, job promotions, selling and buying of real estate, inheritances, etc. Given these unpredictable life changes and the number of customers at an institution, it can be resource-intensive to re-classify individuals into the proper peer groups and use those peer groups as a means to compare certain financial activity in an attempt to detect money laundering (as is what is done in standard practice). This inability to forever re-classify individuals in meaningful peer groups will invariably generate false positive alerts. This makes the practice of reviewing all transactions outside of a customer's profile very costly at larger financial institutions. An emerging issue is how to use these detected deviations in a way that is effective and efficient. Using the risk factor approach in SAS® may resolve this difficulty.

CONCLUDING REMARKS

Data mining and artificial intelligence are vitally important to combating money laundering in a global economy that is electronically linked. The data mining techniques discussed above allows law enforcement and financial institutions to save time; increase leads, and make it easier to comply with the regulatory requirements. The technology also gives insight into money laundering activities from volumes of data that otherwise would be a daunting task for even a team of seasoned investigators.

One major challenge in detecting money laundering is limited amount of time and resources to devote to money laundering activities. In this country, there are only 10 small groups within the FBI that are specifically designated to working on money laundering activity[28]. This difficulty is compounded by the time required to investigate money laundering cases even after they have been identified. It can take years to develop and follow through with leads on a money laundering case.

Another obstacle is manually searching through large data sets in order to find patterns and obtain leads on cases. Data mining technologies can help investigators that may lack training as data analysts to search through large data sets quickly and efficiently.

---

[28] Watkins, R. C., K. M. Reynolds, et al. (2003). "Tracking Dirty Proceeds: Exploring Data Mining Technologies as Tools to Investigate Money Laundering." *Police Practice and Research* 4(2): 163-178.

Chapter 8

MANAGEMENT AND BOARD CHALLENGES COMPLYING WITH BANK SECRECY ACT AND ANTI MONEY LAUNDERING REGULATIONS

***Raj Aggarwal*[1] *and Kamala Raghavan*[2]**

[1] Professor, Kent State University

[2] Assistant Professor, Robert Morris University

INTRODUCTION

In an effort to prevent and deter financing of terrorist activity, bank secrecy laws were revised and new anti-money laundering provisions were enacted following the events of September 11, 2001. This paper explores how the compliance with Bank Secrecy Act (BSA) and anti money laundering (AML) requirements are changing the emphasis of corporate governance and finance functions in financial institutions. The Board of Directors of banking institutions often find themselves unsure about dealing with overlapping and sometimes conflicting requirements imposed by FDICIA of 1991, Bank Secrecy Act (BSA) /Patriot Act/ Anti Money Laundering (AML) of 2001, Sarbanes-Oxley Act of 2002 (SOX), and the Interagency guidance on banking services to MSB of 2005. FDICIA centered on internal controls related to banking operations, SOX concentrated primarily on sound internal controls related to financial reporting based on transactions, and BSA/AML specified due diligence procedures for monitoring foreign correspondent and private banking customer accounts. The Inter-agency Operational risk Supervisory Guidance on Operational Risk Advanced Measurement Approaches issued in 2003 is based on Basel II operational risk framework, and extends the same approach by assigning risk based capital to businesses/products – capital requirements that are partially based on internal controls. Obviously the common thread in these regulations is internal control and compliance monitoring of transactions from all lines of business dealing with all customers, measuring and quantifying the inherent risks, and implementing risk mitigation measures.

The FFIEC publication on uniform examination guidelines for BSA/AML compliance issued in 2005 and the joint note issued by Basel Committee, International Association of Insurance Supervisors (IAIS), and International Organization of Securities Commissions

(IOSCO) on initiatives to combat money laundering and financing of terrorism in late 2003, indicate that examiners are taking a comprehensive, global, and systemic approach to AML. The elements of safety and soundness in FDICIA, the internal control guidelines of Committee of Sponsoring Organizations of the Treadway Commission (COSO) and SOX, and the due diligence and reporting of BSA/AML provide an extensive framework for effective management of operational risk and capital by banking managers. In the current investment environment following major episodes of corporate scandals and mismanagement, the investor community has also begun to use this framework to differentiate between adopters and non-adopters of good corporate management practices.

This chapter outlines the regulatory overlaps and seamless integration possibilities in the internal control structures to comply with the regulations, making it a competitive advantage to the banking institutions. It points out that by emphasizing the integral nature of BSA/AML compliance in overall customer relationship and internal control structure across business lines, the financial institutions can derive maximum value from the compliance efforts.

THE NATURE OF BSA/AML REGULATION

A number of influences have resulted in the current set of BSA/AML regulations that are often confusing and conflicting. While each contributing factor makes sense when examined individually, conflicts and confusion is not unusual given that the BSA/AML regulations developed over a number of years and are enforced by many separate government agencies.

1. A Brief Chronology of the BSA/AML Regulation

One reason why financial institutions have to comply with many often confusing and conflicting requirements is that these regulations were developed at different times in response to varying problems. Thus, it is useful to briefly review this chronology and Exhibit 8-1 summarizes briefly the chronology of the many related regulations

Exhibit 8-1
A BRIEF CHRONOLOGY OF BANK REGULATIONS

1970: Congress passed the Currency and Foreign Transactions Reporting Act commonly known as the "*Bank Secrecy Act*," which established requirements for recordkeeping and reporting by private individuals, banks, and other financial institutions. It was designed to help identify the source, volume, and movement of currency and other monetary instruments transported or transmitted into or out of the United States or deposited in financial institutions. Terrorist networks can use the criminal proceeds to facilitate their activities, corrupt and possibly destabilize communities or entire economies. In both money laundering and terrorist financing, criminals can exploit loopholes and other weaknesses in the financial system to launder criminal proceeds, and support terrorism. BSA was intended to safeguard the U.S. financial system and U.S. financial institutions from the abuses of financial crime including money laundering, terrorist financing, and other illicit financial transactions.

1986: *The Money Laundering Control Act* augmented the effectiveness of BSA, and imposed criminal liability on a person or financial institution that knowingly assists in the laundering of money, or that structures transactions to avoid reporting them. It directed banks to establish and maintain procedures reasonably designed to ensure and monitor compliance with the reporting and recordkeeping requirements of the BSA. On January 27, 1987, all federal banking agencies issued essentially similar regulations requiring banks to develop programs for BSA compliance by the interrelated sections 8(s) and 21 to the Federal Deposit Insurance Act (FDI Act), which apply equally to banks of all charters.

1991: *FDICIA* required banks to document, evaluate, and report on the effectiveness of their internal controls. Independent accountant must attest to management's assertions about internal controls.

1992: *Annunzio-Wylie Anti-Money Laundering Act* (AML) strengthened US Treasury's role and the sanctions for BSA violations.

1994: *Money Laundering Suppression Act* (MLSA) further strengthened the U.S. Treasury role in combating money laundering.

1996: *Suspicious Activity Report (SAR)* required to be filed by any U.S. banking organization that detects a known or suspected criminal violation of federal law or auspicious transaction related to money laundering activity or a violation of the BSA.

2001: In response to the September 11, 2001 terrorist attacks Congress passed the *Patriot Act.* Title III of the Patriot Act is the International Money Laundering Abatement and Anti-Terrorist Financing Act of 2001. The Patriot Act was probably the single most significant anti money laundering legislation since the enactment of BSA. It criminalized the financing of terrorism, and augmented the existing BSA framework by strengthening customer identification procedures; prohibited financial institutions from engaging in business with foreign shell banks; required financial institutions to have due diligence procedures, imposed enhanced due diligence procedures for foreign correspondent and private banking accounts; and improved information sharing between financial institutions and the U.S. government. The implementation of the Patriot Act accomplished the following:

- Expanded the AML program requirements to all financial institutions.
- Increased the civil and criminal penalties for money laundering.
- Provided the Secretary of the Treasury with the authority to impose "special measures" on jurisdictions, institutions, or transactions that are of "primary money laundering concern."
- Facilitated records access and required banks to respond to regulatory requests for information within 120 hours.
- Required federal banking agencies to consider a bank's AML record when reviewing bank mergers, acquisitions, and other applications for business combinations.

2002: In response to the public outcry over the accounting scandals, the *Sarbanes Oxley Act (SOX)* was enacted. It required verification of adherence to enhanced financial reporting requirements, audit procedures, board composition etc; Develop process for documenting risks and controls relating to financial integrity; Buy or build supporting information technology; Monitor off-balance sheet transactions and use of special purpose entities.

2003: The Inter-agency Operational risk Supervisory Guidance on Operational Risk Advanced Measurement Approaches issued in 2003 is based on Basel II operational risk framework, and extends the same approach by assigning risk based capital to businesses/products based on internal controls. Banks are expected to: Implement systems and processes to capture and assess operational risks; Develop and refine AMA qualifying capital model for operational risks; Banks adopting the Advanced Measurement Approaches (AMA) and Internal Ratings Based (IRB) approaches are required to conduct parallel calculations with current accord for 1 year prior to implementation.

As Exhibit 8-1 shows, the current set of BSA/AML regulations are a composite of a number of different legislative acts and regulatory documents developed over time often with imperfect coordination between the latest and earlier regulations. This somewhat disjointed process cannot be expected to result in an optimal or fully consistent set of regulations.

The nature of regulation has also been influenced by the effectiveness (or lack thereof) of existing regulation. For example, BSA/AML requires banking organizations to develop, implement, and maintain effective AML programs to address ever changing strategies of money launderers and terrorists who attempt to gain access to the U.S. financial system. Nevertheless, enforcement actions in the recent years have been mostly due to violations on filing timely and accurate suspicious activity reports (SAR) and currency transaction reports (CTR), ineffective internal control structures, insufficient testing and maintenance of BSA/AML monitoring systems and risk assessments, and inadequate training of personnel.

At the Bond Market Association's Legal and Compliance conference in 2004, Fed Governor Susan Schmidt Bies cited several lapses in internal control in financial institutions showing that enforcing SOX and BSA/AML requirements and holding executives accountable for their fiduciary responsibilities helped in identifying the problems and augmented the effectiveness of FDICIA certifications on internal controls. Some examples of lapses in internal control and applicable regulations are given in Exhibit 8-2.

While these lapses in internal control shown in Exhibit 8-2 and other regulatory violations noted earlier must be corrected and should not happen, these lapses and violations mentioned earlier have so far not provided feedback that is significant in modifying and improving BSL/AML regulation.

2. Government Agencies Enforcing BSA/AML Regulations

A second reason why financial institutions have to comply with many often confusing and conflicting requirements is that many different government agencies play critical roles in implementing BSA regulations, developing examination guidance, ensuring compliance with the BSA, and enforcing the BSA. Some of these international and national government agencies are listed in Exhibit 8-3.

Exhibit 8-2
Examples of Compliance Problems Uncovered (2004)

Problems uncovered	Internal control weaknesses	Regulation
Criminals laundering funds through the banks	Inadequate anti money laundering programs deficiencies in audit and management oversight.	BSA/ AML, SOX
False information entered into the records; Fraudulent fund transfers.	Failure to segregate duties: Inadequate management oversight.	BSA/ AML, FDICIA, SOX
Trading program with phony trades over a number of years resulting in significant losses	Inadequate management oversight; Compensation structures.	FDICIA, SOX, BSA/AML
Improper Transactions with special purpose entities (SPE)	Inadequate identification and management of risks; Inadequate oversight by competent directors.	FDICIA, SOX BSA/ AML
Complex financial transactions initiated by business line managers	Inadequate infrastructure and legal review; Compensation structures.	BSA/AML, FDICIA
Accounting irregularities and resulting financial statements	Aggressive interpretation of accounting restatements of rules; Inadequate board oversight.	FDICIA, SOX BSA/ AML

Exhibit 8-3
Agencies Responsible for Enforcing the BSA/AML Regulations

U.S. Treasury: requires financial institutions (banks, savings associations, and credit unions, but also non-bank financial institutions, such as money services businesses, casinos, brokers/dealers in securities, and futures commission merchants) to establish AML programs, file certain reports, and keep certain records of transactions.

Financial Crimes Enforcement Network (FinCEN), a bureau of U.S. Treasury is the delegated administrator of the BSA. It issues regulations and interpretive guidance, provides outreach to regulated industries, supports the examination functions performed by federal banking agencies, and pursues civil enforcement actions when warranted.

Federal banking agencies (Board of Governors of the Federal Reserve System, Federal Deposit Insurance Corporation, National Credit Union Administration, Office of the Comptroller of the Currency, and Office of Thrift Supervision) are charged with chartering (NCUA, OCC, and OTS), insuring (FDIC and NCUA), regulating, and supervising banks. The agencies require each bank under their supervision to establish and maintain a BSA compliance program. In accordance with the Patriot Act, FinCEN regulations require certain financial institutions to establish an AML compliance program that guards against money laundering and terrorist financing and ensures compliance with the BSA and its implementing regulations. When the Patriot Act was passed, banks under the supervision of a federal banking agency were already required by law to establish and maintain a BSA compliance program that, among other things, requires the bank to identify and report suspicious activity promptly. As part of a strong BSA/AML compliance program, the federal banking agencies seek to ensure that a bank has policies, procedures, and processes to identify and report suspicious transactions to law enforcement. The agencies' supervisory processes assess whether banks have established the appropriate policies, procedures, and processes based on their BSA/AML risk to identify and report suspicious activity and that they provide sufficient detail in reports to law enforcement agencies to make the reports useful for investigating suspicious transactions that are reported.

International agencies (various multilateral government bodies that support the fight against money laundering and terrorist financing).

Financial Action Task Force *(FATF)*, created in 1989 as a part of the US Treasury department, develops and enforces the Anti-money Laundering regulations procedures and some additional requirements added by the US Patriot Act.

Office of Foreign Assets Control (OFAC) administers and enforces economic and trade sanctions based on U.S. foreign policy and national security goals against targeted foreign countries, terrorists, international narcotics traffickers, and those engaged in activities related to the proliferation of weapons of mass destruction. It has the authority to impose controls on transactions and freeze assets under U.S. jurisdiction. OFAC sanctions are based on United Nations and other international mandates, are multilateral in scope, and involve close cooperation with allied governments. OFAC requirements are separate and distinct from the BSA, but because they share a common national security goal. Many financial institutions view compliance with OFAC sanctions as related to BSA compliance obligations; supervisory examination for BSA compliance is logically connected to the examination of a financial institution's compliance with OFAC sanctions.

As this brief review in Exhibit 8-3 indicates, a large number of different national and international governmental and regulatory bodies are responsible for often overlapping aspects of BSA/AML regulations. Financial institutions must satisfy all relevant bodies in attempting to comply with BSA/AML. For example, the US Patriot Act/OFAC guidelines outline specific requirements generally known as the anti-money laundering and customer identification program (ALCIP) for enhanced internal control, customer identification, and periodic assessments and reporting (details of these requirements are available at the website: www.treas.gov/ofac). The European Union has passed similar legislation (Buck, 2005). These regulations mandate that a specific compliance officer is to be designated and identified in each firm that engages in external financial transactions. The compliance officer should maintain US Treasury lists of blocked property and blocked transactions, report suspicious transactions, and ensure compliance and reporting consistent with the requirements of the Anti-money Laundering laws and regulations. At a minimum, an annual internal review and external audit of the ALCIP policies and procedures should be conducted and reported to the appropriate government agency. Firms engaging in significant financial transactions are required to respond within 120 hours to requests for information on accounts and for requests for monitoring and blocking appropriate accounts; report any suspicious account activity; and collect, verify, and maintain identification information provided by new and existing customers under the Anti-money Laundering Customer Identification Program (ALCIP). Clearly the financial institutions need sophisticated monitoring systems to comply with these requirements and are also required to educate selected employees regarding the requirements of ALCIP regulations. Unfortunately, due to market externalities, the best way to ensure that financial institutions disclose the identities of counterparties when they originate through domestic and foreign correspondent banking relationships may be through private incentives rather *than* through regulation (Fitzgerald, 2004). Financial institutions have to comply with multiple new regulations that require them to verify the identity of their customers and report large cash transactions and any other suspicious activity to the government, and most of them have a huge learning curve facing them as they train their staff to comply with these new anti-terrorism regulations.

Thus, as noted in this section, there are at least two major factors that have led to the current state of BSA/AML regulation: the build up of BSA/AML regulation through a series of imperfectly coordinated acts and regulations over a long time period and the large number of different national and international bodies that feel responsible for BSA/AML regulation. Both factors make the current set of BSA/AML regulation a challenge for financial institutions attempting to comply.

Financial Institution Responsibilities and Challenges

The Chief Risk Officer (CRO) is a relatively new role in most financial institutions, and its function is still evolving. The new Basel II requirements mandate the establishment of CRO function and integrated risk management including market, credit, operational, legal and reputation risks in large international financial institutions. Risks faced by businesses that need to be managed can arise from low probability and high loss events, high probability *and* high loss events, or from high probability and low loss events, and optimal procedures to manage each of these risk categories can differ greatly among institutions. The challenges created by terrorism and related regulations have greatly enhanced the role and importance of the CRO.

The Chief Financial Officer (CFO) usually has the responsibilities of Treasurer-related functions that reflect the role of the CFO as a strategic partner for assisting the profitability and growth of business units, and Controller-related functions including internal and external financial reporting, regulatory and tax compliance, and accounting, audit, and other activities designed to ensure the accuracy and integrity of financial information. The passage of the Sarbanes-Oxley Act in the US in 2002, related legislation in the EU in 2002-2003, and the finance-related provisions of the 2001 US Patriot Act in the US and related money laundering legislation in the EU have further emphasized the controller role of the CFO. While Sarbanes-Oxley Act (SOX) has greatly increased the responsibility of the CFO to ensure the integrity of the accounting data used to prepare financial reports with more extensive audit trails and controls, the Patriot Act requires the CFO and CRO to ensure better identification of customers and more extensive reporting to the government of unusually large or suspicious transactions. In the post-SOX and post-BSA/AML era, CFO responsibilities regarding accounting integrity, identification of counter-parties, and reporting transactional activity have increased the reliance on computer information systems and data integrity greatly.

The Chief Information (Technology) Officer (CIO/CTO) must ensure against unintended possible assistance to money-laundering activities or unintended transactions with inadequately identified counterparties. Studies have shown that breaches in computer security at a business are likely to be punished by investors with a loss in market value for the breached firms (Rapoport, 2005). The typical CIO faces many challenges some of which are strategic in nature focusing on the training and deployment of appropriate personnel and the design of secure and integrated systems to detect and report appropriate transactions, and some others are tactical in nature such as ensuring that disaster recovery and contingency plans are implemented.

BSA/AML requirements along with SOX have greatly increased the role and responsibility of the Board of Directors and Audit Committee. Boards of directors must sign off that they have read and understood these complex set of regulations and that they plan to oversee management implementation of these complex BSA/AML regulations. In addition, due to SOX and other regulatory changes boards of directors now also face many additional responsibilities. For example, the audit committee of the board is now responsible for more directly overseeing the audit and risk management functions of the firm. The US Department of Homeland Security has endorsed the 9/11 Commissions recommendations that companies comply with the Emergency Preparedness and Business Continuity Standard (NFPA 1600) developed by the National Fire Protection Association and endorsed by the American National Standards Institute (ANSI). Audit committees and Boards of Directors may face additional liabilities if they ignore this standard. There is some evidence that many audit committees are now integrating their work with risk management and crises planning efforts in their companies (Ernst and Young, 2004).

Clearly, boards of directors and senior managers now face many significant new responsibilities and liabilities. These new requirements are a challenge in many ways. First, it has made the board member's job more demanding and may make it more difficult to recruit qualified directors. Second, management must come up with new and cost efficient approaches to comply with BSA/AML regulation. There is little doubt that now there is a need for a more holistic approach to corporate risk management (Baranoff, 2004). The management of financial institutions has an obligation to identify individuals responsible for managing the various compliance tasks resulting from the new regulations, provide adequate technical and human resources, and provide unambiguous and strategic directives to ensure a robust, integrated risk management platform. The following section provides a roadmap of an approach to implementation of a BSA/AML operations risk model, based on the regulatory guidelines.

An Operational Risk Model for Compliance with BSA/AML

During the Y2K review of critical systems and infrastructures, a clear picture of the financial systems' technological dependence and the inherent complexities of operations risk management emerged. However, the knowledge gained during Y2K was not used to identify, measure, quantify and manage the operations risks in later years. Ignoring past FDICIA compliance efforts during the implementation of SOX, BSA/AML and Basel requirements repeats the historical pattern of not leveraging existing strengths. An earlier section outlined the government agencies that are involved in enforcing BSA/AML, and their responsibilities. The Interagency Interpretive Guidance on providing Banking Services on Money Services Businesses published in April 2005, and the joint note from the BCBS, IAIS and IOSCO issued in June 2003, and the requirements of SOX have been major drivers of improvement in governance and operational risk management in banks worldwide. The operational risk based capital discipline prescribed by the Supervisory Guidance will further enhance and protect shareholder interests by analyzing the institution's risk profile quantitatively, and allocating risk-based capital. The new internal control and governance measures are slowly getting integrated into the activities of the banking institutions, while holding the executives accountable for compliance. A sound BSA/AML compliance program is critical in deterring and preventing these types of activities at, or through, banks and other financial institutions. Financial institutions must develop an integrated, enterprise-wide risk based BSA/AML compliance system, which takes a comprehensive view of the risks across services, geography, customers, and lines of business, as well as the institution's strengths in personnel, technology and corporate culture. The BSA/AML examination manual gives a detailed discussion of the requirements for compliance in specific areas such as correspondent banking, electronic banking, funds transfers, brokered deposits, ATM's, private banking, trust, investment management and others. Appendix J in the manual identifies "Quantity of Risk Matrix" (how active the firm is in a particular activity), and areas identified as "high risk" (trust, investment, electronic banking, secured lending, brokered deposits etc.). It provides a roadmap for institutions to focus their own efforts and resources by comparing the internal risk assessments to regulators' perceptions of "high risk" businesses and activities, and take any remedial action as needed in the BSA/AML compliance structure. A high level overview for developing a comprehensive BSA/AML compliance structure is given below.

- Perform due diligence based on customers and activities, and assign scores based on the risk profiles, similar to credit scores. Identify high-risk business activities, money service businesses, validate names against "terrorist related" lists from the government databases.
- Develop, test and continuously enhance internal control systems tailored to the risk profiles of specific banking activities. In addition to the annual audit, have the system tested by independent experts on a periodic basis.
- Establish continuous monitoring of control systems charged with reviewing and reporting of money laundering activities. Develop/ purchase software to identify customer activity patterns, to be able to detect anomalies. Develop/ contract forensic examination capabilities.

One of the most vulnerable areas in banking institutions has been the technology infrastructure. The steps outlined by Office of comptroller of the Currency in March 1999 to combat infra-structure threats from cyber-terrorists can serve as a model in implementation of BSA/ AML operations risk management model.

- Install a strong intrusion detection system that is resistant to outside attacks. hŸe system should be reviewed periodically. Develop definitions and specifications for industry-wide key risk drivers and key risk indicators (KRI) for each risk type. The guidelines for SOX and FDICIA compliance can be used as the basic framework for this effort.
- Implement disaster recovery plans that are regularly tested and updated.
- Maintain adequate expertise to administer, secure and monitor network security. Plan network design and architecture in terms of connectivity, key components and firewalls.
- Implement physical security program to control access to computing and information resources. Turn audit trails on. Encrypt files and transmissions.
- Incorporate logical access controls to information resources. Conduct regular background checks of employees in sensitive positions.
- Report significant unauthorized access attempts.
- Communicate with peers about best practices. Collect operational loss data and exposures, and management scenarios and self assessments from the lines of business, to build an internal database.
- Commit enough financial resources to operations risk management process including the identification and measurement of operational risks, and developing a robust model to allocate risk based capital to the lines of businesses/ products.
- Design and implement effective management compensation systems based on the level of risk management in the business.

CONCLUSIONS

While terrorism has been around for a long time, it has been receiving greatly increased attention in recent years. The events of September 11, 2001 significantly increased the regulatory requirements facing companies that have large transactions with customers. Concurrent regulatory changes unrelated to terrorism, such as the Sarbanes-Oxley Act in the US and similar legislation elsewhere have further compounded the tasks of risk management and regulatory compliance facing most companies, their senior executives, financial staff, and their boards of directors. Some of the major challenges facing the audit committees of corporate boards and management of financial institutions include the oversight of an enhanced enterprise risk management function, greater emphasis on computer and information system security, and the need for allocating resources to meet the enhanced compliance requirements. These are all significant and important changes. They also have a responsibility to ensure that these changes result in better management of customer relationships and corporate strategies to enhance long term shareholder value, and not mere reactions to comply with regulations. Thus, company boards of directors and senior executives now face some of the most critical and costly changes that they have faced in a long while.

These challenges have many short- and long-term implications. For example, these new responsibilities and liabilities have meant that board directors must spend a great deal more time and effort on their positions than in the past and, in the long run, these additional requirements for boards of directors is likely to shrink the available pool of qualified director candidates. While there is no doubt regarding the need for appropriate BSA/AML regulation, it would be useful to reduce and remove the contradictory aspects of such regulation resulting from lack of consistency over time and across agencies.

REFERENCES

Anonymous, (2005), Costly US laundering rules must change. *International Financial Law Review* (May), p.1-6.

Anonymous, (2005), FINCEN releases 2004 SAR activity report. *Electronic Payments Week* 2 (Jun. 21), pp.1-2.

Anonymous, (2005), Special Report: Looking in the wrong places-Financing Terrorism, *The Economist* 377 (Oct. 22), pp. 82- 87.

Bank for International Settlements, (June 2004), "Basel II: International convergence of capital measurement and capital standards: a revised framework", London.

Baranoff, Etti G., (2004), "Risk Management: A Focus on a More Holistic Approach Three Years after September 11" *Journal of Insurance Regulation* 22 (No. 4, Summer), pp. 71-81.

Basel Committee on Banking Supervision, (2003), "Initiatives by the BCBS, IAIS and IOSCO to combat money laundering and the financing of terrorism", London.

Buck, Trevor, (2005), "New money laundering legislation puts extra onus on EU professions" *Financial Times* (May 27), p. 4.

Ernst and Young, (2004), "Audit Committees and the War on Terror" *Board Matters Quarterly* (December), pp. 7-8.

Federal Financial Institutions Examination Council (FFIEC) (2005), *"Bank secrecy Act/ Anti Money Laundering Examination Manual"* Washington D.C.

Federal Financial Institutions Examination Council (FFIEC) (2003), "Interagency Statement: Supervisory guidance on operational risk: Advanced measurement approaches for regulatory capital. *Federal Register* 68 (no.149, Aug.4).

Financial Crimes Enforcement Network (FINCEN) (2005), "Interagency interpretive guidance on providing banking services to money services businesses operating in the United States", Washington D.C.

Fitzgerald, Valpy, (2004), "Global financial information, compliance incentives and terrorist funding" *European Journal of Political Economy* 20 (No. 2, June), pp. 387-401.

Freeman, David F, (2005), Banking developments. *The Investment Lawyer* 12 (Aug), pp.21-22.

Isaac, William M, (2005), Harsh approach to regulation is backfiring, *American Banker* 170 (Oct.4), pp.1-3.

Office of Comptroller of the Currency (March 5, 1999), *Infrastructure threats from Cyber terrorists*, Washington D.C.

Osborne, Paul R. (2005), BSA/ AML compliance provides opportunity to improve security and enhance customer experience. *ABA Bank Compliance* 26 (no.6, Jul/Aug), pp. 4-5.

Paletta, Damian, (2005), Guidance on MSBs hasn't stemmed pullback; banks still shutting accounts, fearing regulatory scrutiny, *American Banker* 170 (Sept. 26), pp.1-4.

Rapoport, Michael, (2005), "Companies Pay a Price for Security Breaches" *Wall Street Journal* (June 15), p. C3.

Spikes, Sarah (2004), Banks increase spending to fight money laundering. *Wall Street Journal* (Sept. 20), p. A.18A.

Related Web Sites

http://www.occ.treas.gov/BSA/BSAmain.htm
http://www.treas.gov/offices/enforcement/ofac/
http://www.moneylaundering.com

REFERENCES

REFERENCES CITED IN CHAPTERS 1-6

9/11 Commission: See National Commission on Terrorist Attacks

ABN AMRO, Annual Report, 2004.

ABN AMRO, Press Room, "ABN AMRO Announcement Regarding Regulatory Directive," Amsterdam, December 19, 2005.

AmSouth Bancorporation, United States Securities and Exchange Commission, Form 8-K, October 12, 2004.

Amuedo-Dorantes, Catalina, Cynthia Bansak, and Susan Pozo, 'On the Remitting Patterns of Immigrants: Evidence from Mexican Survey Data," Economic Review, Federal Reserve Bank of Atlanta, First Quarter, 2005, 37-58.

Antigua and Barbuda, Finance and Investments, Offshore Financial Sector, http://www.antigua-barbuda.com/finance_investment/offshore_sector.asp; Also see: http://www.antiguabarbuda.gov.ag/business/economy.htm

Arab Bank. First Amended Complaint, Case No. CV 04-5449 (NG) (ASG), U.S. District Court, Eastern District of New York, January 21, 2005.

"Arab Bank Helped Saudi Charity Pay Bomber Families, Suit Says," Bloomberg.com, January 27, 2005.

Ashkanasy, Neal M., Celeste P. M. Wilderom, and Mark F. Peterson, Editors, Handbook of Organizational Culture & Climate, Thousand Oaks, CA, Sage Publications, Inc., 2000.

Baker Botts L.L.P., Internal Investigation on Certain Accounting Matters December 10, 2002 – July 21, 2003, Executive Summary. (See Freddie Mac Release, July 23, 2003: "Freddie Mac Releases Board Counsel's Report,"

Bank for International Settlements, Press Release, "G10 Central Bank Governors and Heads of Supervision Endorse the Publication of the Revised Capital Framework," June 26, 2004. www.bis.org

Basel Committee on Banking Supervision, Consultative Document, "Operational Risk: Supporting Document to the New Basel Capital Accord, January 2001.

Basel Committee on Banking Supervision, "Sound Practices for the Management and Supervision of Operational Risk," No. 96, February 2003. www.bis.org

Basel Committee on Banking Supervision, "Framework for Internal Control Systems in Banking Organizations," September 1998. www.bis.org

Basel Committee on Banking Supervision, "International Convergence of Capital Measurement and Capital Standards: A Revised Framework," No. 107, June 2004, www.bis.org

Baxter, Thomas C., Jr., Testimony before the U.S. House of Representatives, Subcommittee on Oversight and Investigations, Committee on Financial Services, "Risk Management and Regulatory Failures at Riggs and UBS: Lessons Learned," Serial Number 108-91, June 2, 2004.

Beach Bank, Miami Beach Florida, website http://beachbank.com, visited December 2005.

Beckett, Paul, "Banco Popular to Pay Millions in U.S. Fines," The Wall Street Journal, C1, C14.

Biern, Herbert A., Senior Associate Director, Division of Banking Supervision and Regulation. Testimony on The Bank Secrecy Act and U.S.A. Patriot Act, Before the Committee on International Relations, U.S. House of Representatives, November 17, 2004.

Bies, Susan Schmidt, "Trends in Risk Management and Corporate Governance," Remarks by Governor Susan Schmidt Bies at the Financial Managers Society Finance and Accounting Forum for Financial Institutions, Washington, D.C., June 22, 2004.

Biger, Jon, "Glowing Numbers," Money Magazine, November 2000, pp. 112-122.

Blum, Jack A., Michael Levi, R. Thomas Naylor, and Phil Williams, "Financial Havens, Banking Secrecy and Money Laundering," New York, United Nations Office for Drug Control and Crime Prevention, 1999.

Board of Governors of the Federal Reserve System, "Federal Reserve Enforcement Actions," September 19, 2002. http://www.federalreserve.gov/boarddocs/enforcement/

Board of Governors of the Federal Reserve System, Federal Reserve Press Release, February 8, 2000, Enforcement Actions (Bank of New York).

Board of Governors of the Federal Reserve System, Federal Reserve Press Release: March 9, 2000, Enforcement Actions (Banco Popular de Puerto Rico).

Board of Governors of the Federal Reserve System, Federal Reserve Press Release: December 12, 2000, Operation Casablanca Enforcement Actions.

Board of Governors of the Federal Reserve System, Federal Reserve Press Release: May 10, 2004, (Order of Assessment of a Civil Money Penalty Against UBS).

Board of Governors of the Federal Reserve System, Federal Reserve Press Release, "Consent Order to Cease and Desist Against Riggs National Corp and Riggs International Banking Corporation," May 14, 2004

Board of Governors of the Federal Reserve System, "Federal Court Reaffirms Protections for Financial Institutions Filing Suspicious Activity Reports," Interagency Advisory, May 24, 2004.

Board of Governors of the Federal Reserve System, Joint Press Release, "Agencies release supervisory and penalty actions against ABN AMRO Bank N.V." December 19, 2005.

Board of Governors of the Federal Reserve System, "Joint Statement on Providing Banking Services to Money Services Businesses," March 30, 2005.

Board of Governors of the Federal Reserve System, "List of Enforcement Actions" as of 12/31/05; http://www.federalreserve.gov/boarddocs/enforcement/search.cfm

Board of Governors of the Federal Reserve System, Report on the Failure of the Oakwood Deposit Bank Company, by the Office of the Inspector General of the Board of Governors of the Federal Reserve System, October 2002.

Bonner, Robert C., Commissioner, U.S. Customs, Speech to the Egmont Group of Financial Intelligence Units Tracking Terrorist Financing, Washington, D.C., October 31, 2001.

Buckner, Kris, President, Investigative Services, Testimony Before the U.S. Senate Committee on Homeland Security and Governmental Affairs, "Counterfeit Goods, Easy Cash for Criminals and Terrorists," May 25, 2005.

Buffett, Warren E., "To the Shareholders of Berkshire Hathaway Inc." Berkshire Hathaway Inc., 2002 Annual Report, February 21, 2003.

Cañas, Jesus, Roberto Coronado, and Robert W. Gilmer, "U.S., Mexico Deepen Economic Ties," SouthwestEconomy, Federal Reserve Bank of Dallas, January/February 2006, pp. 11-3, 16.

Carroll, Lisa C., "Alternative Remittance Systems Distinguishing Sub-systems of Ethnic Money Laundering in Interpol Member Countries on the Asian Continent," Interpol, December 4, 2002 (Last modification).

Central Intelligence Agency, The World Fact Book, 2005, http://www.cia.gov.

Clearing House Interbank Payments System, http://www.chips.org/

Cohen, Larry, and Felson, Marcus, "Social Change and Crime Trends: A Routine Activities Approach," American Sociological Review, 44: 1979, pp. 588-608.

Committee on Sponsoring Organizations (COSO) of the Treadway Commission, "Fraudulent Financial Reporting, 1987-1997, An Analysis of U.S. Public Companies," 1999, http://www.coso.org/publications.htm

Comptroller of the Currency, The Bank Secrecy Act/Anti-Money Laundering Comptroller's Handbook, Washington, D.C., Consumer Compliance Examination, September 2000, Revised for Web Publication, December, 2000.

Comptroller of the Currency, OCC Bulletin, Guidance on Foreign Official Corruption, OCC 2001-9, February 20, 2001.

Comptroller of the Currency Money Laundering: A Bankers Guide to Avoiding Problems, 2nd ed., June 1993; 3rd ed., December 2002.

Comptroller of the Currency, A Pocket Guide to Detecting Red Flags in Board Reports, October, 2003.

Comptroller of the Currency, New Release, "OCC Assesses $25 Million Penalty Against Riggs Bank N.A." 2004-34, May 13, 2004.

Comptroller of the Currency, OCC Bulletin, Enforcement Guidance for BSA/AML Program Deficiencies, OCC 2004-50, November 10, 2004.

Comptroller of the Currency, New Release, "OCC Issues Cease and Desist Order Against New York Branch of Banco de Chile," NR 2005-11, February 2, 2005.

Comptroller of the Currency, News Release, "OCC Issues Civil Money Penalty Against National Bank Subsidiary," January 4, 2006.

Comptroller of the Currency, Consent Order, The Federal Branch of Arab Bank PLC, New York, New York, AA-EC-05-12, #2005-14, February 24, 2005.

Comptroller of the Currency, News Release, "OCC Issues Order Against the Federal Branch Of Arab Bank PLC," NR 2005-11, February, 25, 2005.

Comptroller of the Currency, New Release, "FinCEN and OCC Assess $24 Million Penalty Against Arab Bank Branch," NR2005-80, August 17, 2005.

Comptroller of the Currency, OCC Bulletin, Interagency Guidance on Providing Banking Services to Money Services Businesses Operating in the United States, OCC 2005-19, May 6, 2005.

Coronado, Roberto, "Workers' Remittances to Mexico," El Paso BusinessFrontier, Federal Reserve Bank of Dallas, Issue 1, 2004.

Council of the European Union, "Directive on Money Laundering and Terrorist Financing," September 20, 2005 (Presse 240). http://ue.eu.int/ueDocs/cms_Data/docs/pressData/en/misc/86283.pdf

Crow, Robert, "Playing With Financial Fire," The Australian Financial Review, February 2, 2004, p. 61.

Customer Due Diligence for Banks, Basel Committee on Banking Supervision, Bank for International Settlements, October 2001.

Deal, Terrence E., and Allan A. Kennedy, Corporate Cultures: The Rites and Rituals of Corporate Life, Reading MA. Addison-Wesley Publishing Co., 1982.

El-Qorchi, Mohammed, "Hawala," Finance and Development, International Monetary Fund, Vol. 39, Number 4, December 2002.

Emerson, Steven, "Terrorism Financing: Origination, Organization, and Prevention," Testimony before the U.S. Senate, Committee on Governmental Affairs, S. Hrg. 108-245, July 31, 2003, pp. 163-170

Emerson, Steven, "Fund-Raising Methods and Procedures for International Terrorist Organizations," Testimony before the House Committee on Financial Services Subcommittee on Oversight and Investigation, Patriot Act Oversight, February 12, 2002.

Emerson, Steven, "Saudi Arabia: Friend or Foe in the War on Terror," Testimony before the U.S. Senate Judiciary Committee, November 8, 2005.

"FAQs regarding Check Cashers," Internal Revenue Service, IRS.gov, http://www.irs.gov/govt/tribes/article/0,,id=108295,00.html

FDIC, Bank Secrecy Act: Registration and De-registration of Money Service Businesses, FIL-20-2006, March 1, 2006.

FDIC, Consumer News, "A Special Guide for Seniors and Families: Fake Documents Used to Steal Homes," Fall 2005.

FDIC, Financial Institutions Letters: "Identity Theft Study on "Account-Hijacking" Identity Theft and Suggestions for Reducing Online Fraud," FIL-132-2004.

FDIC, Financial Institution Letters: Office of Foreign Asset Control Specially Designated Nationals and Blocked Persons, FIL-18-2005, March 17, 2005.

FDIC, Frias, Michael A., "Linking International Remittance Flows to Financial Services: Tapping the Latino Immigrant Market," Supervisory Insights, 2004.

FDIC, Order to Cease and Desist, In the Matter of Beach Bank, Miami Beach, Florida, FDIC-04-233b, May 11, 2004.

FDIC, Press Release PR-70-2004, "Banking Agencies Announce Publication of Revised Capital Framework and Describe U.S. Implementation Efforts," June 6, 2004.

FDIC, Special Alert, SA-192-2005: Fraudulent Information Request, December 21, 2005.

Federal Financial Institutions Examination Council, Bank Secrecy Act/Anti-Money Laundering Examination Manual, June 2005, (FFIEC BSA/AML Examination Manual), www.ffiec.gov/pdf/bsamanual.pdf

Federal Register/Vol. 67, No. 187, September 26, 2002, Rules and Regulations, Department of Treasury, 31 CFR Part 103.

Federal Register/Vol. 71, No. 2, January 4, 2006, 31 CFR Part 103, Financial Crimes Enforcement Network: Anti-Money Laundering Programs; Special Due Diligence Programs for Certain Foreign Accounts: Final Rule and Proposed Rule.

Federal Trade Commission web based resource about identity theft. http://www.consumer.gov/idtheft/#
Ferguson, Roger W., Vice Chairman Federal Reserve, Testimony before the Subcommittee on Financial Institutions and Consumer and Credit, Committee on Financial Services, U.S. House of Representatives, June 19, 2003.
Financial Action Task Force on Money Laundering, "Combating the Abuse of Non-Profit Organizations: International Best Practices," October 11, 2002.
Financial Action Task Force, "Money Laundering & Terrorist Financing Typologies, 2004-2005," June 10, 2005.
Financial Action Task Force on Money Laundering, "1996-1997 Report on Money Laundering Typologies," February, 1997.
Financial Action Task Force on Money Laundering, "1997-1998 Report on Money Laundering Typologies," February 12, 1998.
Financial Action Task Force on Money Laundering, "1998-1999 Report on Money Laundering Typologies," February 10, 1999.
Financial Action Task Force on Money Laundering, "1999-2000 Report on Money Laundering Typologies," February 3, 2000.
Financial Action Task Force on Money Laundering, "2000-2001 Report on Money Laundering Typologies," February 1, 2001.
Financial Action Task Force on Money Laundering, "Report on Money Laundering Typologies, 2001-2002," February 1, 2002.
Financial Action Task Force on Money Laundering, "Report on Money Laundering Typologies, 2002-2003," February 14, 2003.
Financial Action Task Force on Money Laundering, "Report on Money Laundering Typologies, 2003-2004," 2004.
Financial Action Task Force on Money Laundering, "Guidance for Financial Institutions in Detecting Terrorist Financing," April 24, 2002.
Financial Action Task Force on Money Laundering, "The FATF Forty Recommendations," 2003. http://www1.oecd.org/fatf/40Recs_en.htm#Other%20measures
Financial Action Task Force on Money Laundering, "Basic Facts about Money Laundering," February 7, 2004. http://www.fatf-gafi.org/MLaundering_en.htm
Financial Action Task Force on Money Laundering, "Detecting and Preventing Cross-Border Transportation of Cash by Terrorists and Other Criminals, International Best Practices," February 12, 2005.
Financial Crimes Enforcement Network, "Annual Report, Fiscal 2004," Washington, D.C., 2005.
Financial Intelligence Units: An Overview, Washington, D.C., The International Monetary Fund and The World Bank, 2004.
Financial Services Agency (FSA, Japan), "Administrative Actions on Citibank, N.A., Japan Branch" (Provisional Translation), News Release, September 17, 2004.
FinCEN Advisory, "Colombian Black Market Peso Exchange," Issue 9, November 1997.
FinCEN Advisory, "Black Market Peso Exchange Update," Issue 12, June 1999.
FinCEN, Advisory, Informal Value Transfer Systems, Issue 33, March 2003.
FinCEN Annual Report, Fiscal Year 2004.
FinCEN Enforcement Action in the matter of Hartsfield Capital Securities, Inc., No. 2003-05.

FinCEN Fact Sheet, Section 312 of the USA PATRIOT Act, Final Regulation and Notice of Proposed Rulemaking, December, 2005.

FinCEN news, "Insurance Companies Required to Establish Anti-Money Laundering Programs and File Suspicious Activity Reports," October 31, 2005.

FinCENnews, "FinCEN Accesses $2.8 Million Penalty Against Oppenheimer & Co., Inc.," December 29, 2005.

FinCEN, "Suspicious Activities Reported by Casinos," SAR Bulletin, August 2000, Issue 2.

FinCEN, "The SAR Activity Review: Trends, Tips & Issues," Issue 5, February 2003.

FinCEN, "The SAR Activity Review: Trends, Tips & Issues," Issue 7, August 2004.

FinCEN, "The SAR Activity Review: Trends, Tips & Issues," Issue 8, April 2005.

FinCEN, "The SAR Activity Review: Trends, Tips & Issues," Issue 9, October 2005.

FinCEN, "The SAR Activity Review: Trend, Tips, & Issues, Issue 10, May 2006.

FinCEN, "The FinCEN, SAR Activity Review, By the Numbers," Issue 3, December 2004.

FinCENnews, "Dealers in Precious Metals, Stones or Jewels Required to Establish Anti-Money Laundering Programs," June 3, 2005.

"First National Bank of Keystone," ERisk.com Case Study, June 2002.

"Foreign Asset Control Regulations for the Financial Community," U.S. Department of Treasury, November 24, 2004.

Forman, Marcy M. Deputy Assistant Director, Financial Investigations, Immigration and Customs Enforcement, Department of Homeland Security, Statement before the House Government Reform Committee Subcommittee on Criminal Justice, Drug Policy and Human Resources, "Terrorist Financing and Money Laundering Investigations: Who Investigates and How Effective Are They?" May 11, 2004.

Fox, William J., Director, Financial Crimes Enforcement Network, United States Department of Treasury, Statement Before the Senate Committee on Banking, Housing, and Urban Affairs, September 28, 2004

Frank, Robert, "Have $50 million? Come On In," The Wall Street Journal, February 1, 2005, pp. C1, C6.

"Frozen Millions Are Drug Proceeds, Raul Salinas Incriminated by Numerous Witnesses," Office of the Attorney General of Switzerland, Federal Office for Police Matters, Press Office, October 20, 1998.

Garcia, Michael J., Assistant Secretary for Immigration and Customs Enforcement, "Meeting the Threat: A Symposium on Counter-Terrorism, "Duke University Law School, February 4, 2004.

Garner, Bryan A., Ed., Black's Law Dictionary, 7th ed., St. Paul, MN, West Group, 1999.

Glaser, Daniel, L., Deputy Assistant Secretary Office of Terrorist Financing and Financial Crimes, U.S. Department of Treasury, Testimony before the Senate Committee on the Judiciary, November 8, 2005.

"Global Anti-Money Laundering Survey 2004: How Banks are Facing Up to the Challenge," KPMG International, 2004.

Gordon, Marcy, "Banco de Chile to Close Pinochet Accounts," Seattle Post-Intelligencer, February 2, 2005. www.seattlepi.com

Greenberg, Maurice M., "Terrorist Financing," Report of an Independent Task Force Sponsored by the Council on Foreign Relations, New York, Council on Foreign Relations Press, 2002.

Grow, Brian, John Cady, Susann Rutledge, and David Polek, "Gold Rush," Business Week, Investigative Report, January 9, 2006, pp. 69-76.

Grow, Brian, and Bryon MacWilliams, "OnLine Extra: WebMoney and its Customers," BusinessWeek Online, Investigative Report, January 9, 2006.

Gup, Benton E., Targeting Fraud: Uncovering and Deterring Fraud in Financial Institutions, Revised edition, Chicago, Probus Publishing, 1995.

Gup, Benton E., Bank Failures in the Major Trading Countries of the World: Causes and Remedies, Westport, CT., Quorum Books, 1998.

Gup, Benton E., The New Basel Capital Accord, Mason, OH, Thomson-Texere, 2004.

Halper, Evan, "State's Tobacco Revenue Surges," Los Angeles Times, December 27, 2005.

Hamilton, Lee H., Vice Chair, National Commission on Terrorist Attacks, Testimony before The Committee on Financial Services Hearing entitled "The 9/11 Commission Report: Identifying and Preventing Terrorist Financing, August 23, 2004.

Hawke, John D. Jr., Comptroller of the Currency, Testimony before the U.S. Senate Committee on Banking, Housing, and Urban Affairs, June 3, 2004.

Helgerson, John L., Chairman, National Intelligence Council, "The Terrorist Challenge to US National Security," Speech before the Tenth Cosmos Club Spring Symposium, March 23, 2002.

Hutchings, Robert L., Chairman, National Intelligence Council, "Terrorism and Economic Security," Speech before the International Security Management Association, Scottsdale, AZ, January 14, 2004.

"ID-Defusing the Issue: A Progress Report," Financial Crime Sector Report, The Financial Services Authority, London, UK, October 2004.

Idaho Department of Finance, Cease and Desist Order, 97-03-01, Re European Union Bank of Antigua, West Indies, May, 29, 1997.

Idaho Department of Finance, "State Orders Another Offshore Uninsured Bank to Stop Soliciting Deposits on the Internet," Press Release, November 4, 1997.

International Association of Insurance Supervisors, "Guidance Paper on Anti-Money Laundering and Combating the Financing of Terrorism," Guidance Paper No. 5, October 2004.

Investigation into Foreign Exchange Losses at the National Bank of Australia, Sydney, Australia, PricewaterhouseCoopers, March 12, 2004.

Jackson, David, "Mortgage Fraud is The Thing to Do Now," Chicago Tribune, November 5, 2005.

Jackson David, "Scams Build Gang Empire, "Chicago Tribune, November 7, 2005.

Jackson, David, "Even Big Boys Get Scammed," November 8, 2005.

Jackson, David, "How Fraud Became the Nightmare on May St.," Chicago Tribune, November 9, 2005.

Jackson, David, "With Mortgage Fraud, It's Catch 'em if You Can," Chicago Tribune, November 10, 2005.

Jackson, David, "Mortgage Fraud: The New Street Hustle," Chicago Tribune, Broadband, November 2005. http://www.chicagotribune.com.

Jacobellis v. Ohio, 378 U.S. 184, 197 (1964).

Jensen, Michael, C., "The Modern Industrial Revolution, Exit, and the Failure of Internal Control Systems," Journal of Finance, July, 1983, pp. 831 – 880.

Johnson, James E., Testimony on The Colombian Back Market Peso Exchange, Testimony Before the Senate Caucus on International Narcotics Control," June 21, 1999. See U.S. Treasury, Department of Treasury.

Jost, Patrick, Testimony before the U.S. Senate Committee on Banking, Housing, and Urban Affairs, Subcommittee on International Trade and Finance, Hearing on "Hawala and Underground Terrorist Financing Mechanisms," November 14, 2001.

Jost, Patrick M., and Jarjit Singh Sandhu, "The Hawala Alternative Remittance System and Its Role in Money Laundering." Interpol General Secretariat, Lyon, France, January, 2000.

Katzman, Kenneth, "Al Qaeda: Profile and Threat Assessment," CRS Report for Congress, August 17, 2005, Congressional Research Service Order Code RL33038.

Kesmodel, David, "Internet Casinos Get Creative With Ads," The Wall Street Journal, March 2, 2005, p. B2A.

Latynina, Yulia, "Banking Crisis Russian Style," The MoscowTimes.com, July 7, 2004, p. 7. http://www.themoscowtimes.com/stories/2004/07/07/008.html

Laudicina, Paul A, World Out of Balance: Navigating Global Risks to Seize Competitive Advantage," New York, McGraw-Hill, 2005.

Leach, James A., Chairman, Committee on Banking and Financial Services, U.S. House of Representatives, Statement before the Financial Academy, Moscow, Russia, April 25, 2000.

Levey, Stuart A., Under Secretary Terrorism and Financial Intelligence, U.S. Department of Treasury, Testimony before The Committee on Financial Services Hearing entitled "The 9/11 Commission Report: Identifying and Preventing Terrorist Financing, August 23, 2004.

Levey, Stuart A., Under Secretary Terrorism and Financial Intelligence, U.S. Department of Treasury, Testimony before the Senate Committee on Banking, Housing, and Urban Affairs, July 13, 2005.

Levitt, Matthew, Ph.D., Senior Fellow, The Washington Institute for Near East Policy, Testimony Before the U.S. Senate Committee on Homeland Security and Governmental Affairs, "Counterfeit Goods, Easy Cash for Criminals and Terrorists," May 25, 2005.

"List of Al Qaida Inspired Attacks Released," Directgov, July 13, 2005, www.direct.gov.uk/output/Page7930.asp

Matthews, William H., Merle Sharick, Erin E. Omba, Catherine B. Ontero, and D. James Croft, "Seventh Periodic Mortgage Fraud Case Report to the Mortgage Bankers Association," Mortgage Asset Research Institute, Inc., Reston VA, May 2005.

Meyer, Josh, "U.S. Faults Saudi Efforts on Terrorism," Latimes.com. (from the Los Angeles Times), January 15, 2006.

Miller, Mathew, "Catch Me if You Can," Forbes, March 27, 2006, 113 – 125.

Money Transmitter Regulators Association (MTRA), "Ten Year Sentence for Money Laundering and Operating without a Virginia Money Transmission License," November 29, 2005. http://mtraweb.org/news.shtm#ten_year

Morse, Andrew, and Mitchell Pacelle, "Japan Orders Citibank to Halt Private Banking," The Wall Street Journal, September 20, 2004, p. A3.

Morse, Andrew, and Mitchell Pacelle, "Citigroup Submits Plan to Mend Private- Banking Unit in Japan," Wall Street Journal, October 25, 2004, p. C3.

Mowbray, Joel, "The Case Against Arab Bank," The Washington Times, Washingtontimes. com, December 30, 2004.

Napoleoni, Loretta, and Rico Carish, "Terrorist Financing," appears in Confronting Terrorism: The Club de Madrid Series on Democracy and Terrorism, Volume II; The International Summit on Democracy, Terrorism and Security, Madrid, Spain, March 8-11, 2005,

National Board Releases HomeSide Review Outcomes – Wachetell, Lipton, Rosen & Katz Report," National Australia Bank Group, Melbourne, Australia, January 21, 2002.

National Commission on Terrorist Attacks Upon the United States, Monograph on Terrorist Financing, Staff Report by John Roth, Douglas Greenburg, and Serena Wille, 2004, http://www.9-11commission.gov

Newcomb, R. Richard, Director, Office of Foreign Asset Control, U.S. Department of Treasury, Statement before the U.S. Senate, Committee on Governmental Affairs, 108th Cong. 1st. Sess, , Terrorism Financing: Origination, Organization, and Prevention, S. Hrg. 108-245, July 31, 2003.

OECD in Figures: Statistics on Member States, 2004 Edition, OECD Observer, 2004/Supplement 1, Paris, France, July, 2004.

Office of the Comptroller of the Currency – See Comptroller of the Currency.

Office of Federal Housing Enterprise Oversight, Executive Office of the President, Report of Findings to Date Special Examination of Fannie Mae, Washington, D.C., September 17 2004.

Office of National Drug Control Policy, "What America's Users Spend on Illegal Drugs, 1988-2000," December, 2001.

O'Hara, Terence, "6 U.S. Banks Held Pinochet's Accounts," Washington Post.com, March 16, 2005, p. E03.

O'Hara, Terence, "In Cultivating International Clients, Riggs Went down a Perilous Path," Washingtonpost.com, March 21, 2005, p. E01

O'Hara, Terence, "Judge Backs Rigg's $16 million Plea Deal," Washington Post.com, March 30, 2005, p. E02.

Oldfield, Stewart, "NAB Scandal: Trader Hits Back," The Australian Financial Review. January 16, 2004, pp. 1, 63.

Orozco, Manuel, "Remittances to Latin America and the Caribbean: Issues and Perspectives on Development," Report Commissioned by the Organization of American States, Washington, D.C., September 2004.

Orozco, Manuel, "The Remittance Marketplace: Prices, Policy and Financial Institutions," Pew Hispanic Center Report, June 2004.

Parcelle, Mitchell, Martin Fackler, and Andrew Morse, "For Citigroup, Scandal in Japan Shows Danger of Global Sprawl," The Wall Street Journal, December 22, 2004, pp. A1, A10.

Passas, Nikos, "Informal Value Transfer Systems and Criminal Organizations: A study Into So-Called Underground Banking Networks," The Hague, Ministry of Justice (The Netherlands), 1999.

Passas, Nikos, "Informal Value Transfer Systems, Terrorism and Money Laundering: A Report to the National Institute of Justice," November 2003.

Patterns of Global Terrorism, 2003, United States Department of State, April 2004. http://www.state.gov/s/ct/rls/pgtrpt/2003/

Pillar, Paul, "Fighting International Terrorism: Beyond September 11th," National Intelligence Council, November 28, 2001.

Post, Jerold M, "Psychology," appears in Confronting Terrorism: The Club de Madrid Series on Democracy and Terrorism, Volume I; The International Summit on Democracy, Terrorism and Security, Madrid, Spain, March 8-11, 2005,

Powis, Robert E., The Money Launderers, Chicago, Probus Publishing Co., 1992, Chapter 1.

Prados, Alfred B., and Christopher M. Blanchard, Saudi Arabia: Terrorist Financing Issues, CRS Report to Congress, RL32499, Updated March 1, 2005.

Prados, Alfred B., Saudi Arabia: Current Issues and U.S. Relations, CRS Issue Brief for Congress, IB93113, Updated August 4, 2003.

Press Release, "Cease and Desist Order Against Banco de Chile," Enforcement Action, Board of Governors of the Federal Reserve System, February 2, 2005.

Program Performance Report, Fiscal Year 2000, U.S. Department of the Treasury, 2001.

Quirk, Peter J., "Macroeconomic Implications of Money Laundering," International Monetary Fund, Working Paper, WP/96/66-EA, June 1, 1996.

Report into Irregular Currency Trading at National Australia Bank, Australian Prudential Regulatory Authority (APRA), Sydney, Australia, March 23, 2004.

"Report on Correspondent Banking: A Gateway for Money Laundering," Minority Staff of the Permanent Subcommittee on Investigations, U.S. Senate Committee on Governmental Affairs, February 5, 2001. Also Listed under U.S. Senate.

Report On Investigations into the Affairs of National Irish Bank Limited and National Irish Bank Financial Services Limited, By High Court Inspectors, Mr. Justice Blayney and Tom Grace FCA, Appointed 30 March 1998 and 15 June 1998. Published by the High Court, July 30, 2004 (www.odce.ie).

Renyi, Thomas A., Chairman of the Board and CEO of the Bank of New York, Testimony in Panel III of a Hearing of the House Banking and Financial Services Committee Subject: Russian Corruption and Money Laundering, U.S. House of Representatives, September 22, 1999.

"Risks to Insurers Posed by Electronic Commerce," Issue Paper, International Association of Insurance Supervisors, October, 2002. http://www.iaisweb.org/187riskstoinsurers.pdf

Robinson, Phillip L., and Ethan S. Burger, "The Regulatory Framework and Potential Implications of the Bank of New York Money-Laundering Scandal for Russia and the United States," Ludwig & Robinson, P.L.L.C., Washington, D.C. (approx. date 2000).

Rodger, Ian, "Survey of Fraud – Prevention and Detection," Financial Times, October 18, 1994, p. 34.

Saban, Barry, Chief, Counterterrorism Section, Criminal Division, Department of Justice, Testimony before The Committee on Financial Services Hearing entitled "The 9/11 Commission Report: Identifying and Preventing Terrorist Financing, August 23, 2004.

Samor, Geraldo, "Citigroup Parts Ways with Manager in Brazil," Wall Street Journal, March 11, 2005, p. C3

Schroder, William R., "Money Laundering, A Global Threat and the International Community's Response," FBI Law Enforcement Bulletin, May 2001, p. 1-9.

Simson, Glen R., "As Investigations Proliferate, Big Banks Feel Under the Gun," The Wall Street Journal, December 20, 2004, pp. A1, A4.

Simson, Glen R., and John R. Wilke, "Arab Bank to Close Operations In U.S. Amid Inquiry, Lawsuits," The Wall Street Journal, February 9, 2005, p. A2.

Simson, Glen R., "Arab Bank's Link to Terrorism Poses Dilemma for U.S. Policy," The Wall Street Journal, April 20, 2005, pp. A1, A8.

Simson, Glen R., "ABN Amro to Pay $80 Million Fine Over Iran, Libya," The Wall Street Journal, December 20, 2005, pp. A3, A6.

Simson, Glen R., "How Top Dutch Bank Plunged Into World of Shadowy Money," The Wall Street Journal, December 30, 2005, p. A1, A7.

Snyder, Barry R., Letter to The Honorable Susan S. Bies, October 25, 2002, in connection with the Board of Governors of the Federal Reserve System, Office of Inspector General, Report on the Failure of the Oakwood Deposit Bank Company, October 2002.

Sportingbet., Plc, *http://www.sportingbet.com/content/home.asp; http://www.sportingbet.com /info/aboutus.asp*

Stahlmann, Chatherine, "Check Cashers and Money Transmitters, Serious Risks or Just Misunderstood?" International Supervision and Regulation, Federal Reserve Bank of Atlanta, May 2003.

State of Iowa, Iowa Department of Pubic Safety, Intelligence Bureau "Money Laundering Threat Assessment," January 2004.

State of New York Banking Department, Regulatory Action, "Banking Department Fines Western Union $8 Million for Violating Bank Secrecy, USA Patriot, New York Banking Laws," December 20, 2002.

State of New York Banking Department, Regulatory Action, "Bandco Check Cashing Services, Inc., a licensed casher of checks, has entered into a Settlement Agreement with the Superintendent of Banks which includes the payment of a $50,000 fine," April 12, 2004.

"Statement of Purpose of the Egmont Group of Financial Intelligence Units," The Hague, June 13, 2001. http://www1.oecd.org/fatf/Ctry-orgpages/org-egmont_en.htm

Statistical Abstract of the United States, 2004-2005, U.S. Census Bureau, Washington, D.C., 2005.

Stedman (Lieutenant), John, Sheriff's Department, County of Los Angeles, Testimony Before the U.S. Senate Committee on Homeland Security and Governmental Affairs, "Counterfeit Goods, Easy Cash for Criminals and Terrorists," May 25, 2005.

Stipano, Daniel P., Deputy Counsel, OCC, Testimony Before the Subcommittee on Oversight and Investigations of the Committee on Financial Services, U.S. House of Representatives, June 2, 2004.

"Terrorism Financing: Origination, Organization, and Prevention," Hearing before the Committee on Governmental Affairs, U.S. Senate, (S. Hrg. 108-245), July 31, 2003.

"The Holy Land Foundation for Relief and Development, Update," Anti-Defamation League, July 27, 2006. Http://www.adl.org/israel/holyland.asp

The International Money Laundering Abatement and Financial Anti-Terrorism Act of 2001, Pubic Law 107-56, Sec. 302, (31 USC 5311 note) October 26, 2001.

The SAR Activity Review. See FinCEN.

The World Bank, "General Principals for International Remittance Services, Committee on Payment and Settlement Systems," Consultative Report, March 2006.

"Three Guilty, Three Innocent of Laundering Money for Drug Cartel," Las Vegas Review-Journal, June 12, 1999.

Tischler, Bonni, Assistant Commissioner, U.S. Customs Service, "The Colombian Black Market Peso Exchange," Testimony Before the Senate Caucus on International Narcotics Control," June 21, 1999.

Transparency International Press Release: New Index Highlights Worldwide Corruption Crisis, Says Transparency International," Paris, June 27, 2001.

Transparency International Press Release: Russian, Chinese, Taiwanese and S. Korean Companies Widely Seen Using Bribes in Developing Countries," Berlin, May 14, 2002.

Trapani, John, Team Leader, BSA/AML Risk Specialist Unit, Federal Reserve Bank of Chicago, "Money Laundering," Presented at the 2005 Financial Management Association Annual Meeting, Chicago, IL, October 13, 2005.

United Nations, "General Assembly Reaffirms Strong Support for Global Certification Scheme," Press Release GA/10319, December 15, 2004.

U.S. Census Bureau, American FactFinder, "United States 2004 American Community Survey, Data Profile Highlights," http://factfinder.census.gov

U.S. Customs Service, "Black Market Peso Exchange: A Trade Based Money Laundering System," June 1999.

U.S. Customs Service, Press Release, "Manhattan Bank Pleads Guilty to U.S. Criminal Charges for Failure to Report $123 Million in Suspicious Cash Deposits," November 27, 2002.

U.S. Department of Housing and Urban Development, News Release, "HUD Announces Landmark $41 million Settlement Against ABN AMRO," January 4, 2006.

U.S. Department of Justice, Bureau of Justice Statistics, Press Release, "Over 18,000 Charged with Federal Money Laundering From 1994 Through 2001," July 17, 2003.

U.S. Department of Justice and U.S. Department of Treasury, 2002 National Money Laundering Strategy, July 2002.

U.S. Department of Justice and U.S. Department of Treasury, 2003 National Money Laundering Strategy, 2003.

U.S. Department of Justice, Drug Enforcement Agency, News Release, "Colombian Drug and Money Laundering Ring Shattered, Black Market Peso Exchange Used Illegally to Funnel Drug Money," June 14, 2005.

U.S. Department of Justice, Federal Bureau of Investigation, Press Release, "FBI Announces Arrest of British Arms Dealer," August 13, 2003.

U.S. Department of Justice, Federal Bureau of Investigation, Press Release, "FBI Announces Operation Continued Action Targeting Financial Institution Fraud," September 17, 2004.

U.S. Department of Justice, Motivans, Mark, "Money Laundering Offenders, 1994-2001," Bureau of Justice Statistics, Special Report, July 2003.

U. S. Department of Justice, "Al Qaeda Training Manual," February 23, 2004.

U.S. Department of Justice, "Banco Popular de Puerto Rico Enters into Deferred Prosecution Agreement with U.S. Department of Justice," January 16, 2003.

U.S. Department of Justice, News Release, "Holy Land Foundation, Leaders, Accused of Providing Material Support to Hamas Terrorist Organization," July 27, 2004.

U.S. Department of Justice, Press Release, "Riggs Bank Sentenced to Pay $16 Million for Criminal Violation of the Bank Secrecy Act," March 29, 2005.

U.S. Department of Justice, Press Release, "Eleven Defendants Indicted on Domestic Terrorism Charges," January 20, 2006.

U.S. Department of Justice, United States Attorney Northern District of Illinois, "U.S. Indicts Chicago Dentist Allegedly Linked to Providing Luxury Autos and Marina Towers Condos to Nationwide Prostitution Ring," January 18, 2005.

U.S. Department of State, "International Narcotics Control Strategy Report – 2003, Released by the Bureau for International Narcotics and Law Enforcement Affairs, March 2004.

U.S. Department of State, International Narcotics Control Strategy Report -2003, Released by the Bureau for International Narcotics and Law Enforcement Affairs, March 2004.

U.S. Department of State, "Money Laundering and Financial Crimes," No date, www.state.gov/documents/organization/8703.pdf

U.S. Department of State, Patterns of Global Terrorism 2003, 2004, http://www.state.gov/s/ct/rls/pgtrpt/2003/

U.S. Department of State, Philip Zelikow, Counselor for the Department; John Brennan, National Counterterrorism Center Interim Director, "Remarks on Release of 'Country Reports on Terrorism' for 2004, April 27, 2005.

U.S. Department of Treasury, "U.S. Customs Service Takes Down Major Drug Traffickers, Corrupt Banks and Bankers in Largest Drug Money Laundering Case Ever," Press Release, PR-2452, May 18, 1998.

U.S. Department of Treasury, The National Money Laundering Report for 1999," September 1999.

U.S. Department of Treasury, "Treasury Under Secretary for Enforcement James E. Johnson Before the Senate Caucus on International Narcotics Control," Press Release, RR-3214, June 21, 1999.

U.S. Department of Treasury, "Treasury Department Assistant Secretary David Medina, House Banking Subcommittee on Financial Services and Consumer Credit," Press Release, LS-623, May 15, 2000.

U.S. Department of Treasury, "Statement of John B. Taylor," Press Release, PO-771, November 7, 2001.

U.S. Department of Treasury, "Treasury Announces Signing of Multilateral Recommendations for Combating the Black Market Peso Exchange, System," Press Release, PO-2001, March 14, 2002.

U.S. Department of Treasury, Financial Crimes Enforcement Network, In the matter of AmSouth Bank, Assessment of Civil Money Penalty, No. 2004-2, October 12, 2004.

U.S. Department of Treasury, Office of Foreign Asset Control, "Diamond Trading: What You Need to Know About U.S. Sanctions, An Overview of the Rough Diamonds Control Regulations, Title 31 Part 592 of the U.S. Code of Federal Regulations," November 5, 2004.

U.S. Department of Treasury, "Treasury Designates Mexican Money Laundering Cell," Press Release JS-2191, January 12, 2005.

U.S. Department of Treasury, "Financial Crimes Enforcement Network; Amendment to the Bank Secrecy Act Regulations- Imposition of Special Measures Against VEF Banka," Federal Register, Vol. 70, No. 79, April 26, 2005, pp. 21369-21376.

U.S. Department of Treasury (and other U.S. Government agencies, bureaus, and offices), U.S. Money Laundering Threat Assessment, December, 2005.

U.S. Department of Treasury, "Treasury Issues Final Rule Against Bank of Syria, U.S. Financial Institutions Must Terminate Correspondent Accounts," Press Release, JS4105, March 9, 2006.

U.S. District Court for the District of Columbia, United States of America v. All funds seized from or on deposit in SunTrust account number xxxxx8359, in the name of Gold and Silver Reserve, Inc., and all funds on deposit in Regions Bank account number xxxxx4851 in the name of Gold and Silver Reserve, Inc., filed 13/30/2005.

U.S. General Accountability Office, International Remittances: Different Estimation Methodologies Produce Different Results, GAO-06-210.[1]

U.S. General Accounting Office, Combating Money Laundering: Opportunities Exist to Improve the National Strategy, GAO-03-813, September 2003

U. S. General Accounting Office, Failed Banks: Accounting and Auditing Reforms Urgently Needed, Washington, DC., GAO/AFMD-91-43, April 1991.

U.S. General Accounting Office, International Affairs: Information on U.S. Agencies' Efforts to Address Islamic Extremism, GAO-05-853, September 2005.

U.S. General Accounting Office, Interim Report on Internet Gambling, GAO-02-1101R, September 23, 2002.

U.S. General Accounting Office, Internet Gambling: An Overview of the Issues, GAO—03-89, December 2002.

U.S. General Accounting Office, Private Banking: Raul Salinas, Citibank, and Alleged Money Laundering, Statement for the Record of Robert H. Hast, Acting Assistant Comptroller General for Investigations, Report to the Ranking Minority Member, Permanent Subcommittee on Investigations, Committee on Governmental Affairs, U.S. Senate, GAO/OSI-99-1, October 1998.

U.S. General Accounting Office, Money Laundering: Observations on Private Banking and Related Oversight of Selected Offshore Jurisdictions, Statement for the Record of Thomas J. McCool, Director, Financial Institutions and Markets Issues, General Government Division, Before the Permanent Subcommittee on Investigations, Committee of Government Affairs, U.S. Senate, GAO/TGGD-00-32, November 9, 1999.

U.S. General Accounting Office, Private Banking: Raul Salinas, Citibank, and Alleged Money Laundering, Statement for the Record of Robert H. Hast, Acting Assistant Comptroller General for Investigations, Office of Special Investigations, Testimony Before the Permanent Subcommittee on Investigations, Committee on Governmental Affairs, U.S. Senate, GAO/T-OSI-003, November 9, 1999.

U.S. General Accounting Office, "Suspicious Banking Activities: Possible Money Laundering by U.S. Corporations Formed for Russian Entities," Report to the Ranking Minority Member, Permanent Subcommittee on Investigations, Committee on Governmental Affairs, United States Senate, GAO-01-120, October 2000.

U.S. General Accounting Office, Terrorist Financing: U.S. Agencies Should Systematically Assess Terrorists' Use of Alternative Financing Mechanisms," GAO-04-163, November 2003.

U.S. General Accounting Office, D'Agostino, Davi M., Director, Financial Markets and Community Investment, "Anti-Money Laundering: Issues Concerning Depository Institution Regulatory Oversight," Testimony Before the U.S. Senate Committee on Banking, Housing, and Urban Affairs, GAO-04-833T, June 3, 2004.

[1] Effective July 7, 2004, the Government Accounting Office became the Government Accountability Office.

U.S. House of Representatives, Subcommittee on Oversight and Investigations, Committee on Financial Services, "Risk Management and Regulatory Failures at Riggs and UBS: Lessons Learned," Serial Number 108-91, June 2, 2004.

U.S. Immigration and Customs Enforcement, News Release, "Delta National Bank & Trust Company Pleads Guilty After ICE Investigation," October 1, 2003.

U.S. Immigration and Customs Enforcement, News Release, "ICE Undercover Investigation Dismantles International Drug Money Laundering Organization," October 15, 2004.

U.S. Immigration and Customs Enforcement, News Release, "Former High-Ranking Official from Holy Land Foundation Ordered Removed from the United States," February 8, 2005.

U.S. Immigration and Customs Enforcement, News Release, "ICE Arrests 14 Charged with Operating an Unlicensed Money Remitting Business and Extortionate Loan Scheme, More than $5 million Smuggled to Yemen," March 28, 2006.

U.S. Money Laundering Threat Assessment, December 2005. (See U.S. Dept. of Treasury)

U.S. Secret Service, "Public Awareness Advisory Regarding '4-1-9' or 'Advance Fee Fraud' Schemes, No date, http://www.secretservice.gov/alert419.shtml

U.S. Senate, Permanent Subcommittee on Investigations, Committee on Homeland Security and Governmental Affairs, "Money Laundering and Foreign Corruption: Enforcement and Effectiveness of the Patriot Act, Supplemental Staff Report on U.S. Accounts by Augusto Pinochet," March 16, 2005.

U.S. Senate, Committee on Governmental Affairs, "Terrorism Financing: Origination, Organization, and Prevention," S. Hrg. 108-245, July 31, 2003.

U.S. Senate, Permanent Subcommittee on Investigations, Committee on Governmental Affairs, "Private Banking and Money Laundering: A Case Study of Opportunities and Vulnerabilities," S. Hrg. 106-428, November 9, 10, 1999.

U. S. Senate, Permanent Subcommittee on Investigations, Committee on Governmental Affairs, "Minority Staff of the Permanent Subcommittee on Investigations Report on Correspondent Banking: A Gateway for Money Laundering," February 5, 2001.

U. S. Senate, Permanent Subcommittee on Investigations, Committee on Governmental Affairs, "Role of U.S. Correspondent Banking in International Money Laundering," March 1, 2, 6, 2001.

U. S. Senate, Permanent Subcommittee on Investigations, Committee on Governmental Affairs, "Money Laundering and Foreign Corruption: Enforcement and Effectiveness of the Patriot Act, Senate Hearing 108-633, July 15, 2004.

U. S. Senate, Permanent Subcommittee on Investigations, Committee on Governmental Affairs, "Money Laundering and Foreign Corruption: Enforcement and Effectiveness of the Patriot Act, Case Study Involving Riggs Bank," Report prepared by the Minority Staff of the Permanent Subcommittee, July 15, 2004.

U. S. Senate, Current Trends in Money Laundering, Report prepared for the Permanent Subcommittee on Investigations of the Committee on Government Affairs, 102nd Cong., 2nd Sess. S Hrg. 102-123, December 1992.

U. S. Senate, Current Trends in Money Laundering, Report prepared for the Permanent Subcommittee on Investigations of the Committee on Government Affairs, 102nd Cong., 2nd Sess. S. Hrg. 102-579, February 27, 1992.

United States of America Before the Board of Governors of the Federal Reserve System, Washington, D.C., Office of Foreign Asset Control, U.S. Department of The Treasury,

State of Illinois Department of Financial and Professional Regulation, New York State Banking Department, New York, New York, In the Matter of ABN AMRO BANK N.V., Amsterdam, The Netherlands, ... New York Branch, and Chicago Branch, FRB Dkt No. 05-35-CMP-FB, Order of Assessment of Civil Money Penalty…., December 19, 2005.

United States of America, Department of The Treasury, Financial Crimes Enforcement Network, In the Matter of the New York Branch, ABN AMRO BANK N.V., New York, New York, Number 2005-5, December 19, 2005.

United Nations Office on Drugs and Crime, "Global Programme Against Money Laundering," April 4, 2005.

United Nations Office on Drugs and Crime, "The Ten Fundamental Laws of Money Laundering," April 4, 2005.

US v. Afshari, U.S. 9th Circuit Court of Appeals, Case number 02-50355, 12/20/04.

US v. Giraldi, 86 F. 3d 1368 (5th Cir. 1996)

US v. Uddin, No 04-CR-80192 (E. D. Mich. April 11, 2005)

Uzun, Hatice, Samuel H. Szewczyk, and Raj Varma, "Board Composition and Corporate Fraud," Financial Analysts Journal, May/June 2004, pp. 33- 43.

Want, Jerry, "Corporate Culture- Illuminating the Black Hole," Journal of Business Strategy, 24 (4), 2003, pp. 14-21.

Warren, Mary Lee, Deputy Assistant Attorney General, Criminal Division, United States Department of Justice, Testimony before the Permanent Subcommittee on Investigations of the Committee on Governmental Affairs of the United States Senate, March 6, 2001.

Welcome to FINTRAC, What Must Be Reported, Suspicious Transactions, http://www.fintrac.gc.ca/publications/brochure/may-2003/pamphlet2_e.asp

Winer, Jonathan M., Alston & Bird LLP, Testimony, "Terrorism Financing: Origination, Organization, and Prevention," Hearing before the Committee on Governmental Affairs, U.S. Senate, (S. Hrg. 108-245), July 31, 2003.

White House, Executive Order 13224 on Terrorist Financing: Blocking Property and Prohibiting Transactions With Persons Who Commit, Threaten to Commit, or Support Terrorism, September 24, 2001. http://www.whitehouse.gov/news/releases/2001/09/print/20010924-1.html

White House Executive Order 13312, Implementing the Clean Diamond Trading Act, July 29, 2003.

White House News Release, "Fact Sheet on Shutting Down the Terrorist Financial Network," December 4, 2001.

World Bank. See The World Bank

World Council of Credit Unions, "International Remittance Network (IRnet)," https://www.woccu.org/prod_serv/irnet/index.php;https://www.woccu.org/prod_serv/irnet/faq.php

Yousef, Tarik M., Testimony before the U.S. Senate Committee on Banking, Housing, and Urban Affairs, Subcommittee on International Trade and Finance, Hearing on "Hawala and Underground Terrorist Financing Mechanisms," November 14, 2001.

Zarte, Juan Carlos, Assistant Secretary Terrorist Financing and Financial Crimes, U.S. Department of Treasury, Testimony before the House Financial Services Committee on Domestic and International Monetary Policy, Trade and Technology And Oversight and Investigations," September 30, 2004.

Zarte, Juan Carlos, Assistant Secretary Terrorist Financing and Financial Crimes, U.S. Department of Treasury, Testimony before the House Financial Services Committee on Domestic and International Monetary Policy, Trade and Technology And Oversight and Investigations," February 16, 2005.

12 U.S.C. 1818, 1819; 31 U.S.C. 5318; Part 353 appears at 61 Fed. Reg. 6099 (Suspicious Activity Reports)

31 CFR Part 103, RIN 1506-AA36, Financial Crimes Enforcement Network: Amendment to the Bank Secrecy Act Regulations – Requirement that Insurance Companies Report Suspicious Activity. FinCEN Final Rule

31 CFR Part 103, RIN 1506-AA70, Financial Crimes Enforcement Network: Amendment to the Bank Secrecy Act Regulations-Anti-Money Laundering Programs for Insurance Companies, Final Rule.

Online Sources of Information

Asia Pacific Group on Money Laundering (APG): http://www.apgml.org

AUSTRAC, Australia's anti-money laundering, crime, and tax evasion regulator; http://www.austrac.gov.au/

Basel Committee on Banking Supervision, Bank for International Settlements (BIS): http://www.bis.org

Board of Governors of the Federal Reserve: http://www.federalreserve.gov

Caribbean Financial Action Task Force: http://www.cfatf.org

Clearing House Interbank Payments System, http://www.chips.org/

Egmont Group of Financial Intelligence Units, http://www1.oecd.org/fatf/Ctry-orgpages/org-egmont_en.htm; http://www.egmontgroup.org/

Federal Deposit Insurance Corporation, FDIC: http://www.fdic.gov

Federal Financial Institutions Examination Council, FFIEC, http://www.ffiec.gov

Federal Trade Commission web based resource about identity theft. http://www. consumer. gov/idtheft/#

Financial Action Task Force (FATF): http://www.fatf-gafi.org/index.htm

Financial Crimes Enforcement Network, FinCEN: http://www.fincen.gov

Financial Transactions and Reports Analysis Centre of Canada (FINTRAC): http://www.fintrac.gc.ca/intro_e.asp

International Association of Insurance Supervisors: http://www.iaisweb.org/.

International Organization of Securities Commissions (IOSCO): http://www.iosco.org

Interpol: http://www.interpol.int

Money Transmitter Regulators Association (MTRA): http://www.mtraweb.org/

MSB. Gov, (FinCEN website for Money Service Businesses): http://www.msb.gov/

National Criminal Justice Reference Service (Administered by the U.S. DOJ): http://www.ncjrs.org/

Office of the Comptroller of the Currency, OCC: http://www.occ.treas.gov

Office of Foreign Asset Control, OFAC, http://www.treas.gov/offices/enforcement/ofac/

Office of National Drug Control Policy, Executive Office of the President, http://www.whitehousedrugpolicy.gov/

Organization for Economic Co-Operation and Development (OECD): http://www.oecd.org
State of New York Banking Department (Regulatory Actions): http://www.banking. state. ny.us/index.htmt
Suspicious Activity Reports (SAR) http://www.fdic.gov/regulations/laws/rules/2000-7500.html
U.S. Customs and Border Protection, http://www.cbp.gov.
U.S. Department of Homeland Security, http://www.dhs.gov/dhspublic/
U.S. Department of Justice, http://www.usdoj.gov/
U.S. Department of State, Bureau for International Narcotics and Law Enforcement Affairs, http://www.state.gov/g/inl/rls/nrcrpt/2003/vol2/html/index.htm
U.S. Immigration and Customs Enforcement (ICE), http://www.ice.gov/graphics/index.htm; http://www.bice.immigration.gov/graphics/index.htm
U.S. Secret Service: http://www.secretservice.gov/index.shtml
U.S. Department of Treasury: http://www.treas.gov
Wolfsberg Principles: http://www.wolfsberg-principles.com

ABBREVIATIONS (CHAPTERS 1-6)

AIAI	Terrorist group Al-Itihaad Al-Islamiya
AIM	The London Stock Exchange's Alternative Investment Market for small growth companies.
AKA	Also known as
ALF	Animal Liberation Front
AML	Anti-money laundering programs
APG	Asia Pacific Group on Money Laundering
APT	Asset protection trust
ARS	Alternative Remittance Systems (see IVTS)
ATM	Automatic teller machines
AUSTRAC	Australian Transaction Reports and Analysis Centre
BCCI	Bank of Commerce and Credit International
BMPE	Black Market Peso Exchange
BSA	Bank Secrecy Act
BSA/AML	Bank Secrecy Act/Anti-money laundering programs
C&D	Cease and desist order
CDD	Customer due diligence
CIP	Customer identification programs
CFT	Combating the financing of terrorism
CHIPS	Clearing House Interbank Payments System
CMIR	Currency or Monetary Instruments Report
CMP	Civil money penalty
CTR	Currency Transaction Reports
CTRC	Currency Transaction Reports by Casinos
d/b/a	Doing business as
ECI	Extended custodial Inventory
ELF	Earth Liberation Front
EO	Executive Order by the President
FARC	Fuerzas Armadas Revolusionaria de Colombia (a designated foreign terrorist organization)
FATF	Financial Action Task Force
FBI	Federal Bureau of Investigation
FFIEC	Federal Financial Institutions Examination Council

FinCEN	Financial Crimes Enforcement Network
FIU	Financial Intelligence Units
FHA	Federal Housing Administration
FTO	Foreign Terrorist Organization
FSA	Financial Services Agency (Japan)
GDP	Gross Domestic Product
HIDTA	High Intensity Drug Traffic Areas
HIFCA	High Intensity Financial Crime Area
IAIS	International Association of Insurance Supervisors
IBC	International Business Corporation/Company
ICE	Bureau of Immigration and Customs Enforcement
IOSCO	International Organization of Securities Commissions
IPR	Intellectual Property Rights
IRnet	International Remittance Network of the World Council of Credit Unions (WOCCU)
IRS	Internal Revenue Service
IVTS	Informal value transfer system
KPCS	Kimberley Process Certification Scheme
KYC	Know your customer
MEK	Mujahedin-e Khalq, a designated terrorist organization.
MSB	Money Service Business
MTRA	Money Transmitter Regulators Association
NGO	Non-governmental organization
NPO	Non-profit organization
OCC	Office of the Comptroller of the Currency
OECD	Organization for Economic Co-operation and Development
OFAC	U.S. Department of Treasury's Office of Foreign Asset Control
PEPS	Politically exposed persons
PTA	Payable through account
PIC	Private investment companies, also called shell companies
RICO	Racketeer-Influenced and Corrupt Organizations
SAR	Suspicious Activity Reports
SDGT	Specially Designated Global Terrorist
SDN	Specially Designated Nationals
SDT	Specially Designated Terrorist
SDNTK	Specially Designated Narcotics Trafficker Kingpins
UAE	United Arab Emirates
WAMY	World Assembly of Muslim Youth
WOCCU	The World Council of Credit Unions

DEFINITIONS OF SELECTED TERMS (CHAPTERS 1-6)

Alternative Remittance Systems, See Informal Value Transfer System, and Hawala.

Beneficial owner. An individual or group that controls an account.

Black Market Peso Exchange. The largest money laundering system in the Western Hemisphere used by Colombian drug traffickers to launder the proceeds from their drug sales in the U.S. to their Colombian bank accounts.

Cash transactions. The BSA, the Internal Revenue Code (Title 26), and the money laundering criminal statutes (Title 18) requires any person engaged in trade or business who receives more than $10,000 in a single transaction or related series of transactions to file a "Report of Cash Payments over $10,000 Received in Trade or Business" report with the Internal Revenue Service (IRS). This is only one example of cash transactions that must be reported to FinCEN and/or the IRS. (See Transactions)

Computer e-cash. E-cash exists only in cyberspace and it is used for virtual transactions. E-cash consists of electronic units that can be used in place of currency or credit cards for internet transactions. For example, e-cash/digital funds can be placed on a smart card or hard drive.

Concentration account. A concentration account for a business is used to commingle funds that are subsequently transferred to other accounts.

Correspondent account. Accounts established by one bank with another bank that provide regular services, dealings, and other financial transactions

Correspondent banking is one bank that provides services to another bank (respondent bank).

Endorsed/third party check is a check payable to somebody other than the drawer, who transfers the check to someone else by endorsing the check and writing "pay to the order of" another party.

Enforcement actions. "The Federal Reserve takes formal enforcement actions against the above entities for violations of laws, rules, or regulations, unsafe or unsound practices, breaches of fiduciary duty, and violations of final orders. Formal enforcement actions include cease and desist orders, written agreements, removal and prohibition orders, and orders assessing civil money penalties"[1]

---

[1] "Federal Reserve Enforcement Actions," Board of Governors of the Federal Reserve System, September 19, 2002. http://www.federalreserve.gov/boarddocs/enforcement/

Executive Order 13224. Executive Order on Terrorist Financing: Blocking Property and Prohibiting Transactions With Persons Who Commit, Threaten to Commit, or Support Terrorism issued by President George W. Bush

Federal Financial Institutions Examination Council (FFIEC) is comprised of five banking agencies: The Board of Governors of the Federal Reserve System, Federal Deposit Insurance Corporation, National Credit Union Administration, Office of the Comptroller of the Currency, and Office of Thrift Supervision.

Financial Action Task Force (FATF) is an inter-governmental body whose purpose is the development and promotion of national and international policies to combat money laundering and terrorist financing.

Financial institutions, in the context of BSA/AML, include banks (e.g. commercial banks, all subsidiaries of bank holding companies, Edge and Agreement corporations, U.S. branches and agencies of foreign banks, savings and loan associations, credit unions), federally regulated securities brokers, dealers and investment companies, money service businesses (MSBs, currency dealers or exchangers; check cashers, issuers of traveler's checks, money orders, or stored value; sellers or redeemers of traveler's checks, money orders, or stored value; and funds transmitters), persons subject to supervision by state or federal bank supervisory authority, casinos, card clubs, futures commission merchants, introducing brokers, commodity pool operators, and commodity trading advisors. Also included in the definition of financial institutions are any individuals or groups engaged in conducting, controlling, directing or owning informal value transfer systems (IVTS) in the United States. In 2006, insurance companies offering selected products to the list of financial institutions.

Front companies. Illegal funds are represented as income (commingled) from companies such as legitimate real estate agencies and pizzerias. Front companies also may be dummy corporations, such as jewelry stores and precious metal dealers, established for the express purpose of laundering or hiding assets.

Hawala means "transfer" in Arabic. It is a traditional informal value transfer system (IVTS) or alternative remittance system (ARS). Hawala requires four participants: the sender of funds in one country, the receiver in another, and IVTS operators in both countries facilitate the transfer or remittance. IVTS operators are also called **hawaladars**.

Informal Value Transfer System (IVTS) refers to any non-bank system where someone receives money for the purpose of making those funds, or an equivalent value, available to someone else in a different geographic location. IVTS is also known as an Alternative Remittance Systems (ARS)

Insurance sector includes insurers, reinsurance companies, their agents, brokers, or mediators who operate on their behalf.

International Business Corporation/Company. Antigua and Barbuda enacted the International Business Corporations Act of 1982. (Also called Shell corporations). IBCs are corporations established in an offshore jurisdiction and are generally licensed to conduct business only outside the country of incorporation. They are often established in jurisdictions with little or no taxation or regulation, and secrecy laws that shield the identity of the owners.

Kimberley Process Certification Scheme (KPCS). A United Nations resolution dealing with "conflict diamond" or "rough diamonds" that are used to fund armed conflicts in selected African countries.

Know Your Customers (KYC). Banks must make reasonable efforts to determine who the borrower is, the credit history, the purpose of a loan, and other relevant information. KYC is closely linked with customer identification programs (CID).

Money laundering is the conversion of the monetary proceeds of criminal activity into funds with an apparently legal source and without revealing the true nature, source, or ownership of those proceeds.

Money Service Business (MSB) includes five distinct types of financial service providers and the U.S. Postal Service: 1) currency dealers or exchangers; 2) check cashers; 3) issuers of traveler's checks, money orders, or stored value; 4) sellers or redeemers of traveler's checks, money orders, or stored value; 5) money transmitters.

Nested accounts/correspondents are foreign or shell banks that use their correspondent's bank accounts in say, the U.S., without the U.S. bank's knowledge or consent.

Office of Foreign Assets Control (OFAC) of the U.S. Department of the Treasury administers and enforces U.S. economic and trade sanctions against targeted foreign countries, terrorists, and others.

Offshore banks are banks with licenses limited to transacting business with persons outside of the country where the bank is licensed, or banks that are bared from transacting business using the local currency where the bank is licensed.

Payable through accounts (PTAs) are also known as "pass-through" or "pass-by." In a PTA, the foreign bank provides its customers with checks that allows them to draw funds from the foreign institution's account at the U.S. bank.

Politically exposed persons (PEPs) are public figures including heads of states, politicians, senior executives of corporations, and high level political figures.

Private banking is the term used for "preferential treatment and services" given to high net worth individuals. Such services may include asset management, trust, investment services, etc. The minimum amount of funds or assets is $1 million or more.

Private investment companies (PIC) are shell companies incorporated in financial secrecy jurisdictions that are used for various tax or trust related purposes.

Quit claim deeds are used to remove someone from or add someone to the titles of residential real estate or other property.

Remittance. The term remittance refers to funds being sent by someone living in one country to someone else in a different country.

Respondent bank. See correspondent bank.

Shell banks are institutions with no physical presence in the jurisdiction where they are incorporated, and they are not affiliated with a regulated financial group.

Shell corporations also called International Business Corporations (IBCs), are similar to front companies, but they may be chartered offshore to hide the identities of the owners, and they may exist on paper only. They have no independent assets or operations of their own. They are used to conduct or maintain control of other companies. In addition, they can be used to transfer funds in what may or may not be legitimate transactions. See private investment companies (PICs).

Smurfing is defined as two or more persons conducting related financial transactions that could have been completed in a single transaction.

Terrorism can be defined as premeditated, politically motivated violence perpetrated against noncombatant targets by sub-national groups or clandestine agents, usually intended to influence an audience. The term **international terrorism** refers to citizens in more than one country. A **terrorist group** refers to any group or subgroup that practices international terrorism.

Transactions, in the context of BSA/AML programs include deposits, withdrawals, transfers between accounts, extensions of credit, buying and selling stocks, bonds, CDs, or other monetary instruments or investment securities, or any other payment or transfers made by or to a bank.

Travel Rule. All financial institutions must include certain customer information in transmitting orders for funds of $3000 or more. See 31 CFR 103.33, and/or the FFEIC BSA/AML Examination Manual for additional details.

Tri-border area, where Argentina, Brazil, and Paraguay converge, has been a safe haven for Hezbollah and Hamas to fund their activities in the Middle East.

Wire transfers refers to any financial transaction carried out for a person through a financial institution by electronic means, and making that amount of money available to a person at another financial institution.

Wolfsberg Group is a private association of twelve global banks, which aims to develop financial services industry standards, and related products, for Know Your Customer, Anti-Money Laundering and Counter Terrorist Financing policies.

ABOUT THE AUTHOR

Benton E. Gup, Ph.D.
Chair of Banking
The University of Alabama

Dr. Benton E. Gup has a broad background in finance. His undergraduate and graduate degrees are from the University of Cincinnati. After receiving his Ph.D. in economics, he served as a staff economist for the Federal Reserve Bank of Cleveland. He currently holds the Robert Hunt Cochrane/Alabama Bankers Association Chair of Banking at the University of Alabama, Tuscaloosa, Alabama, U.S.A. He also held banking chairs at the University of Virginia and the University of Tulsa. He worked in bank research for the Office of the Comptroller of the Currency while on sabbatical in 1997.

Dr. Gup is the author or editor of the following books: Money Laundering, Financing Terrorism, and Suspicious Activity (forthcoming), Capital Market, Globalization, and Economic Development (2005); Commercial Banking: The Management of Risk, 3rd. ed., (with J. Kolari, 2005);The New Basel Capital Accord (2004); Too-Big-To-Fail: Policies and Practices in Government Bailouts (2004); Investing Online (2003); The Future of Banking (2003); Megamergers in a Global Economy - Causes and Consequences (2002); The New Financial Architecture: Banking Regulation in the 21st Century (2000); Commercial Bank Management, 2nd ed. (with D. Fraser and J. Kolari); International Banking Crises; Bank Failures in the Major Trading Countries of the World; The Bank Director's Handbook; Targeting Fraud; Interest Rate Risk Management (with R. Brooks); The Basics of Investing, 5th ed.; Bank Fraud: Exposing the Hidden Threat to Financial Institutions; Bank Mergers; Cases in Bank Management (with C. Meiburg); Principles of Financial Management; Financial Institutions; Financial Intermediaries; Personal Investing: A Complete Guide; Guide to Strategic Planning; and How to Ask for a Business Loan.

Dr. Gup's articles on financial subjects have appeared in The Journal of Finance, The Journal of Financial and Quantitative Analysis, The Journal of Money, Credit, and Banking, Financial Management, The Journal of Banking and Finance, Financial Analysts Journal, and elsewhere.

He is an internationally known lecturer in executive development and graduate programs in Australia (University of Melbourne, University of Technology, Sydney), New Zealand

(University of Auckland), Peru (University of Lima), and South Africa (Graduate School of Business Leadership). He has been a visiting researcher at the Bank of Japan, and at Macquarie University, Sydney, Australia. Finally, he serves as a consultant to government, industry, and the IMF.

Dr. Gup's current research interests include banking issues and corporate valuation. He is currently working on a book dealing with money laundering and financing terrorism.

Benton E. Gup, Ph.D.
Chair of Banking
University of Alabama
Box 870224, Room 200 Alston Hall
Tuscaloosa, AL. 35487 USA

Phone 205-348-8984
FAX 205-348-0590
e-mail bgup@cba.ua.edu

CONTRIBUTING AUTHORS

Prof. J. Michael Hardin
Dept. of Information Systems, Statistics, and Management
300 Alston Hall
P.O. Box 870226
Tuscaloosa, AL 35487
205- 348-6085

Billie S. Anderson
Dept. of Information Systems, Statistics, and Management
300 Alston Hall
P.O. Box 870226
Tuscaloosa, AL 35487
205- 348-6085

Tim Lutz
SAS Institute Inc.
100 SAS Campus Dr.
Cary, NC 27513
(919)677-8000

David Stewart
SAS Institute Inc.
100 SAS Campus Dr.
Cary, NC 27513
(919)677-8000

Prof. Raj Aggarwal
Kent State University
BSA 434
Kent, Ohio 44242
330-672-1219

Prof. Kamala Raghavan
Robert Morris University
Dept. of Accounting and Taxation
Pittsburgh, PA 15108
412-269-3970

INDEX

C

D

E

H

I

N

O

P

Q

R

S

T

U

V

W

Y